Optimize English Legal System

OPTIMIZE LAW REVISION

Titles in the series:
Contract Law
The English Legal System
Equity and Trusts
EU Law
Land Law
Public Law

Forthcoming:
Criminal Law
Tort Law

The Optimize series' academic advisors are:

– Michael Bromby, Higher Education Academy Discipline Lead for Law 2011–2013, Reader in Law, GCU

'The use of visualisation in Optimize will help students to focus on the key issues when revising.'

– Emily Allbon, Law Librarian and creator of Lawbore, City University

'Partnering well-explained, comprehensive content with visual tools like maps and flowcharts is what makes the Optimize series so unique. These books help students take their learning up a notch; offering support in grappling with the subject, as well as insight into what will help make their work stand out.'

– Sanmeet Kaur Dua, Lecturer in Law, co-creator of Lawbore, City University

'This series sets out the essential concepts and principles that students need to grasp in a logical way by combining memorable visual diagrams and text. Students will find that they will not easily forget what they read in this series as the unique aim higher and interaction points will leave a blueprint in their minds.'

– Zoe Swan, Senior Lecturer in Law, University of Brighton.

'The wide range of visual material includes diagrams, charts, tables and maps enable students to check their knowledge and understanding on each topic area, every step of the way... When combined with carefully explained legal principles and solid, understandable examples, students will find this series provides them with a win- win solution to the study of law and developing revision techniques.'

Optimize English Legal System

Odette Hutchinson and Angela Stanhope

Routledge
Taylor & Francis Group

LONDON AND NEW YORK

First published 2014
by Routledge
2 Park Square, Milton Park, Abingdon, Oxon OX14 4RN

and by Routledge
711 Third Avenue, New York, NY 10017

Routledge is an imprint of the Taylor & Francis Group, an informa business
© 2014 Odette Hutchinson and Angela Stanhope

British Library Cataloguing in Publication Data
A catalogue record for this book is available from the British Library

Library of Congress Cataloging in Publication Data
A catalogue record for this book has been requested

ISBN: 978-0-415-70229-4 (pbk)
ISBN: 978-1-315-84899-0 (ebk)

Typeset in TheSans
by RefineCatch Limited, Bungay, Suffolk

Printed and bound in Great Britain by
CPI Group (UK) Ltd, Croydon, CR0 4YY

Contents

Optimize – Your Blueprint for Exam Success

Why Optimize?

In developing the *Optimize* format, Routledge have spent a lot of time talking to law students like you, and to your lecturers and examiners about assessment, about teaching and learning, and about exam preparation. The aim of our series is to help you make the most of your knowledge to gain good marks – to optimize your revision.

Students

Students told us that there was a huge amount to learn, and that visual features such as diagrams, tables and flowcharts made the law easier to follow. Learning and remembering cases was an area of difficulty, as was applying these in problem questions. Revision guides could make this easier by presenting the law succinctly, showing concepts in a visual format and highlighting how important cases can be applied in assessment.

Lecturers

Lecturers agreed that visual features were effective to aid learning, but were concerned that students learned by rote when using revision guides. To succeed in assessment, they wanted to encourage them to get their teeth into arguments, to support their answers with authority, and to show they had truly understood the principles underlying their questions. In short, they wanted them to show they understood how they were assessed on the law, rather than repeating the basic principles.

Assessment criteria

If you want to do well in exams, it's important to understand how you will be assessed. In order to get the best out of your exam or essay question, your first port of call should be to make yourself familiar with the marking criteria available from your law school; this will help you to identify and recognise the skills and knowledge you will need to succeed. Like course outlines, assessment criteria can differ from school to school and so if you can get hold of a copy of your own criteria, this will be invaluable. To give you a clear idea of what these criteria look like, we've collated the most common terms from 64 marking schemes for core curriculum courses in the UK.

research

reading

Evidence

Understanding

Structure   Critical Argument

Engagement

Application   Use   sources

Organization

Analysis   Accuracy   Originality

Knowledge

Presentation

Common Assessment Criteria, Routledge Subject Assessment Survey

Optimizing the law

The format of this Optimize Law volume has been developed with these assessment criteria and the learning needs of students firmly in mind.

- ❖ **Visual format:** Our expert series advisors have brought a wealth of knowledge about visual learning to help us to develop the books' visual format.
- ❖ **Tailored coverage:** Each book is tailored to the needs of your core curriculum course and presents all commonly taught topics.
- ❖ **Assessment led-revision:** Our authors are experienced teachers with an interest in how students learn, and they have structured each chapter around revision objectives that relate to the criteria you will be assessed on.
- ❖ **Assessment led-pedagogy:** The Aim Higher, Common Pitfalls, Up for Debate and Case precedent features used in these books are closely linked to common assessment criteria – showing you how to gain the best marks, avoid the worst, apply the law and think critically about it.
- ❖ **Putting it into practice:** Each chapter presents example essay or problem questions and template answers to show you how to apply what you have learned.

Routledge and the Optimize team wish you the very best of luck in your exams and essays!

Guide to Using the Book and the Companion Website

The Routledge Optimize revision series is designed to provide students with a clear overview of the core topics in their course, and to contextualise this overview within a narrative that offers straightforward, practical advice relating to assessment.

Revision objectives

These overviews are a brief introduction of the core themes and issues you will encounter in each chapter.

Chapter Topic Maps

Visually link together all of the key topics in each chapter to tie together understanding of key issues.

Illustrative diagrams

A series of diagrams and tables are used to help facilitate the understanding of concepts and interrelationships within key topics.

Up for Debate

Up for Debate features help you to critique current law and reflect on how and in which direction it may develop in the future.

Case precedent boxes

A variety of landmark cases are highlighted in text boxes for ease of reference. The facts, principle and application for the case are presented to help understand how these courses are used in legal problems.

Aim Higher and Common Pitfalls

These assessment-focused sections show students how to get the best marks and avoid the most common mistakes.

Table of key cases

Drawing together all of the key cases from each chapter.

Companion Website

www.routledge.com/revision

Visit the Law Revision website to discover a comprehensive range of resources designed to enhance your learning experience.

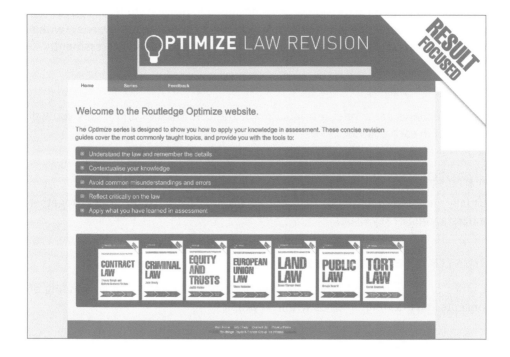

Resources for Optimize Law revision

❖ Revision tips products
❖ Topic overview podcasts
❖ Subject maps for each topic
❖ Downloadable versions of chapter maps and other diagrams
❖ Flashcard Glossary
❖ MCQ questions

Table of Cases and Statutes

■ Cases

■ Statutes

■ Statutory Instruments

◼ European Legislation

1

Introduction

Revision objectives

Understand the law

- Do you understand the introductory principles in this chapter?

Remember the details

- Can you categorise the areas of law that you are studying in your first year as an undergraduate?

Reflect critically on areas of debate

- Why do we have laws and what are their purpose?

Contextualise

- Can you see how the topics in this chapter underpin all your other subject areas?

Apply your skills and knowledge

- You will be applying the principles in this chapter throughout your studies – do not forget the basics!

Chapter Map

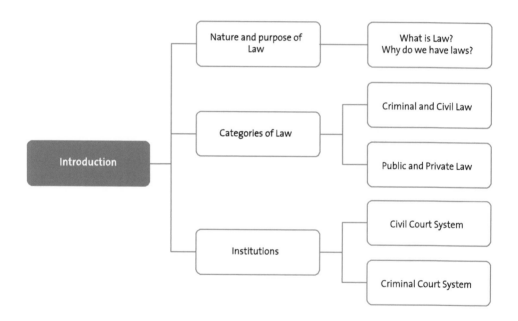

Introduction

Welcome to your **Optimize English Legal System** book. We hope very much that you enjoy reading it and it helps in guiding you towards success in your ELS assessments.

The study of the English legal system is one of the first topics you will study on your undergraduate programme, and it will normally be taught over one term. Students can sometimes dismiss this area, feeling it is not as important as their other topics, but a good understanding in this module will give you the tools you need to be successful in your other law modules. The topic of legal skills, and in particular **the lack of legal skills demonstrated by students**, has become a rather hot topic recently so you will be pleased to find a chapter (Chapter 11) in this book dedicated to that area. You are fortunate in that this chapter contains 'real' feedback from lecturers teaching ELS in universities right now. This chapter tells you what the lecturers think about why bright students are not always achieving the marks they deserve.

There is no substitute for hard work when you do your degree. There are no shortcuts. It is through clear understanding and application of the law that great marks can be achieved.

You need to read, so make sure you have your own copy of an **up-to-date** ELS textbook – your lecturer should have advised which one to buy. If money is an issue check if you can buy a second-hand copy, but do not buy an out-of-date textbook, as **it is out of date for a reason!**

We will continue in this introduction by considering three topics.

These are:

❖ Nature and purpose of law
❖ Categories of law
❖ Institutions

Nature and purpose of law

Under this heading we will explore 'what is law and why do we have it?'

Laws are often thought of as a set of rules that all citizens must abide by in order to ensure the safety and smooth running of society as a whole. They regulate the behaviour of those who are subject to them; in our case, those who live in the UK. They can be as simple as requiring everyone to drive on the left, or more complicated rules such as deciding who inherits a person's wealth if they die intestate (without a will).

Enforcement of the rules is also a key part of the legal process. You will see as you work through this book that this involves not only the traditional court system but also tribunals and other methods of Alternative Dispute Resolution (you will find a chapter dedicated to ADR in this book).

You will see in many of your textbooks that the English courts have an adversarial system. This means the lawyers are there to do the best job they can for their client. It may be helpful to think of them as being in competition with each other. This system is often contrasted with the inquisitorial style adopted by those in other countries. In the inquisitorial system the judge plays a much more active role in extracting the facts to arrive at a conclusion.

Aim Higher

Consider whether the adversarial system makes 'winning' the object of the action. Consider if it stifles the search for the truth.

This is something that is not confined to academic comment. In 2003 the detective involved in the Damilola Taylor trial questioned whether we should adopt the inquisitorial system, especially where vulnerable witnesses are involved.

See http://news.bbc.co.uk/1/hi/uk/3132193.stm for a snapshot of how the system works in this country and how an increased inquisitorial approach would be of benefit to those most vulnerable in the system.

Aim Higher

For further reading (and an article that brings together some other issues in this book), see:

Geoffrey Bindman, 'Justice in the Balance' (2013) 163 NLJ 6 (available on Lexis Library).

In this article Bindman discusses whether we can save the rule of law, the impact of the recent legal aid cuts and the reform of the adversarial system.

Categories of law

There are various ways in which law can be categorised.

We will consider the following two in this chapter.

Public and Private Law

The charts below illustrate the main differences between the two branches.

Public Law is concerned with the relationship between the **state** and **its citizens**. It covers the three areas outlined below.

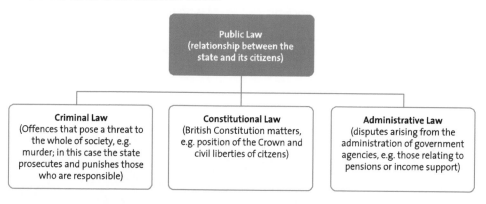

Private Law can be broken down into five main areas:

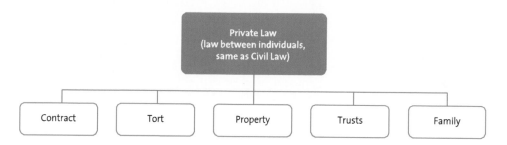

Criminal and Civil Law

The main differences between these two branches is illustrated in the following diagram.

	Criminal Law	Civil Law
Covers	Crimes against the state	Disputes between individuals
Parties to the action	The state prosecutes the defendant. Cases are brought in the name of the Crown, e.g. *R v Smith*	A claimant brings an action against the defendant. Cases are in the names of the parties, e.g. *Smith v Jones*

	Criminal Law	Civil Law
Courts used	Criminal Courts	Civil Courts or Alternative Dispute Resolution
Standard and Burden of Proof	Beyond reasonable doubt. The accused is either convicted or acquitted.	On the balance of probabilities. The claimant either wins or loses.
Punishment	Imprisonment, fine, community service. Aim is to punish the offender and protect society.	Damages, injunctions, specific performance. Aim is to compensate those who have suffered loss or injury due to another's actions.
Examples	Murder, theft, assault.	Contract, tort, property, trusts, family.

Aim Higher

What you can see from the table above is that there are key differences between the civil and criminal branches of the law. It is not uncommon for students, at least initially, to get confused and use civil terminology when dealing with criminal litigation and vice versa.

To help you avoid making mistakes with your use of terminology, we have created a number of flashcards and multiple choice questions which you can find located on the companion website. We would encourage you to test your knowledge throughout the duration of the course. Remember, precision is everything in law and inaccurate or incorrect use of terminology does matter!

Institutions

Under this heading we will consider both civil court and criminal court structures

NB: The European courts have been omitted here as you will cover these in your other first-year subjects.

The Civil Court structure

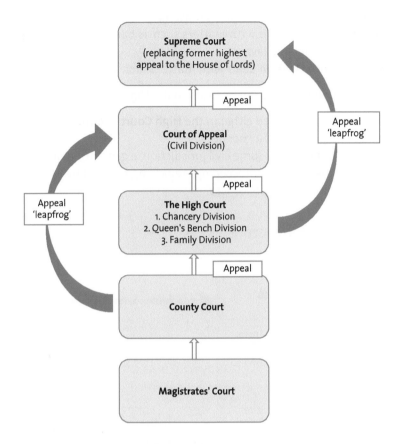

The **Supreme Court** is the highest appeal court in the UK.

❖ It hears appeals from the **Court of Appeal** and from the **High Court** in a 'leapfrog' action.
❖ Parties are allowed to 'leapfrog' the **Court of Appeal** if the **Supreme Court** gives permission, all parties agree and an important point of law is involved.

The **Court of Appeal** is split into two divisions: the **Civil Division** and the **Criminal Division**.

❖ The **Court of Appeal (Civil Division)** hears appeals from the **High Court**.
❖ The **Court of Appeal** may also hear a 'leapfrog' action from the **County Court** (if an important point of principle or practice is in issue).

The **High Court** is divided into three divisions:

- ❖ The **Family Division** deals with family matters.
- ❖ The **Chancery Division** deals with matters such as bankruptcy, mortgages, company and partnership law.
- ❖ The **Queen's Bench Division** deals with matters such as contract and tort.

Appeals from the **County Court** can be heard in the **High Court**.

- ❖ Civil proceedings are started either in the **High Court** or **County Court** (see the chapter on civil justice for further details).
- ❖ The **Magistrates Court** has some civil jurisdiction, e.g. granting order for protection against violence, proceedings regarding the welfare of children, or those relating to granting of licences.

The Criminal Court structure

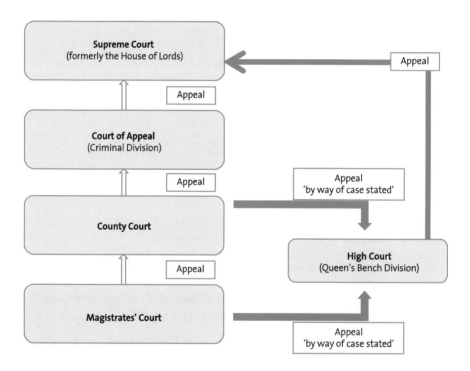

All proceedings are started in the **Magistrates' Court** but not all are heard there.

- ❖ The **Magistrates Court** will commit the more serious offences to the **Crown Court** (see the chapter on Criminal Justice for further details).
- ❖ An appeal can be made from the **Magistrates' Court** directly to the **High Court (Queen's Bench Division)** by way of case stated. Alternatively an appeal can be made to the **Crown Court** against either **conviction** or **sentence**.

- Appeals can also be made from the **Crown Court** to **the High Court (Queen's Bench Division)** if the case was first tried in the **Magistrates' Court** and then an appeal has been made to the **Crown Court**.
- Appeals from the **Crown Court** to the **Court of Appeal (Criminal Division)** can be against either sentence or conviction.
- Appeals can be made from the **Court of Appeal (Criminal Division)** or from the **High Court (Queen's Bench Division)** to the **Supreme Court**.

Aim Higher – revision tip

An understanding of the court structure in the English legal system is going to be fundamental to your understanding of the operation of key areas of any English legal system course. For example:

- the operation of the doctrine of binding judicial precedent
- the operation of the criminal justice system
- the operation of the civil justice system and ADR
- the judiciary.

You may find it helpful therefore to print off a copy of the court structure (available for download on the companion website). You can then refer to it when covering relevant topics, plus the more you see the structure the more ingrained it will become in your memory – and that will help at revision time!

Core issues checklist

Law can be summarised as a series of rules that exist for the good of society as a whole	✔
The UK has an adversarial (rather than an inquisitorial) system.	✔
Law can be categorised in different ways. For example, Criminal and Civil Law or Public and Private Law	✔
The Court System is divided into Civil Courts and Criminal Courts.	✔
Some of these courts (Supreme and Court of Appeal) are common to both systems.	✔

Useful websites

Topic	Website
Lawbore is an invaluable website with a range of great resources	http://lawbore.net/

@ Visit the book's companion website to test your knowledge

❖ Resources include a subject map, revision tip podcasts, downloadable diagrams, MCQ quizzes for each chapter, and a flashcard glossary

❖ www.routledge.com/cw/optimizelawrevision

2

Rule of Law and Human Rights

Revision objectives

Understand the law
- Are you able to explain what is meant by the rule of law?

Remember the details
- Can you articulate the different ways in which human rights can be protected?

Reflect critically on areas of debate
- Can you confidently address the issues in the 'Up for debate' boxes?

Contextualise
- Can you see where knowledge of this subject will help you in other areas of your studies? For example, when studying precedent, statutory interpretation and sources of law.

Apply your skills and knowledge
- Can you complete the 'Putting it into practice' question?

Chapter Map

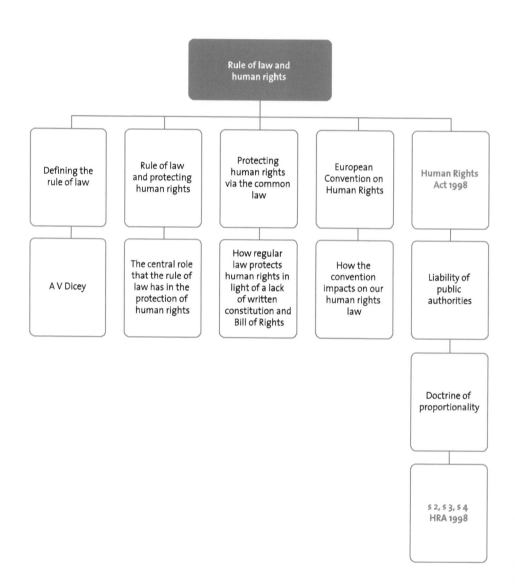

'It is the function of the courts to uphold the rule of law and to secure fundamental human rights.'

Analyse this statement and state whether you agree that the passing of the Human Rights Act 1998 has allowed the domestic courts to carry out that role more effectively.

You will find an outline answer at the end of this chapter.

Introduction

In this chapter we will consider the relationship between the **rule of law** and **the protection of human rights**.

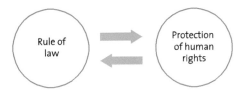

This is a complicated area of law; it is not straightforward and this presents certain challenges for students. Work through each of the sections below to build up your knowledge bit by bit, thereby ensuring you have covered everything you need to know.

Due to the nature of this series it has not been possible to expand on all the relevant case authority. Where appropriate, I have included additional cases which you should use if you wish to undertake further, independent reading.

When studying this area of law, one of the first things you must grasp is the idea that if our legal system upholds the rule of law, this will ensure the law is open and clear, and that citizens will be free from arbitrary or unfair rules and the misuse of governmental power.

This, in turn, will ensure the protection of our basic liberties and fundamental human rights.

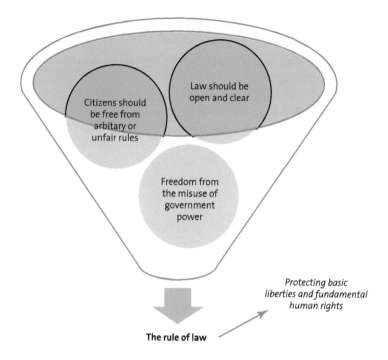

Protecting basic
liberties and fundamental
human rights

The rule of law

Defining the rule of law

Common Pitfall

Students should be careful to show their understanding of the rule of law in the context of the protection of human rights. Do not just repeat information about the rule of law that you have learnt in other contexts. Stress the importance of control of power and equality in securing the freedom and rights of the individual.

Let us begin by helping you gain a firm understanding of the rule of law. This is not an easy task due to several theorists developing their own ideas. A **common thread**, however, is the need for everyone, especially the government, to be **subject to the law** and for **all disputes to be resolved within the law**.

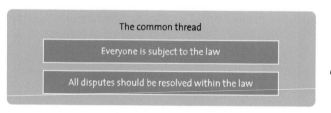

The common thread

Everyone is subject to the law

All disputes should be resolved within the law

All theorists
believe in this
common thread

Professor A V Dicey

Although several theorists exist, the **most important** is **Professor A V Dicey**, and we will look briefly at his definition of the rule of law. **This is important** because unless you understand the rule of law you will have difficulty in understanding the human rights issues.

Dicey identified two features which characterised the political institutions of England.

❖ **Supremacy of Parliament**
❖ **Rule or supremacy of law**

These, in Dicey's view, protected us from arbitrary governmental rule.

It is the **second characteristic** (*rule or supremacy of law*) that we will concentrate on.

Dicey subdivided the second characteristic into **three** further concepts.

1. *The supremacy of regular law as opposed to the influence of arbitary power.*

In simple terms this means that no one can be punished or interfered with unless the law authorises it – as Dicey stated, for a distinct breach of the law; a man can be punished for breach of the law but he cannot be punished for anything else – and that all actions of government bodies have to be authorised by law (see *Entick* below).

Aim Higher

You can contrast this principle with a case where a government can do as it pleases and there are no controls over its actions; thus Dicey gives the examples of arbitrary arrest or temporary imprisonment.

Dicey considered how wide the powers of government should be, and the dangers of allowing discretionary or arbitrary powers.

Case precedent – *Entick v Carrington* (1765)

Facts: Carrington, along with three other of the King's messengers forced their way into Entick's home in an attempt to confiscate papers of a seditious nature. Entick sued for trespass and Carrington claimed he was acting under a warrant given by Lord Halifax, which purported to act on the grounds of 'state necessity'. It was held that Lord Halifax had no legal right to issue the warrant.

Principle: assessing the scope of executive power.

Application: this case illustrates that governmental power must derive from the 'regular' (common) law as opposed to the discretion of government itself. Lord Camden CJ held that if the rule (on state necessity) was law it will be found in our books. The case also illustrates Dicey's other two principles, below.

2. *No man is above the law (every man, whatever his rank or condition, is subject to the ordinary law).*

Here, Dicey is insisting on equality for all – including the government – before the law. This simply means that all sections of society should be subject to the ordinary law of the land, administered by the ordinary law courts, with no exemptions for those in power – see *Entick*, above.

3. *That the general principles of the constitution result from judicial decisions from the courts.*

Dicey argued that having an unwritten constitution did not matter with respect to the protection of our rights, and in fact it was to our advantage. He stated that in a country with a written constitution, personal liberty flows or is secured by the constitution, wheras in England personal liberty becomes part of the constitution when it is secured by the decision of the courts, as in *Entick*.

In summary,

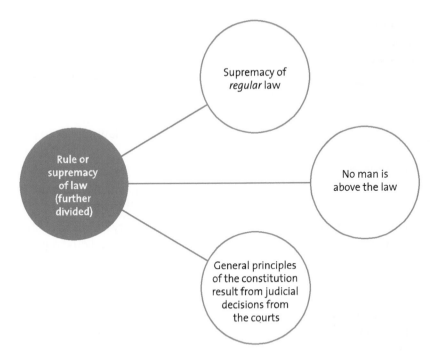

Feeling confident that you understand Dicey's rule of law, we must now consider how the rule of law is **central to the protection of human rights**.

Aim Higher – suggested reading

❖ Young, J, 'The politics of the **Human Rights Act**' (1999) 26(1) JLS 27
❖ Keating, D, 'Upholding the Rule of Law' (1999) 149 NLJ 533

Remember there are always extra marks available where you demonstrate that you have read beyond the core textbook!

The rule of law and protecting human rights

Under the rule of law government needs to be regulated by an independent judiciary, whose central role is to safeguard the individual from arbitrary power. Thus, s 6 of the Human Rights Act 1998 makes it unlawful for a public authority to violate Convention rights. This ensures that individuals enjoy rights equally, that government power is restricted and that international human rights law is followed. However, the domestic, and European, courts show proper respect to parliament, government and domestic law.

Let us have a look at these in more detail.

1	**Government power needs to be regulated**	Government power that impacts on individual liberty and rights needs to be regulated by clear, accessible and reasoned law – human rights law insists that any interference with rights must be 'prescribed by law' and 'necessary in a democratic society'.
2	**s 6 Human Rights Act 1998**	Under s 6 most human rights law applies to public bodies and authorities.
3	**Independent judiciary**	Central to this regulation is the independence and impartiality of the judiciary, which will ensure that government acts by and within the law.
4	**Central role of the judiciary**	The central role of the judiciary is thus to control arbitrary power and to secure individual rights – in domestic law this has been done via the common law but is now supported by the Human Rights Act 1998.
5	**Some rights are based on the rule of law**	Accordingly, some human rights – the right to a fair trial and freedom from retrospective criminal law – are based on the idea of the rule of law, the independence of the judiciary and the rules of natural justice.
6	**Equal treatment for all citizens**	Human rights law insists on the equal treatment of all citizens with respect to their human rights and their right to be free from discrimination.
7	**International human rights law**	These principles are contained in international human rights law – the European Convention for the Protection of Human Rights (1950) – and domestic law – common law and the Human Rights Act 1998.
8	**'Judicial Deference' and 'Margin of Appreciation'**	However, the court's role in upholding the rule of law must be combined with their duty to respect the separation of powers and the sovereignty of a democratically elected Parliament – in national law this is known as 'judicial deference' and in international law as the 'margin of appreciation'.

Protection of human rights via the common law

Consider this section under the following headings.

Common Pitfall

Many students confuse the European Convention on Human Rights, and the European Court of Human Rights, with EU law and the European Court of Justice. Ensure that you appreciate the difference, and relationship, between the two.

Protection of individual human rights without a written constitution

- The UK, lacking a written constitution and a Bill of Rights, protected individual human rights by the regular law, with such rights being safeguarded by the courts and the democratic process.

A V Dicey

- This method was favoured by A V Dicey, above, who preferred our rights to be protected by court decisions (*Entick v Carrington* (1765); see above).

Strengthening by the **HRA 1998**

- This method has now been strengthened by the passing of the **Human Rights Act 1998**, below, but is still employed in the absence of a formal Bill of Rights.

Interpretation

- The courts have always been able, subject to parliamentary sovereignty, to interpret legislation in a human rights friendly manner (*Waddington v Miah* [1974]) and to subject government decisions to strict judicial review where human rights have been violated (*R v Ministry of Defence, ex parte Smith* [1996]).

Legislation

- Parliament can pass legislation to control official powers (**Police and Criminal Evidence Act 1984**), to secure equality and freedom from discrimination (**Equality Act 2010**) and to respect certain rights, such as privacy (**Regulation of Investigatory Powers Act 2000**).

Criticisms

- This traditional method was subject to a number of criticisms and was very often not consistent with the UK's obligations under the European Convention on Human Rights (1950); see below. In particular, the individual often had to go to the European Court of Human Rights in Strasbourg to get justice – see, for example, *Malone v United Kingdom* (1984).

The **1998 Act**

- The **Human Rights Act 1998** (see later) was passed to give greater and further effect to the rights contained in the European Convention, and the Act now works with the common law system to secure human rights.

Aim Higher

When answering a question in this area, ensure you appreciate the relationship between the rule of law, the judiciary and human rights. Also ensure your awareness of the common law protection of human rights by the courts, in addition to the **Human Rights Act 1998**, below.

The European Convention on Human Rights (1950)

Introduction

The European Convention on Human Rights (1950) is an **international treaty for the protection of individual human rights**. It possesses its own machinery (**the European Court of Human Rights**) to ensure that Member States (including the UK) abide by their obligations under the treaty. Under Art 1 of the treaty all 'High Contracting Parties must secure to everyone within their jurisdiction the rights and freedoms defined in the Convention'.

The Convention has several effects on UK human rights law:

First	Second	Third
• Decisions of the European Court against the UK are binding on the UK in international law and the government is bound to alter its domestic law in compliance with that ruling (Art 46). • Note: unlike the decisions of the European Court of Justice, the decisions of the European Court of Human Rights do not have an overriding force and do not automatically overrule inconsistent domestic law.	• The rights in the Convention are given further effect by the Human Rights Act 1998, which allows domestic courts to apply Convention principles and case law to interpret and apply legislation in compliance with such rights (see ss 2 and 3 HRA).	• The UK Parliament, although strictly sovereign, will attempt to legislate in line with the Convention. • See Police and Criminal Evidence Act 1984, Gender Recognition Act 2004 and Regulation of Investigatory Powers Act 2000.

The European Convention Rights

The rights guaranteed are contained in s 1 of the Convention, in Arts 2–14 and a number of optional protocols. Many of these rights are also now contained in s 1 of the Human Rights Act 1998.

Rights include:

Article 2	❖ The right to life: everyone's right to life shall be protected by law
Article 3	❖ Prohibition of torture and inhuman and degrading treatment and punishment
Article 4	❖ Prohibition of slavery and forced labour
Article 5	❖ Liberty and security of the person
Article 6	❖ The right to a fair and public hearing

Article 7	❖ Prohibition of retrospective criminal law and penalties
Article 8	❖ Right to private and family life, home and correspondence
Article 9	❖ Freedom of thought, conscience and religion
Article 10	❖ Freedom of expression
Article 11	❖ Freedom of assembly and association
Article 12	❖ The right to marry
Article 1 of the First Protocol	❖ The right to property
Article 2 of the First Protocol	❖ The right to education
Article 3 of the First Protocol	❖ The right to free elections

In addition Art 13 provides that everyone whose Convention rights are violated shall have an effective remedy before a national authority; and Art 14 provides that the enjoyment of such rights shall be secured without discrimination on any ground such as sex, race, colour, or other status.

The Human Rights Act 1998

We will consider the above Act under the following headings.

Introduction to the Act — Liability of public authorities — Doctrine of proportionality — s 2 HRA — s 3 HRA — s 4 HRA

Introduction

The Human Rights Act 1998 allowed domestic courts to apply Convention principles and case law directly, reducing the need for citizens to seek the assistance of the European Court. In brief, the Act gives effect to the rights contained in Part 1 of the European Convention (s 1) and makes it unlawful for public authorities to violate Convention rights (s 6). The Act then allows 'victims' to rely on Convention rights in domestic proceedings and for the courts to award just satisfaction (ss 7–9). Note that under s 11 an individual is still entitled to petition the European Court of Human Rights.

The Act generally only applies to acts or decisions of public authorities taking place after the coming into operation of the Act (*R v Lambert, Ali and Jordan* (2001)); violations taking place before are subject to the traditional method of protection (*Secretary of State for the Home Department v Wainwright* (2003)).

The Convention rights guaranteed under the Act are those listed above, with the exception of Arts 1 and 13 (duty to secure rights and effective remedies). Section 14 of the Act allows derogations to be made in times of emergency.

Liability of public authorities under the Act

As highlighted above, an essential aspect of the rule of law is the control of arbitrary government power and the government's observance of human rights.

Section 6 of the Act provides that it is unlawful for a **public authority** to act in a way that is inconsistent with a Convention right.

'Public authority' includes a court or tribunal, but does not include either of the Houses of Parliament (s 6(3)). It also includes any person certain whose functions are functions of a public nature (s 6(3)(b)). The Act thus makes a distinction between public authorities and private bodies or individuals, the Act only applying, directly, to public authorities (contrast *Heather, Ward and Callin v Leonard Cheshire Foundation* (2002) with *Poplar Housing and Regeneration Community Association Ltd v Donoghue* (2001) and *Parochial Church Council of the Parish of Aston Cantlow and others v Wallbank* (2003).

The doctrine of proportionality

The Act allows the domestic courts to use the doctrine of proportionality when adjudicating on human rights disputes, ensuring that any interference with Convention rights meets a pressing social need and is proportionate. This contrasts with the traditional approach of the courts, which was to challenge a decision only if it was irrational (*Wednesbury* unreasonableness). See Lord Steyn in *R v Secretary of State for the Home Department, ex parte Daly* (2001).

Case precedent – *A and others v Secretary of State for the Home Department* (2004)

The question was whether the detention of foreign nationals suspected of terrorism under s 21 of the Anti-Terrorism, Crime and Security Act 2001 was compatible with liberty of the person (Art 5) and the government's power of derogation under Art 15. The House of Lords held that the provisions were disproportionate to the threat of terrorism and discriminatory.

Lord Bingham noted that the traditional *Wednesbury* approach was no longer appropriate and the domestic courts had to form a judgment whether a Convention right was breached.

Note: the decision was upheld by the European Court of Human Rights in *A v United Kingdom* (2009).

Section 2 **HRA 1998**: use of Convention case law by the domestic courts

Section 2 of the Act provides that when a court is determining a question involving any Convention right, it must take into account any judgment, decision, declaratory or advisory opinion of the European Court of Human Rights, so far as it is relevant to the proceedings.

Note, s 2 does not insist that the courts have to *apply* such decisions, merely 'take them into account'.

The domestic courts will generally follow European Court case law where the European jurisprudence is clear and would involve domestic law being inconsistent with the Convention.

> ### Case precedent – *R v Secretary of State for the Home Department, ex parte Taylor and Anderson* (2001)
>
> The Court of Appeal held that it would be improper for the domestic courts to decide a case in a way that was contrary to the application currently being applied by the European Court of Human Rights.
>
> The question was whether the Home Secretary should set sentences for mandatory life sentence prisoners. This used to be allowed by the European Court of Human Rights (*Wynne v United Kingdom* (1995)), but the European Court later overruled that case (*Stafford v United Kingdom* (2002)), and so the House of Lords declared the powers incompatible with **Art 6**.

However, the courts may choose to follow binding domestic law, where the European Court has not ruled directly on the legal issue.

> ### Case precedent – *Re P and others* (2008)
>
> In *Re P and others* (2008), the House of Lords held that where the European Court has not laid down a definitive interpretation of the article's application the domestic courts were not bound to follow those decisions, and could give their own interpretation to them.

Section 3 HRA 1998: interpreting statutory provisions in the light of the Convention

Section 3 of the Act states that so far as it is possible to do so, primary legislation and subordinate legislation must be read and given effect in a way which is compatible with Convention rights. This covers legislation passed before or after the Act.

> This is an important point because our constitution and legal system is based on the supremacy of Parliament – that it can make such law as it chooses – and we will deal with this issue again in relation to sources of law

Parliamentary sovereignty is preserved – the courts have no power to set aside an Act of Parliament and must follow it when it is not possible to interpret its compatibly with Convention rights – s 3(2).

Section 3 should preserve the distinction between radical interpretation of statutes and judicial legislation.

> ### Case precedent – *R v A (Complainant's sexual history)* (2001)
>
> The House of Lords held that s 3 applied even where there was no ambiguity and that the court must strive to find a possible interpretation compatible with Convention rights. Section 3 required the courts to proceed on the basis that the legislature would not, if alerted to the problem, have wished to deny the right to an accused to put forward a full and complete defence.

However, the provision does not allow the courts to read words into a statute that are clearly not there, or involve itself in judicial legislation (*Poplar Housing and Regeneration Community Association Ltd v Donoghue* (2001)); *Re W and B (Children: Care Plan); In Re W (Child: Care Plan)* (2002)

In appropriate cases the domestic courts will leave necessary legislative changes to Parliament. For example, in *Bellinger v Bellinger* (2003) the House of Lords refused to interpret the words 'man and woman' to include a person who had undergone gender reassignment, leaving it to Parliament to make such radical changes to family law: Parliament subsequently passed the Gender Recognition Act 2004.

Section 4 HRA 1998: declarations of incompatibility

Section 4(2) of the Act provides that if a court is satisfied that the provision of primary legislation is incompatible with a Convention right, it may make a declaration of incompatibility.

This is another important point as the Act allows the courts to question, but not strike down, clear legislation which is contrary to Convention rights. We will revisit it when we deal with statutory interpretation. Demonstrating an understanding of this will attract more marks, particularly in relation to a question on statutory interpretation.

Further, s 4(4) states that If a court is satisfied that the provision of secondary legislation is incompatible with a Convention right **and that the primary legislation concerned prevents removal of the incompatibility** it may make a declaration of incompatibility. Thus, s 4 of the Act allows courts to declare both primary and secondary legislation incompatible with Convention rights of the European Convention.

See the diagram below.

The Declaration of Incompatibility process

Last resort: this provision will be used once the court has failed to use its interpretation powers, under s 3, to achieve compatibility

↓

Parliamentary sovereignty is preserved and courts are not allowed to strike down clear parliamentary legislation even if it is incompatible with Convention rights or case law (see Bellinger, above). It will be expected that offending legislation will be amended so as to comply with the government's obligations under the Convention

↓

Incompatible legislation continues with respect to validity, continuing operation and enforcement despite the declaration (s 4(6))

↓

Issuing courts: s 4 restricts the power to issue such declarations to courts including the High Court and above

↓

Amendment of legislation: Incompatible legislation can be addressed and amended by Parliament, and s 10 of the Act allows for a fast-track procedure to allow this

↓

Statement in Parliament: under s 19(1) a Minister of the Crown in charge of a Bill in either House must, before the Second Reading of the Bill, make a statement of either compatibility or incompatibility

↓

Pre-1998 legislation: declarations cannot be granted in respect of any breach of Convention rights caused by the legislation taking place before the Act came into operation (*Wilson v First County Trust Ltd (No 2) (2003)*)

↓

Relevance of legislation: a declaration will not be granted where the relevant legislation is not likely to affect any particular 'victim' (*R v Attorney-General, ex parte Rusbridger and another (2003)*)

Since the Act came into force there have been a number of declarations of incompatibility made by the domestic courts:

❖ *Bellinger v Bellinger* (2003) – the House of Lords held that the refusal of domestic law to recognise a marriage celebrated between a man and a transsexual who had been born a male was contrary to Arts 8 and 12 (private life and the right to marry), following the decision of the European Court of Human Rights in *Goodwin v United Kingdom* (2002).

❖ *A and others v Secretary of State for the Home Department* (2004) above – detention without trial of foreign terrorist suspects incompatible with Arts 5 and 15.

However, the court will refuse to interfere where it believes that the legislation is within the margin of appreciation allowed by the Convention and the case law of the European Court:

❖ *R v DPP, ex parte Pretty and another* (2001) – s 2(1) of the Suicide Act 1961 making unlawful any assistance in taking a person's life was not incompatible with the European Convention, as any interference with those rights was necessary and proportionate (The decision was upheld by the European Court of Human Rights: *Pretty v United Kingdom* (2002).)

Aim Higher

Ensure you have a solid understanding of the **Human Rights Act 1998**: why it was passed; its central provisions and case law, the legal and constitutional problems that it has caused; its relationship with the common law and parliamentary sovereignty.

Core issues checklist

The most important theorist is A V Dicey. He believed everyone should be subject to the law and all disputes should be resolved within the law.	✔
Human Rights can be protected via the common law.	✔
The European Convention on Human Rights helps to protect individual human rights.	✔
The Convention includes certain rights, e.g. right to life, right to private and family life	✔
The Human Rights Act 1998 allows our domestic courts (see your introductory chapter) to apply Convention principles.	✔
The Act allows domestic courts to apply the doctrine of proportionality.	✔

Up for Debate

Do you think that the **Human Rights Act 1998** achieves the right balance between upholding the rule of law and individual rights on the one hand, and respecting the will of parliament and the power of government on the other?

Useful websites

Topic	Website
The Council of Europe	http://hub.coe.int
The Equality and Human Rights Commission	www.equalityhumanrights.com
European Court of Human Rights	www.echr.coe.int

Putting it into practice – example essay question

'It is the function of the courts to uphold the rule of law and to secure fundamental human rights.'

Analyse this statement and state whether you agree that the passing of the Human Rights Act 1998 has allowed the domestic courts to carry out that role more effectively.

Answer plan

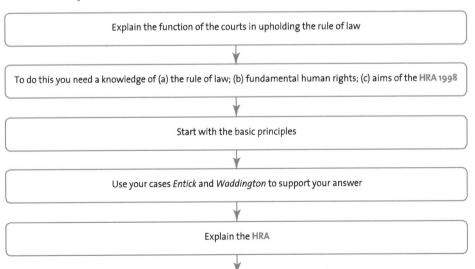

Explain the function of the courts in upholding the rule of law

To do this you need a knowledge of (a) the rule of law; (b) fundamental human rights; (c) aims of the HRA 1998

Start with the basic principles

Use your cases *Entick* and *Waddington* to support your answer

Explain the HRA

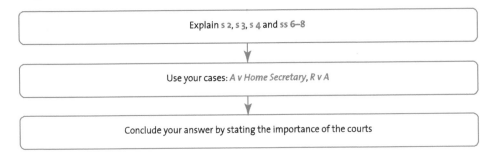

Explain s 2, s 3, s 4 and ss 6–8

Use your cases: *A v Home Secretary, R v A*

Conclude your answer by stating the importance of the courts

Outline answer

The question is asking you to explain the central function of the courts in upholding the rule of law and, in particular, in safeguarding and securing individual liberty and fundamental rights. It will require a knowledge and understanding of the basic concepts of the rule of law, fundamental human rights and liberty and the provisions and aims of the Human Rights Act 1998.

* Begin by identifying the basic concepts and principles of the rule of law – its independence from government, requirements of equality, clarity, openness and procedural fairness, etc.
* Analyse and explain the importance of the independence and impartiality of judges in upholding the above principles and give examples where the courts have controlled executive power and safeguarded individual liberty by developing the common law (*Entick v Carrington*) or by interpreting statues (*Waddington v Miah*).
* Explain the central provisions of the Human Rights Act 1998, why it was passed, and how it was intended to enhance the protection of human rights in the UK.
* Identify provisions of the Act which allow the courts increased powers to uphold human rights and to control governmental power (s 2, power to use proportionality; s 3, increased powers of interpretation; s 4 declarations of incompatibility; ss 6–8 to hold public authorities to account).
* Provide case examples where these powers have been used by the courts (*A v Home Secretary; R v A; Ghaidan v Mendoza*).
* Conclude on the importance of the courts in upholding the rule of law and human rights, and the impact of the Human Rights Act in that respect.

Table of key cases referred to in this chapter

Case name	Area of law	Principle
A and others v Secretary of State for the Home Department [2004] UKHL 56	Application of the principles of proportionality in emergency situations	Duty of courts to carefully scrutinise interferences with individual liberty even in the context of terrorism

R (Countryside Alliance) v Attorney General	Whether the Hunting Act was incompatible with any convention rights (s 4 HRA)	Due respect shown by the courts to parliamentary decisions and legislation
R v A (Complainant's sexual history)	'Possible' interpretations of domestic legislation to ensure compatibility (s 3 HRA)	Statutory duty on courts to achieve compatibility wherever possible so as to achieve the objectives of the 1998 Act
R v Secretary of State for the Home Department, ex parte Daly [2001] UKHL 26	s 2 HRA - Application of *Wednesbury* and Proportionality principles	More intense review of decision-making under the Human Rights Act 1998
R v Secretary of State for the Home Department, ex parte Taylor and Anderson citation	Duty to take into account decisions of the European Court of Human Rights (s 2 HRA)	General practice of following the most recent jurisprudence of the European Court
Re P and others [2008] UKHL 38	Whether Convention rights can be expanded by domestic courts	Right of domestic courts to expand such rights where European Court case law does not preclude it

---

@ **Visit the book's companion website to test your knowledge**

❖ Resources include a subject map, revision tip podcasts, downloadable diagrams, MCQ quizzes for each chapter, and a flashcard glossary

❖ www.routledge.com/cw/optimizelawrevision

3

Sources of Law I – Legislation, EU Law and Statutory Interpretation

Revision objectives

Understand the law
- Can you identify the different sources of law in the English legal system?
- Are you able to identify the most significant sources of law?

Remember the details
- Can you explain the different types of legislation and the way in which they come into force?
- Can you give appropriate illustrations to support your work?

Reflect critically on areas of debate
- Can you critically appraise the different types of legislation and the different legislative processess?
- Are you able to support your reflections by reference to academic opinion?

Contextualise
- Do you understand the relationship between the different types of legislation?
- Do you undertand the relationship and interplay between legislative sources of law and other sources of law?

Apply your skills and knowledge
- Are you able to structure an answer to the 'Putting it into Practice' question?

Chapter Map

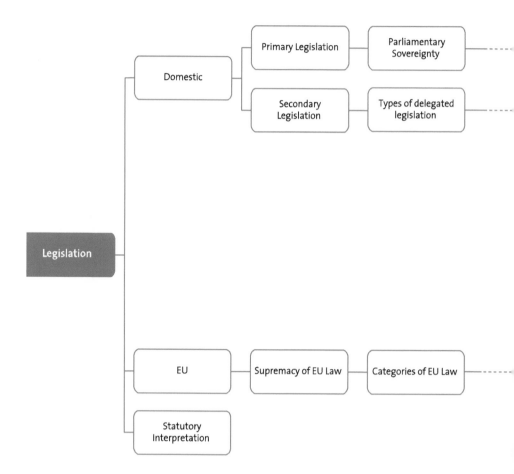

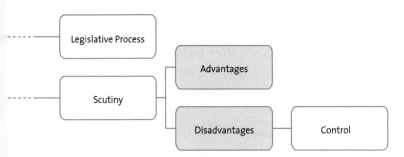

Legislative Process

Scutiny

Advantages

Disadvantages

Control

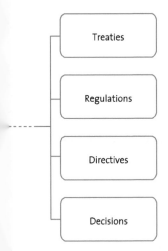

Treaties

Regulations

Directives

Decisions

Introduction

In this chapter and the following one, we are going to consider the different sources of law in the English legal system. This is a particularly popular area with examiners and, in order to perform well, students must demonstrate an understanding not only of the different sources of law, but of relationship and interplay between them.

The English legal system is a common law system and as such our body of law consists of the following:

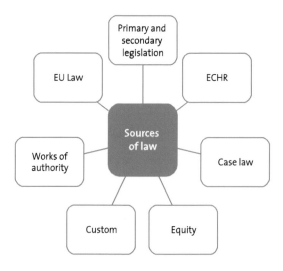

In this first chapter on sources of law will focus on domestic and European legislation. We will examine the following areas:

Legislation in the English Legal System

In a common law system the decisions of the superior courts are an important source of law. However, the main source of law in the English legal system, is legislation.

Key term: legislation

❖ Legislation is an umbrella term. It is most frequently used to describe the following:
❖ Acts of Parliament
  ❖ Statutes
  ❖ Secondary legislation, or delegated legislation. This is legislation that is created under the authority of a Parent Act or Enabling Act.
❖ It is worth noting that textbooks and your lecturers will use these terms interchangeably.

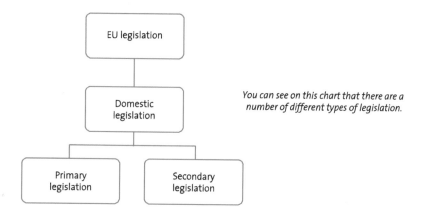

You can see on this chart that there are a number of different types of legislation.

In the next section we will consider primary domestic legislation. Before we do, we need to explore a key concept in the English legal system and the doctrine of Parliamentary Sovereignty.

Parliamentary Sovereignty

Parliament is the supreme law-making body in the English legal system. This means that Parliament has the power to enact, revoke or amend any law it wants.

Parliament cannot however, bind its successors. This means that no Parliament can enact a law that cannot be revoked or amended by Parliament in the future.

Statutes or Acts of Parliament are supreme; they override all existing common law provisions. The courts are subordinate to the legislature (Parliament). In the event of conflict between an Act of Parliament and case law, the Act of Parliament prevails.

Primary legislation

The origins of legislation

The government in the English legal system is responsible for generating, and enacting, most legislation that becomes law. It is possible, however, for individual Members of Parliament to propose legislation. This can happen in one of three ways:

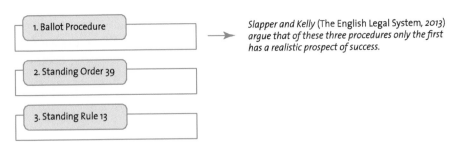

1. Ballot Procedure

2. Standing Order 39

3. Standing Rule 13

Slapper and Kelly (The English Legal System, 2013) argue that of these three procedures only the first has a realistic prospect of success.

All statutes begin life as a Bill. A Bill may start life as a government consultation paper. There are two types of government consultation papers that you will need to be aware of these are:

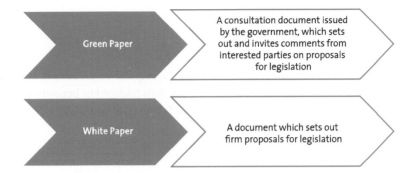

The following two Cabinet committees determine which Bills will be placed before Parliament in any parliamentary session:

1. **The Future Legislation Committee**
2. **The Legislation Committee**

In order for a Bill to become an Act of Parliament it must be debated in the House of Commons and the House of Lords. It must then receive Royal Assent.

What or who is Parliament?

Parliament consists of three distinct elements:

A Bill must be given three readings in both the House of Commons and the House of Lords before it can be presented for Royal Assent.

When a Bill receives Royal Assent it becomes an Act of Parliament and comes into force on that day, unless the Act has a different commencement date.

With the exception of Money Bills, which must commence proceedings in the House of Commons, the legislative process can commence in either the House of Commons, or the House of Lords.

You can see from the following diagram that once a Bill has passed to the House of Lords it has:

❖ A first reading
❖ A second reading

* A committee stage
* A report stage
* A third reading

What should be evident at this juncture is that the legislative process is a lengthy one. It is also a process that is time bound. If a Bill is to succeed in becoming an Act of Parliament, it must, in most cases, pass through these various stages during one parliamentary session.

The passage of a Bill commencing in the House of Commons

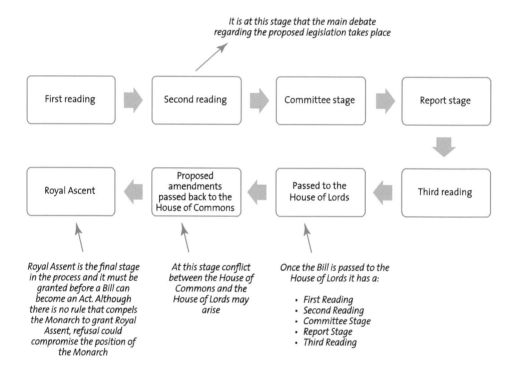

It is at this stage that the main debate regarding the proposed legislation takes place

First reading → Second reading → Committee stage → Report stage

Royal Ascent ← Proposed amendments passed back to the House of Commons ← Passed to the House of Lords ← Third reading

Royal Assent is the final stage in the process and it must be granted before a Bill can become an Act. Although there is no rule that compels the Monarch to grant Royal Assent, refusal could compromise the position of the Monarch

At this stage conflict between the House of Commons and the House of Lords may arise

Once the Bill is passed to the House of Lords it has a:

* *First Reading*
* *Second Reading*
* *Committee Stage*
* *Report Stage*
* *Third Reading*

Resolving conflict

The legislative process requires that a Bill passes through, and is approved by, both Houses of Parliament. This presents a potential conundrum: what if the two Houses cannot agree on the content of a Bill, or proposed amendments? The Bill could in theory be passed back and forth between the two Houses with no resolution or agreement.

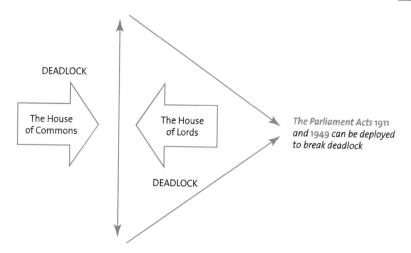

The House of Commons is a democratically elected chamber and as such this chamber has greater power and arguably legitimacy. In 1911 the Parliament Act was introduced with the aim of reducing the House of Lords' power to veto a Bill. It also reduced the power that the House of Lords has to delay a Bill by up to two years. This ability was further reduced to one year by the Parliament Act 1949.

The delaying powers of the House of Lords can therefore be summarised as follows:

Money Bills	After a one-month delay by the House of Lords these Bills can be enacted without the approval of the House of Lords.
Other Bills	Other Bills can be delayed by the House of Lords for only one year.

Once the House of Lords has rejected a Bill twice the House of Commons can use the Parliament Acts to 'force' a Bill through. If this happens the Bill will simply require the approval of the Monarch.

In reality the House of Commons has used the Parliament Acts sparingly to force through legislation. Only a handful of statutes have been passed using The Parliament Acts. If you are answering an assessment question on the legislative process, make sure that you can provide one or two illustrations of statutes that have been enacted using the Parliament Acts. We have given you some examples in the diagram on the following page.

Examples of legislation passed using the **Parliament Acts 1911** and **1949**

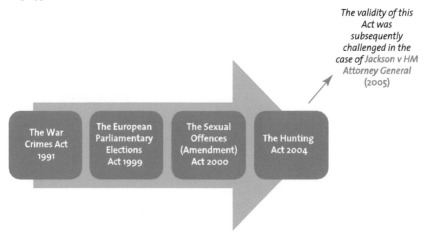

The validity of this Act was subsequently challenged in the case of Jackson v HM Attorney General (2005)

The War Crimes Act 1991

The European Parliamentary Elections Act 1999

The Sexual Offences (Amendment) Act 2000

The Hunting Act 2004

Case precedent– *Jackson v HM Attorney General* [2005] 3 WLR 733

Facts: the appellants in this case claimed that the 1949 Parliament Act was invalid. They argued that as the 2004 Hunting Act had been passed using the 1949 Parliament Act, the 2004 Hunting Act must by association be invalid also.

Principle: the appellants were unsuccessful in their challenge; the Parliament Act 1949 was valid, and so too was the Hunting Act 2004.

Application: this case can be used in an assessment as an illustration of a recent challenge to the validity of the Parliament Acts following the enactment of the Hunting Act 2004.

Categorising legislation

As is frequently the case, there are several different ways of classifying legislation, e.g. by subject matter.

Public Acts (Public Bills and Private Members Bills)	These Acts concern matters that affect the general public.
Private Acts	These Acts concern the interests of particular individuals or institutions.
Enabling Legislation	Enabling legislation is legislation that enables a particular person, or body to define the detail of implementation with the aim of achieving the purpose stated in the Parent Act.

Common Pitfall

When using the word Act you must remember in the context of legislation the word ALWAYS has a capital A. For a law student to get this wrong is a silly and careless mistake. If an examiner has to correct this mistake repeatedly through your work, it does not create a good impression.

Another way of classifying Acts of Parliament is according to the function that they perform:

Consolidating legislation	Consolidating legislation brings together provisions from a number of different Acts. Consolidating legislation does not make changes to the content of those provisions.
Codifying legislation	Codifying legislation brings together provisions in different Acts and gives effect to common law rules – putting the common law on a statutory footing.
Amending legislation	Amending legislation as the name suggests makes alterations to existing legal provisions.

Harmonising legislation with EU Law: section 19 of the Human Rights Act 1998

Following the enactment of the Human Rights Act (HRA) 1998:

❖ Ministers with responsibility for specific Bills must issue a declaration of compatibility with the European Convention on Human Rights. You will find more detail on this point in Chapter 2.
❖ If they cannot issue a declaration of compatibility they must make a statement to Parliament acknowledging incompatibility with the European Convention on Human Rights but stating that the Government nonetheless intends to proceed despite incompatibility.

Remember that Parliament is supreme and under the doctrine of parliamentary sovereignty it can enact any legislation it wishes, even if it is incompatible with the European Convention on Human Rights.

Secondary legislation

**Key Term:
secondary
legislation**

❖ Secondary legislation is another broad umbrella term. Secondary legislation is legislation that is created under the authority of a Parent Act or Enabling Act by a body other than Parliament.
❖ The following terms are used interchangeably:
  ❖ Secondary legislation
  ❖ Delegated legislation
  ❖ Subordinate legislation.
❖ It is important that you are familiar with interchangeable terms, as this will help you identify assessment questions accurately and reduce the chances of misinterpreting the focus of a question.

Secondary legislation is made by a person or body that Parliament has delegated power to. This form of legislation has the same legislative force as primary legislation. The power to legislate, and the extent of that power, is conferred by an Enabling Act, which is sometimes referred to as the Parent Act.

The significance of secondary legislation

Secondary legislation is particularly important in the modern English legal system, because the volume of delegated legislation far exceeds the production of primary legislation by Parliament. There are several thousand pieces of secondary legislation enacted each year.

There are a number of different types of delegated legislation, each of which has its own strengths and weaknesses.

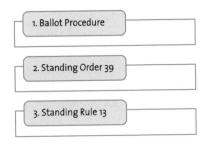

1. Ballot Procedure

2. Standing Order 39

3. Standing Rule 13

1. *Orders in Council: are made by the Legislative Committee of the Privy Council and are used in emergency situations to bring legislation in quickly.*

2. *Statutory Instruments: are created under the power of an enabling Act, which provides the broad framework for the delegated legislation, a minister or government department is given the power to bring in legislation.*

3. *Bylaws: these are made by local authorities, public and nationalised bodies.*

Advantages of delegated legislation

❖ Time saving
❖ Speed
❖ Utilising particular expertise or particular local knowledge
❖ Flexibility

Disadvantages of delegated legislation

- ❖ Accountability
- ❖ Undemocratic
- ❖ Scrutiny
- ❖ Bulk
- ❖ Sub-delegation

Control over delegated legislation

Common Pitfall

Students answering questions on delegated legislation frequently remember to consider the advantages and disadvantages of delegated legislation. However, they seldom address the critical issue of control over delegated legislation. Remembering to include this in your answer will 'round off' your essay well. For more marks you might want to consider how effective these controls are.

The critical question in relation to delegated legislation, is in relation to controls over it.

Parliamentary control
New delegated legislation is laid before Parliament before coming into force.

- ❖ Some provisions require **positive resolution** before they become law; that is, they must be placed before the House of Commons and the House of Lords.
- ❖ Most delegated legislation requires **negative resolution**. This is a requirement that provisions are simply laid before Parliament and if, after 40 days, a resolution to annul them is not made, then the provisions automatically become law.

Judicial control
Delegated legislation can be challenged through a process known as judicial review on the following basis:

- ❖ **Procedural *ultra vires*:** this is a claim that the procedures established by the Parent Act have not been followed.
- ❖ **Substantive *ultra vires*:** this is a claim that the person or body that Parliament delegated power to, has acted in excess of the power granted to them by Parliament. A good example of this procedure in action is the case of *HM Treasury v Mohammed Jabar Ahmed* (2010).

Delegated legislation and the **Human Rights Act 1998**
The courts cannot declare primary legislation invalid; they can, however issue a declaration of incompatibility. **This rule does not apply to delegated legislation.** The

courts can declare secondary legislation invalid on the basis that it conflicts with rights provided under the ECHR.

Aim Higher

The **Human Rights Act 1998** has considerably increased the courts power in relation to the control of delegated legislation. Following the enactment of the **HRA 1998**, the courts are able to question the validity of delegated legislation on the following two grounds:

1. Procedure
2. Compatibility with the ECHR

You will find more information in Chapter 2 in relation to the second route.

European Law

Another important source of law in the English legal system is EU law. When the UK joined the EEC in 1973 it passed the power to make legislation affecting the UK and its citizens to European institutions. The focus of this section will be how EU law impacts on the English legal system. You will study EU law in much detail later on in your course.

It is worth noting that EU law has had a particular impact on domestic law the following areas:

❖ The free movement of workers and goods
❖ Employment law – particularly discrimination and equal rights
❖ Commercial law
❖ Consumer law
❖ Environmental law

Key quote
'EU law is like an incoming tide. It flows into the estuaries and up the rivers. It cannot be held back.' Lord Denning in *HP Bulmer Ltd v J Bollinger SA (No 2)* 1974

Institutions of the EU

When examining sources of EU law it is important to be aware of the different institutions of the EU and how they are governed. Following the **Lisbon Treaty**, the following are institutions of the EU:

Institution	Role	Governed by
The Commission	The role of The Commission is to: ❖ initiate legislation ❖ represent the EU internationally ❖ enforce EU law ❖ implement policy and the EU budget.	**Articles 244–250 Treaty on the Functioning of the European Union**
The Council	The role of The European Council is to: ❖ exercise legislative functions ❖ approve the EU budget ❖ co-ordinate the economic policy of the EU ❖ develop common foreign and security polices ❖ co-ordinate the co-operation of Member States justice systems ❖ form international agreements.	**Articles 237–243 Treaty on the Functioning of the European Union**
The European Council	The role of the European Council is to: ❖ provide the Union with the necessary impetus for development ❖ define the general political guidelines.	**Articles 235–236 Treaty on the Functioning of the European Union (TFEU)** and **Article 15 Treaty on the European Union (TEU)**
The European Parliament of the European Union	The European Parliament has several functions: 1. It has a legislative function. 2. It has a supervisory role over the EU institutions. 3. It has budgetary powers.	**Articles 123–234 TFEU**
The Court of Justice of the European Union	The role of the ECJ is to: ❖ ensure that EU law and the interpretation of EU law is observed. ❖ provide a dispute resolution forum for Member States and individuals. ❖ protect individual rights.	**Articles 251–281 TFEU**
The European Central Bank	The European Central Bank has responsibility for monetary policy in the EU.	**Articles 282–284 TFEU**

Supremacy of EU Law and domestic law

In joining the EU, Parliament has effectively limited its own sovereignty in areas which are governed by EU law. Section 2(1) of the European Communities Act 1972 provides that English law should be interpreted and have effect subject to the principle that EU law is supreme.

In short, EU law takes precedence over all other sources of domestic law.

Case precedent – *Factortame Ltd v Secretary of State Transport (No. 2)* [1991]

Facts: in this case there was a claim by Spanish fishermen that provisions within the Merchant Shipping Act 1988 contravened EU law.

Principle: the ECJ held that the provisions in the Merchant Shipping Act 1988 contravened Art 52 of the **TEC**. In the event of conflict between national law and EC law, EC law is supreme.

Application: this case can be used in an assessment as authority for the proposition that where conflict between EU law and domestic law arises, EU law prevails.

This case has particular constitutional significance because it is a key statement of supremacy by the ECJ of the supremacy of EU law over national law. It illustrates that in passing the European Communities Act 1972, the UK has voluntarily agreed that EU law takes precedence over domestic law where there is conflict.

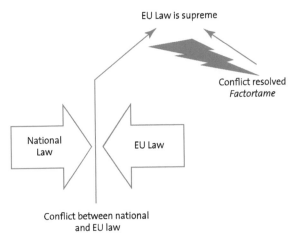

Conflict: the doctrine of Parliamentary Supremacy

The notion that EU law is supreme contravenes the principle of Parliamentary Supremacy discussed earlier in this chapter. It should, however, be noted that, in theory at least, Parliament could repeal the European Communities Act 1972 – extremely unlikely though!

Revision tip

Initially when faced with a conflict between an Act of Parliament and EU law the approach adopted by English judges was to try their best to interpret national law as in harmony with EU law, e.g. *Pickstone v Freemans plc* (1988).

This approach was simply untenable where Parliament had subsequently legislated in a way which was clearly in direct conflict with EU law. In this situation the doctrine of Parliamentary Supremacy would suggest that subsequent legislation revokes earlier EU provisions. In *Macarthys v Smith* [1979] WLR 1189 the court held that the doctrine of Parliamentary Supremacy in this situation would require the court to give effect to national law.

However, the case of *Factortame* altered this position. The principle of EU supremacy is now well established in the English legal system. See discussion above.

Aim Higher – suggested reading

The supremacy of EU law is a complicated area, particularly if you have not yet studied public/constitutional and administrative law and or EU law. For more information on this topic Chapter 8 of *Unlocking EU Law* (2011) by Storey and Turner has excellent coverage of the area. It also has a really useful suggested solution to an essay question on this topic at the end of the chapter.

If you really want to impress your lecturer with your independent research and depth of knowledge, you might want to look at the following reading suggestions:

❖ Craig P, '**The European Union Act 2011**: Locks, Limits and Legality' (2011) 48 CMLRev 1915
❖ Lanaerts K and Corthaut T, 'Of Birds and Hedges: the Role of Primacy in Invoking Norms of EU Law' (2006) 31 ELRev 287
❖ Walker N, 'The Idea of Constitutional Pluralism (2002) 65 MLR 317

Sources of EU Law

There are a number of different types of EU law, which can be identified as follows:

❖ Treaties
❖ Regulations

❖ Directives
❖ Decisions

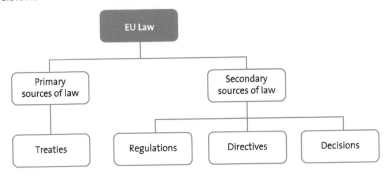

When considering the impact of EU legislation on national law it is important to draw a distinction between provisions which are **directly applicable** and those which have **direct effect**.

Key terms

Key Term: directly applicable	❖ These provisions immediately become part of the national law of Member States.

Key Term: direct effect	❖ Provisions that have direct effect create individual rights, which must be protected by the national courts of Member States
	❖ There are two types of direct effect:
	  ❖ **Vertical direct effect:** this provides rights to individuals against governments.
	  ❖ **Horizontal direct effect:** this provides rights against other individuals and organisations.
	❖ The case of *Van Gend en Loos* established that Treaties, Regulations and Directives will have direct effect only if they meet the following criteria:
	  ❖ they are clear
	  ❖ the provision is unconditional and
	  ❖ the provision requires no further legislation to implement it in Member States.

Treaties

The Treaties are the most significant source of EU law. They are a primary source of law and all subsequent law must fulfil the objectives that are laid down in the Treaties.

❖ Treaties have immediate applicability
❖ They are binding on all Member States and individuals

❖ Treaties can have vertical direct effect: *Van Gend en Loos v Nederlandse Administratie der Belastingen* (1963)
❖ Treaties can have horizontal direct effect: *Defrenne v Sabena (No 2)* (1976)

Case precedent – *Van Gend en Loos v Nederlandse Administratie der Belastingen* [1963] ECR 1

This case established that Treaty provisions can have direct effect (horizontal and vertical), if they are:

❖ unconditional
❖ clear
❖ precise and
❖ there is no discretion as to whether Members States may implement them.

Key Treaties of the EU are:

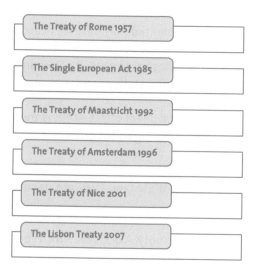

The Treaty of Rome 1957

The Single European Act 1985

The Treaty of Maastricht 1992

The Treaty of Amsterdam 1996

The Treaty of Nice 2001

The Lisbon Treaty 2007

Regulations

Regulations are a secondary source of EU law. They are defined in **Art 288** of the **Treaty on the Functioning of the European Union**:

'A regulation shall have general application. It shall be binding in its entirety and directly applicable in all Member States'.

❖ Regulations are of 'general application' or 'general applicability' – this simply means that the measures apply to all Member States.
❖ Member States are bound by the Regulation in its entirety.
❖ They are 'directly applicable or directly applicable' – the measures become law automatically in each Member State.

❖ Regulations can have vertical direct effect: *Leonesio v Italian Ministry of Agriculture Case 93/71* [1972] ECR 287, CJEC
❖ Regulations can have horizontal direct effect: *Antonio Munoz Cia SA v Frumar Ltd* Case C-253/00 [2002] ECR-I/7289, CJEC

Directives
Article 288 of the TFEU defines Directives in paragraph 3:

'A Directive shall be binding, as to the result to be achieved, upon each Member State to which it is addressed, but shall leave to the national authorities the choice of form and method.'

❖ Directives are a secondary source of EU law.
❖ Directives are aimed at Member States and have the primary aim of harmonising law in the EU.
❖ They instruct Member States to introduce their own national version of the Directive within a specific time frame.
❖ Directives are not directly applicable.
❖ Directives which are not implemented may have vertical direct effect provided that they meet the criteria laid down in *Van Gend en Loos.*
❖ An individual who has suffered loss as the result of non implementation of a directive may be entitled to sue the state, *Francovitch and Bonifaci v Italy* [1991] ECRI 5357.
❖ Directives do not have horizontal direct effect – that is they are not enforceable against individuals or organisations: *Facci Dori* [1995] All ER (EC).

Decisions
Decisions are a secondary source of EU law. They are defined in paragraph 4 of Art 288 of the TFEU.

'A decision shall be binding in its entirety. A decision which specifies those to who it is addressed shall be binding on only them.'

❖ Decisions can be directed at individuals, Member States or an organisation.
❖ They are not intended to have general effect.
❖ They are only enforceable against the individual to whom the decision is addressed.
❖ They are capable of having direct effect.

Other secondary sources of EU Law
These include:

❖ Recommendations
❖ Opinions
❖ 'Soft law': This may include Commission guidelines or notices.

The interpretation of legislation

Topic map

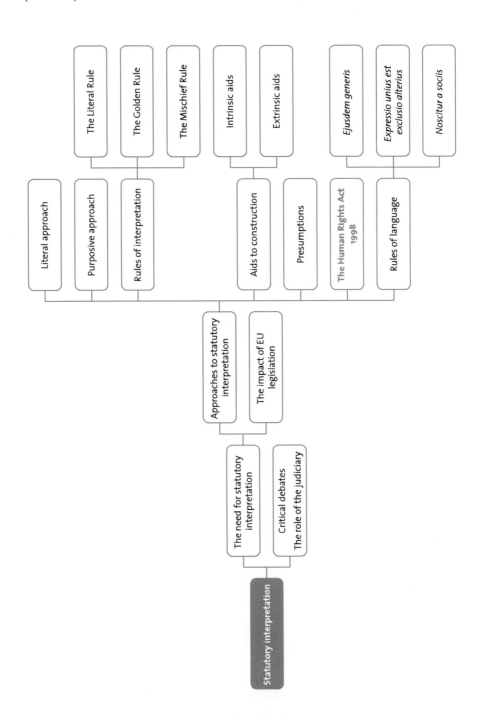

Introduction

In the previous section we considered the process by which the legislature makes law. Once law has been created, it must be applied to real situations. It is impossible for Parliament to spell out how a statute should apply in every situation. It is therefore necessary for the judiciary to interpret the framework provided by Parliament and give effect to their words.

The need for statutory interpretation

Before considering the way that judges interpret legislation, it is important to understand the range of factors that can create uncertainty as to statutory meaning. The starting position is to acknowledge the inherent limitations of language, as even plain, clear language can convey a variety of different meanings. *Bennion On Statute Law* (Longman, 1990) identifies a number of factors which can cause uncertainty as to statutory meaning.

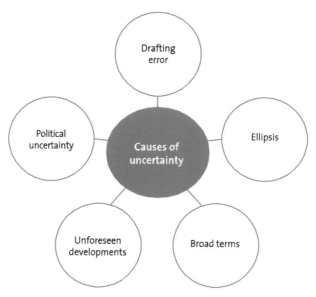

In addition to the factors identified by Bennion, uncertainty as to the interpretation of a statute can arise where:

1. Words have more than one potential meaning.
2. The meaning of a particular word has changed.
3. The meaning of a word is derived from the context in which that word is used.

Discovering the intention of Parliament

The primary objective of statutory interpretation is the courts' discovery of the 'will or intention of Parliament'. Parliament as a legislative body consists of the monarch and two chambers, each of which contains many members. Each chamber and the monarch must give their consent if a Bill is to become law. Against this backdrop the concept of a single, unified 'intention/will of Parliament' is problematic.

Key quote

'We often say that we are looking for the intention of Parliament, but that is not quite accurate. We are seeking the meaning of words, which Parliament used. We are seeking not what Parliament meant but the true meaning of what they said . . .' Lord Reid in *Black-Clawson International Ltd v Papierwerke* [1975] 1 All ER 810 at 814

Aim Higher

Cownie, Bradney and Burton, in *The English Legal System in Context* (OUP, 2010), argue that there is a significant gap between following the words of a statute and 'finding the will of Parliament'.

It is certainly worth familiarising yourself with the critical themes in statutory interpretation, if for no other reason than that it is an area that students usually neglect when dealing with this topic. Remember that supported, well-considered arguments will always attract more marks.

In circumstances where the meaning of a statute is unclear, a judge has a range of rules, aids and presumptions, which can assist with interpretation.

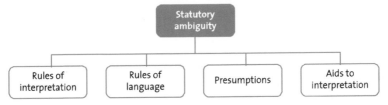

The traditional view

The doctrine of Parliamentary Sovereignty asserts a hierarchical structure, in which Parliament is positioned above the judiciary.

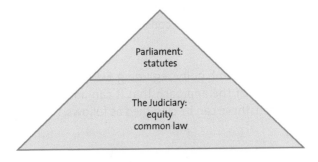

The traditional view is that the constitutional role of the judiciary is to interpret and apply the law; it is for Parliament to make law. This view, as we will see, is over-simplistic. The truth of the matter is that there is scope in the English legal system for:

* judicial creativity; and
* judicial discretion (we will address some of these issues in more detail in Chapter 4 when we consider the doctrine of precedent).

There are two primary concerns with the notion of judicial creativity and the excise of judicial discretion. They are:

1. Members of the judiciary are not democratically elected and accountable. As such, they should not be making law.
2. The discretion judges have when interpreting statutes may reflect their own personal beliefs and prejudices, subverting the wishes of Parliament (who are democratically elected).

Approaches to statutory interpretation

There are two contrasting views with respect to how judges should go about determining the meaning of a statute.

The literal approach	* Judges should look at the words of the legislation in order to determine meaning.

The purposive approach	* This approach is typical of civil law systems. * Faced with ambiguity, the judge should look beyond the words of the statute. The meaning of words should be considered in accordance with the purpose of the statute.

The interpretation of EU legislation

The UK's membership of the EU has had an impact on the interpretation of legislation and it seems appropriate, while EU law is still fresh in your mind, to deal with this here, before moving on to consider the interpretation of domestic legislation.

When faced with legislative ambiguity regarding EU law, a court has a range of options available in terms of the approach that it can adopt in order to establish meaning. Broadly defined, these can be classified as follows:

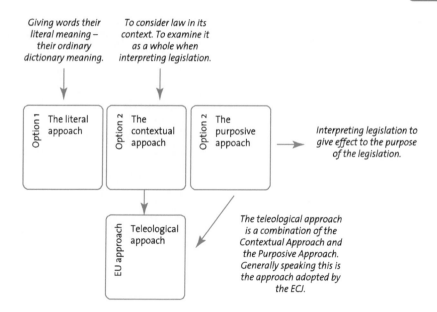

European Union legislation is drafted in the continental, civil law manner. What this means is that EU legislation sets out the general principles and leaves the fine detail of the legislation to be determined in cases, by the judiciary. The impact of this approach to legislative drafting is that the meaning of legislation can be determined only on the basis of a purposive approach. What you can see from the diagram above is that the ECJ uses a teleological approach to statutory interpretation; that is, a combination of the purposive approach and the contextual approach.

The purposive approach to the interpretation of statutes is not in keeping with the traditional literal approach adopted by judges in the English legal system. However, in order to interpret EU legislation, members of the judiciary in the UK have had to adopt a purposive approach. An illustration of this approach is seen in the case of *Pinkstone v Freemans plc* (1998). As a direct result the purposive approach is now being adopted more frequently in the context of the interpretation of domestic legislation.

The Human Rights Act 1998

The Human Rights Act 1998 requires all legislation, as far as is possible, to be construed in such a way as to be compatible with the **European Convention on Human Rights**. The impact of this requirement is that the judiciary have much wider powers of interpretation than those afforded to them by the traditional rules of interpretation: *R v A* (2001).

We will now consider the traditional rules or approaches to statutory interpretation. You need to be comfortable with these rules and understand how the application of different rules can produce very different outcomes.

Aim Higher

In terms of assessment, there are two typical ways in which a question on statutory interpretation could be posed.

1. The first is by posing a traditional essay question. Statutory interpretation may be the sole focus of the question, or it may be paired with other topics. A popular pairing is 'judicial creativity', in which the examiner is inviting a discussion regarding statutory interpretation and precedent.
2. The second popular way of examining statutory interpretation is by way of a problem-style question that requires you to interpret a real, or fictitious piece of legislation and apply the various possible interpretations to the scenario that you have been given.

The three rules of interpretation

The Literal Rule

This rule requires the judge to give the words of the statute their ordinary and natural meaning – even if the effect of the literal interpretation is to produce an unjust, or undesirable, result. *Fisher v Bell* [1960] 3 All ER 731

The Golden Rule

This rule is considered to be an extension of the Literal Rule. It is applied where an application of the Literal Rule would result in an absurdity. The Golden Rule may take one of two forms:

❖ *The narrow meaning:* this approach is adopted when a word has potentially two different meanings. The narrow approach of the Golden Rule determines that priority is given to the meaning that does not produce a manifest absurdity. *Adler v George* (1964)
❖ *The wider meaning:* this approach is adopted when there is only one possible meaning of a given word, but a literal interpretation will result in a manifest absurdity, inconsistency or inconvenience. *Re Sigsworth* (1935)

The Mischief Rule

This is the most flexible rule. It allows the court to consider the words of the statute in the context of the 'mischief' that the legislation was intended to resolve. According to *Heydon's case* (1584).

The following table illustrates some of the advantages and disadvantages of the different rules of interpretation. It is important that you understand how these rules would be applied in practice.

Rule of interpretation	Advantage	Disadvantage	Illustrations
The Literal Rule	The literal rule respects the constitutional position of the judiciary. Their role is limited to stating the law and applying the law.	An application of the literal rule may lead to an absurdity. The rule fails to account for drafting errors, ambiguous language and broad terms. The meaning of language can change over the passage of time.	*Fisher v Bell* (1960)
The Golden Rule	The court must find genuine difficulties with construction before the golden rule is applied. This rule allows for departure from the literal interpretation when the result would be a manifest absurdity.	The rule involves the judiciary attempting to determine what they consider the statute should have said in reality. How is an absurdity determined?	*Adler v George* (1964)
The Mischief Rule	This rule is the most flexible approach to statutory interpretation.	This rule does not conform to the traditional depiction of the 'constitutional role' of the judiciary. The mischief rule emphasises the scope for judicial discretion and creativity.	*Heydon's Case* (1584) *Royal College of Nursing v DHSS* (1981)

Aids to interpretation

In addition to the rules on interpretation the judiciary may also make use of aids to interpretation. As was the case with the rules of interpretation a judge has the discretion to decide which of these aids, if any, they wish to utilise. The aids to statutory construction are categorised as follows

Internal aids to interpretation

As the name suggests, internal aids to construction are derived from the statute itself. They include:

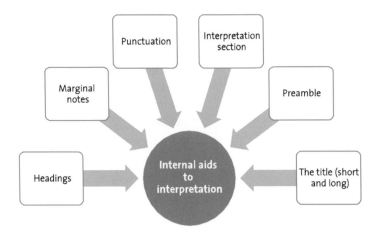

External aids to interpretation

External or extrinsic aids to interpretation are sources outside the Act itself:

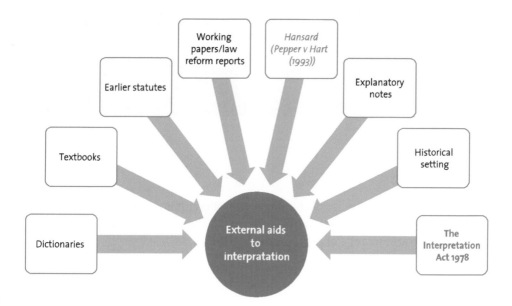

A more recent and controversial addition to the list of external aids to interpretation is the addition of Hansard (the official record of debates and proceedings held in Parliament).

Case precedent – *Pepper v Hart* (1993)

Facts: this case involved the tax liability owed by employees of a fee-paying school. The employees were entitled to send their children to the school at a greatly reduced fee. The difficulty was with calculating how this 'benefit' should be taxed. The legislation was unclear and ambiguous.

Principle: the courts can refer to Hansard as an aid to interpretation.

Application: this case illustrates a departure from the previous ban on the use of Hansard as an aid to interpretation. The use of Hansard is only permitted where:

- ❖ there is ambiguity as to the meaning of a statute; and
- ❖ there are clear statements made by the Bill's promoter or Minister.

Aim Higher

The rule in *Pepper v Hart* (1993) was extended in *Three Rivers DC v Bank of England (No 2)* (1996), to include situations in which there is no ambiguity, but where a statute may be ineffective in its intention to give effect to an EC Directive.

The use of Hansard is not without its drawbacks. A good student will be able to demonstrate a critical understanding of the arguments for and against the use of Hansard. There is good coverage of this issue in Chapter 3 of *The English Legal System 2013/14*, by Elliot and Quinn.

Presumptions

The courts may also make use of certain presumptions. It is important to remember that these presumptions may be rebutted with the use of express words. The diagram illustrates a range of presumptions.

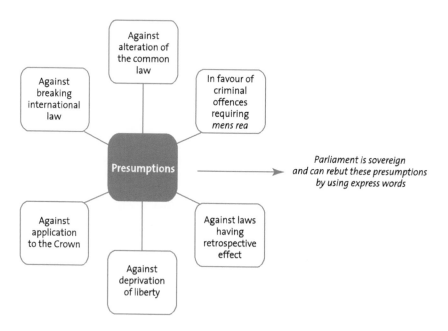

Rather than provide a very long list of explanations, we have decided to focus on four presumptions here. This is a sensible approach to adopt in your assessments. As a general rule examiners are not looking for a long list of examples but accurate detail and good use of illustrations and authority.

1. *Against alteration of the common law:* in the absence of express wording to the contrary, it will be assumed that a statute does not intend to alter the common law. When faced with alternatives, one of which alters the common law and one of which does not, the preferred interpretation will be the one that does not alter the common law.

❖ Illustration: *R (Rottman) v Commissioner of Police* (2002)

2. *Against retrospective effect:* the courts presume that statutes are not intended to be retrospective in nature. This is particularly important in the context of criminal offences and contractual agreements.

❖ Illustration: *Home Secretary v Wainwright* (2002)

3. *In favour of criminal offences requiring mens rea:* where a statute is silent with reference to *mens rea* (the mental element required in order to construct criminal liability for an offence), the presumption that Parliament did not intend to create an offence of strict liability will prevail in the absence of express words to the contrary.

❖ Illustration: *Sweet v Parsley* (1970)

4. *Against deprivation of liberty:* in the absence of express words to the contrary the courts presume that Parliament does not intend to deprive an individual of their liberty.

❖ Illustration: *R v Secretary of State for the Home Department ex p Khawaja* (1983)

Rules of language

In addition to presumptions there are a number of rules of language that can assist in constructing statutory meaning. The rules of language are as follows:

1. *Ejusdem generis:* general words should be interpreted in line with the list of previous examples.

❖ Illustration: *Powell v Kempton Park Racecourse* (1899)

2. *Expressio uniius exclusion alterius:* where a statute establishes a closed list of what is covered by the statute, anything not expressly included in the list is excluded.

❖ Illustration: *R v Inhabitants of Sedgley* (1831)

3. *Noscitur a sociis:* a word is to be construed as being similar to the other objects in the list.

❖ Illustration: *IRC v Frere* (1969)

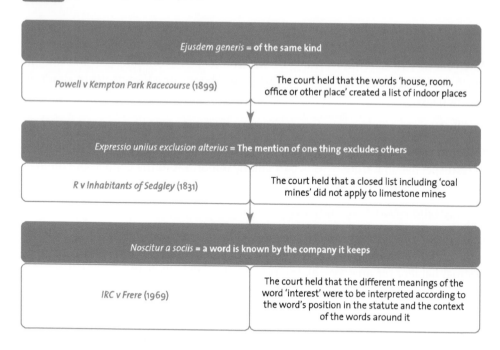

Ejusdem generis = of the same kind	
Powell v Kempton Park Racecourse (1899)	The court held that the words 'house, room, office or other place' created a list of indoor places

Expressio uniius exclusion alterius = The mention of one thing excludes others	
R v Inhabitants of Sedgley (1831)	The court held that a closed list including 'coal mines' did not apply to limestone mines

Noscitur a sociis = a word is known by the company it keeps	
IRC v Frere (1969)	The court held that the different meanings of the word 'interest' were to be interpreted according to the word's position in the statute and the context of the words around it

Core issues checklist

There are a number of different sources of law in the English legal system. EU law is now an important source of law in the ELS.	✔
Domestic legislation can be split into primary and secondary legislation.	✔
In order to become an Act of Parliament a Bill must pass through and be approved by the House of Commons and the House of Lords. It must also receive Royal Assent.	✔
Delegated legislation is made under the authority of a Parent or Enabling Act. There are a number of different types of delegated or secondary legislation. Delegated legislation is controlled in two distinct ways.	✔
Parliament is sovereign, it can enact, amend or repeal legislation as it sees fit. Parliament cannot bind its successors.	✔
There are a number of different types of EU legislation including Treaties, Regulations, Directives and Decisions.	✔
In joining the EU the UK has eroded its supremacy by passing law-making powers to wider EU institutions. It is settled law that EU law is supreme in relation to matters concerning the EU.	✔
The courts must interpret and apply legislation. There are a number of different situations that can give rise to statutory ambiguity.	✔

In attempting to discover the intention of parliament the courts use a number of different rules: the Literal Rule, the Golden Rule and the Mischief Rule. The courts also have access to a range of intrinsic and extrinsic aids to interpretation.	✔
The courts also apply a number of rules of language and presumptions in attempting to discover the intention of parliament.	✔

Useful websites

Topic	Website
Acts of Parliament	www.legislation.gov.uk
Parliament website	www.parliament.uk
Website of the EU	http://europa.eu/

Putting it into practice – example essay question

'Consider the different forms of legislation in the English legal system and how the courts go about interpreting legislation.'

Answer plan

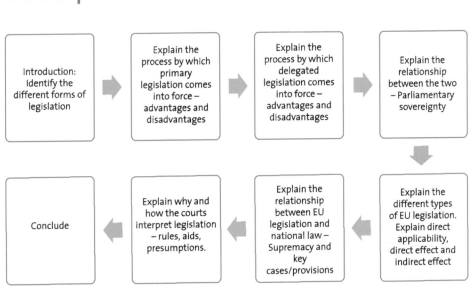

Outline answer

❖ The question is asking you to consider all of the different types of legislation in the English legal system. The key here is to remember that EU law is an important source of law and should be included in your answer.

❖ This question is effectively a two-part question. The first part considers the different types of legislation and the second part why and how legislation is interpreted by the courts.

❖ It makes sense to compartmentalise your coverage and you might want to do this under subheadings.

❖ You will need to consider primary legislation and the legislative process in particular. You should consider the Parliament Acts 1911 and 1949 and how they operate to resolve conflict or impasse between the House of Lords and the House of Commons.

❖ You could then consider delegated legislation or secondary legislation. It is important to consider the different types of secondary legislation. Where possible you should give illustrations. You can also consider the strengths and weaknesses of delegated legislation and the different controls over it.

❖ A good answer will address the significance of the Human Rights Act 1998 and issues in relation to scrutiny and democratic accountability.

❖ You should then move on to consider EU legislation and why it needs to be included in any discussion on legislative sources of law in the ELS.

❖ Make sure that you remember to deal with the meaning of direct applicability, direct effect (horizontal and vertical) and what indirect effect means.

❖ Once you have explained the different forms of EU law you need to deal with the issue of supremacy again, this time in relation to EU law and national law.

❖ The second part of the question requires you to explore how the courts interpret legislation. You will need to consider the different approaches to statutory interpretation – literal v purposive.

❖ You will need to explore the rules to interpretation giving appropriate examples where possible.

❖ You also need to consider the different rules of language and presumptions that the courts employ.

❖ It is important to consider intrinsic and extrinsic aids to interpretation.

❖ Because of the nature of the question it would be sensible to make reference to the interpretation of EU law in particular.

❖ Your conclusion could make reference to the most significant forms of legislation in terms of importance or perhaps in terms of proliferation!

Aim Higher

Process words: consider

When an essay question is asking you to 'consider' a topic, you are being asked to think carefully about the subject. You will need to provide an explanation of the area/topic and provide relevant illustrations and authorities. You will also need to consider key themes that relate to the topic that you have been asked to consider. If you are writing from a committed standpoint you will need to remember that you must support your position by reference to academic argument and opinion.

Table of key cases referred to in this chapter

Case name	Area of law	Principle
Adler v George [1994] 1 All ER 628	Rules of statutory interpretation. Illustration of the Golden Rule.	Illustration of the Golden Rule. This rule is considered an extension of the Literal Rule if it would result in an inconstancy or absurdity.
Faccini Dori v Recreb Srl (Case C-91/92) [1994] ECR I-3325	This case concerns the direct effect of Directives.	Directives do not have horizontal direct effect – that is they are not enforceable against individuals or organisations.
Factortame Ltd v Secretary of State Transport (No 2) [1991] 2 All ER 679	This case concerns the supremacy of EU law over national law.	In the event of conflict between national law and EU law, EU law is supreme.
Fisher v Bell [1961] 1 QB 394	Rules of statutory interpretation. Illustration of the Literal Rule.	Illustration of words being given their ordinary and natural meaning.
Francovitch and Bonifaci v Italy [1991] ECRI 5357	This case concerns the non-implementation of directives.	An individual who has suffered loss as the result of non-implementation may be entitled to sue the state.

Case name	Area of law	Principle
HM Treasury v Mohammed Jabar Ahmed [2010] UKSC 2	This is an illustration of a challenge to the validity of delegated legislation via judicial review.	This is an illustration of substantive *ultra vires*: a claim that the person or body that Parliament delegated power to has acted in excess of the power granted to them by Parliament.
IRC v Frere [1969] 3 WLR 1193	Rule of language, *noscitur a sociis* in statutory interpretation.	A word is known by the company it keeps.
Jackson v HM Attorney General [2005] 3 WLR 733	This case can be used as an illustration of a recent challenge to the validity of the Parliament Acts following the enactment of the Hunting Act 2004.	It is not necessary to have the consent of the House of Lords to enact a Bill. The Parliament Act 1949 was valid, thus so too was the Hunting Act 2004.
Pepper v Hart [1993] 1 All ER 42	Statutory interpretation in particular extrinsic aids to interpretation. Hansard can be referred to.	The use of Hansard is permitted only where: ❖ there is ambiguity as to the meaning of a statute; and ❖ there are clear statements made by the Bill's promoter or Minister.
Powell v Kempton Park Racecourse [1899] AC 143	Rule of language, *ejusdem generis*.	This simply means 'of the same kind'.
R v Inhabitants of Sedgley [1831] 2 B & Ad 65	Rule of language, *expressio uniius exclusio alterius* in statutory interpretation.	The mention of one thing excludes others.
Royal College of Nursing v DHSS [1981] AC 800	Rules of statutory interpretation. Illustration of the mischief rule.	Illustration of an application of the Mischief Rule. The Mischief Rule allows the court to consider the words of the statute in the context of the 'mischief' that the legislation was intended to resolve.

Three Rivers DC v Bank of England (No 2) [1996] 2 All ER 363	Extrinsic aids to interpretation. The extension of the rule in *Pepper v Hart*.	Hansard can now be referred to in situations in where there is no ambiguity, but where a statute may be ineffective in its intention to give effect to an EU Directive.
Van Gend en Loos v Nederlandse Administratie der Belastingen [1963] CLR 105	This case concerns the direct effect of EU law.	This case established that Treaty provisions can have direct effect (horizontal and vertical), if they are: ❖ unconditional; ❖ clear; ❖ precise; and ❖ there is no discretion as to whether Members States may implement them.

@ **Visit the book's companion website to test your knowledge**

❖ Resources include a subject map, revision tip podcasts, downloadable diagrams, MCQ quizzes for each chapter, and a flashcard glossary

❖ www.routledge.com/cw/optimizelawrevision

4

Sources of Law II – The Common Law, Equity and Judicial Precedent

Revision objectives

Understand the law
- Do you understand the development of the common law, and the development of equity?
- Do you understand how the doctrine of precedent operates?

Remember the details
- Can you remember the origins of the different sources of law and how they relate to the sources of law in the previous chapter?

Reflect critically on the law
- Can you reflect critically on the different sources of law discussed in this chapter?

Contextualise the law
- Are you able to explain the relationship between the different sources of law in this chapter?

Apply your skills and knowledge
- Can you apply your knowledge, using relevant examples to complete the 'Putting it into practice' questions at the end of each section?

Equity
Topic Map

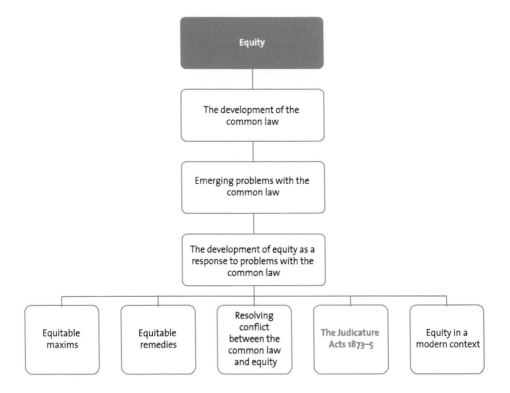

Introduction

In this chapter we are going to continue our consideration of the different sources of law in the English legal system. This chapter will be separated into several different sections. It is important to remember that an examiner could ask a general question about sources of law and/or ask a question on a specific source of law.

We will consider the following topics in this chapter:

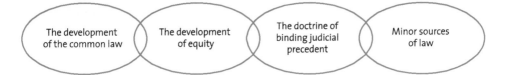

| The development of the common law | The development of equity | The doctrine of binding judicial precedent | Minor sources of law |

The common law and equity

We have created separate learning objectives for the different sections of this chapter, given the popularity of these topics with examiners.

Understand the law
- Can you explain the different meanings of the term 'the common law'?
- Can you explain the historical development of the common law?
- Can you explain the development of equity?

Remember the details
- Can you remember and explain the issues that gave rise to the development of equity?
- Can you explain a selection of maxims of equity, giving relevant case examples to illustrate your answer?

Reflect critically on areas of debate
- Can you reflect on the way in which conflict between the common law and equity was resolved?
- Can you reflect on the significance of equity and equitable remedies in the modern legal system?

Contextualise
- Can you explain the significance of the Judicature Acts 1873–75?

Apply your skills and knowledge

- Can you apply your knowledge using relevant authorities and illustrations to answer the 'Putting it into practice' question?

Putting it into practice – example essay question

'Using examples and authority, discuss critically the development of equity in the English legal system.'

An outline answer is available at the end of this section.

Introduction

As discussed in the last chapter, the English legal system is a common law system and as such judicial decision-making plays a significant role in the development and refinement of the law.

It is worth noting that the term 'common law' has several different meanings, so it is important that you look at the context in which the term is being used, in order to determine the correct meaning. This is particularly important in the context of an examination, or assessment question, where adopting the wrong meaning could cost you valuable marks.

The common law

The diagram bellow illustrates some of the most common meanings of the term the 'common law'. It is only through reading 'around' a subject that you will become comfortable with these various and interchangeable meanings.

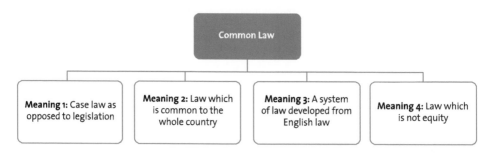

Common Law

| Meaning 1: Case law as opposed to legislation | Meaning 2: Law which is common to the whole country | Meaning 3: A system of law developed from English law | Meaning 4: Law which is not equity |

The development of the common law

Prior to the Norman Conquest in 1066 there was no unified legal system in England and Wales. Different regions had different practices, which were influenced by local customs and conventions. Law enforcement was the responsibility of regional Lords and Sheriffs. There was no recognisable central government at this time.

When William the Conqueror came to the throne following the Battle of Hastings, he sought to establish a single, unified legal system and a centralised government. He achieved this unification by travelling throughout the country with his itinerant justices, to hear disputes and administer justice. These travelling courts were called the *Curia Regis*. The King and his itinerant justices carefully selected laws and customs from different areas of the country and began to apply them consistently throughout the realm. In historical terms this is the origin of the 'common law system': a legal system which is 'common' to the country as a whole (**Meaning 2,** on the diagram above).

Difficulties with the common law
As the common law was gradually developed it slowly became more and more rigid until eventually its development stalled. The factors that caused this rigidity are outlined below:

1. The restrictive operation of the doctrine of stare decisis
The early common law operated on the basis of a restrictive form of *stare decisis* (see the section on 'The Doctrine of Binding Judicial Precedent' below). This strict form of precedent meant that judges were bound to follow decisions made in earlier cases. There were inadequate mechanisms available to avoid 'bad' decisions, and as a consequence the law became stale and inflexible.

> Note: demonstrating an understanding of the difficulties that emerged as the common law matured is very important. Make sure you remember to give specific details of the issues as outlined here.

2. A lack of appropriate remedies
The only available remedy at the time was damages (which is simply another way of saying monetary compensation). While this remedy was certainly appropriate in many cases, there were cases in which the award of damages was an inappropriate remedy.

3. The operation of the writ system
The common law operated a writ system, in which a party wanting to start legal proceedings against another, would have to select the right writ to commence proceedings. The Provisions of Oxford in 1258 limited the creation of new writs, and the existing writs were highly prescriptive. Many litigants found that their particular problem or issue did not fit neatly within the confines of the defined writs; as a result many were left without a cause of action.

Remedying the defects: the development of equity

As a result of these defects and other inefficiencies in the common law system, many individuals were left without adequate means of redress. Individuals began to petition the King as the 'fountain of justice', requesting the resolution of their unique dispute. As the number of petitions increased the King delegated the responsibility of hearing these disputes to the Lord Chancellor, who was free to determine individual cases without recourse to the common law, or the doctrine of *stare decisis*. Cases were decided on their merits with a view to achieving justice where the common law had failed. Notions of equity and fairness prevailed in the Courts of Chancery.

A body of distinct rules began to emerge from the Courts of Chancery, known as the 'rules of equity'. The courts of equity also developed a number of innovative remedies; know as 'equitable remedies'.

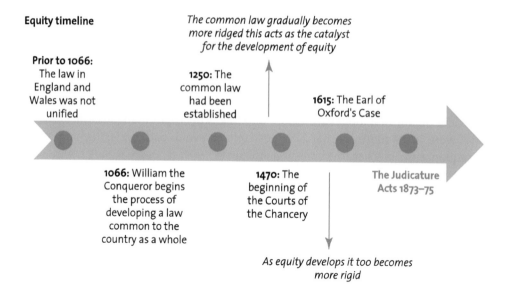

Equity timeline

The common law gradually becomes more ridged this acts as the catalyst for the development of equity

Prior to 1066: The law in England and Wales was not unified

1250: The common law had been established

1615: The Earl of Oxford's Case

1066: William the Conqueror begins the process of developing a law common to the country as a whole

1470: The beginning of the Courts of the Chancery

The Judicature Acts 1873–75

As equity develops it too becomes more rigid

Equitable maxims

Initially the development of equity was rather unpredictable, and this gave rise to the expression 'equity varies with the length of the Chancellor's foot'. Gradually a system of consistent rules to govern the operation of equity emerged. These rules of equity are also referred to as the 'maxims of equity' or 'qualities of equity'. These are guiding principles that govern the operation of equity in practice.

	Maxim	Meaning	Case illustration
1	'He who comes to equity must come with clean hands'.	A party that is seeking equity must have behaved well; individuals that have behaved in an unconscionable manner will not be granted an equitable remedy.	*D&C Builders v Rees* (1996)
2	'Equity is equality'.	In the absence of evidence to the contrary property/assets should be divided in equal shares.	*Burrough v Philcox* (1840)
3	'Equity acts *in personam*'.	Equitable remedies apply to the person not their property.	*Norris v Chambres* (1861)
4	'Equity looks at the substance rather than the form'.	Equity draws a distinction between matters of substance and matters of form. If by insisting on the form, the substance will be defeated, it is inequitable to allow a person to insist on such form.	*Parkin v Thorold* (1852)

It is important at this juncture to note that this is not an exhaustive list of equitable maxims; there are in fact a number of other maxims, although there is disagreement as to whether a definitive list of maxims exists at all. When revising the maxims of equity you will see that there is a good degree of overlap between some of these maxims.

By the nineteenth century equity had developed a body of principles, rules and remedies and had become as rigid as the common law.

Aim Higher

If you decide to attempt a question on equity you will want to distinguish your answer from a descriptive overview of the historical development of equity and the common law. There are a number of ways in which you can attract more marks:

❖ Consider the significance of equity in a modern context. You might want to focus here on the creation of a range of flexible remedies. You could also discuss the development of trusts and mortgages.
❖ Enhance the quality of your answer by reference to academic works.

Equitable remedies

A significant contribution that equity has made to the modern English legal system is the development of a range of 'equitable remedies', which supplement those available at common law.

Equitable remedies include:

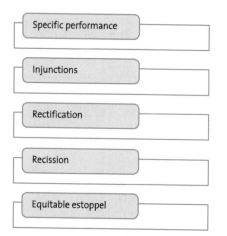

- Specific performance
- Injunctions
- Rectification
- Recission
- Equitable estoppel

These remedies are not available as of right. They are discretionary.

Aim Higher

If you want to find out more about the development of equity you will find extended coverage of the subject by looking in an Equity and Trusts Law Textbook. You will probably find there is much richer detail here than in any textbook on the English legal system!

The most important point to note in relation to equitable remedies is that they are discretionary in nature. This can be contrasted with damages that are available as of right. The decision to award an equitable remedy will therefore be informed by the conduct of the parties.

Where an equitable remedy is ordered by the court it must be acted upon. A failure to do so is Contempt of Court.

Conflict between the common law and equity

A particular problem that arose as a result of the development of equity was the operation of two bodies of law within one, apparently unified system. The common law had one body of rules that were applied only in the common law courts. Equity had an entirely different body of rules, available only in the Chancery Courts.

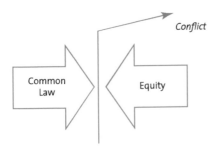

Conflict

This situation inevitably led to conflict, which was eventually resolved in the *Earl of Oxford's Case* (1615). You will need to make reference to this case if you are answering a question on Equity.

> **Case precedent – *The Earl of Oxford's Case* (1615)**
>
> **Facts:** in this case judgment was obtained initially in the Common Law Courts and then later in the Courts of the Chancery. The two judgments conflicted and the matter was referred to the Monarch.
>
> **Principle:** the King decided that in the event of conflict between the common law and equity, equity will prevail.

Fusion and the Judicature Acts

In circumstances where a claimant requested an equitable remedy it was essential that they commenced proceedings in the Courts of Equity. Common law courts were unable to administer equitable principles and remedies. Eventually it was decided that there was no need for equitable principles and common law principles to operate in separate courts. Nor was it necessary for the common law courts and the courts of equity to operate different procedures. The Judicature Acts of 1873–75 provided that equitable and common law principles and remedies would now operate in all courts. This represented a significant development in terms of efficiency for litigants.

It is worth noting that the Judicature Acts did not fuse equity and the common law. This is an important point and it is not uncommon for assessment questions to be posed by examiners that focus on the issue of fusion. In reality, the Judicature Acts simply brought together the administration of equity and the common law. The common law and equity therefore continue to exist as separate bodies of law (Meaning 4 on the diagram on page 72).

Core issues checklist

❖ The origins of the common law can be traced back to the Norman Conquest in 1066. Prior to the Norman Conquest different areas of the country had different rules or laws. These regional laws were influenced by local customs and laws imported by invaders.	✔
❖ The common law was developed by William the Conqueror and his itinerant justices through the *Curia Regis*. A unified law common to the country a whole began to emerge.	✔
❖ Defects in the common law began to emerge – and equity developed in the Courts of the Chancery as a response to these defects. This new body of law was referred to as 'equity'. Equity is governed by a number of maxims.	✔
❖ Conflict between these two bodies of law was eventually resolved in the *Earl of Oxford's Case*. The Judicature Acts 1873–75 brought together the administration of equity and the common law, enabling common law rules and equity to be administered in the same courts.	✔
❖ Equity and the common law still exist, however, as distinct bodies of law. Equity has real relevance in the modern English legal system, particularly in relation to the law of trusts and in relation to equitable remedies.	✔

Useful websites

Topic	Website
Her Majesty's Courts Service	www.justice.gov.uk/about/hmcts

Putting it into practice – example essay question

'Using examples and authority, discuss critically the development of equity in the English legal system.'

Answer plan

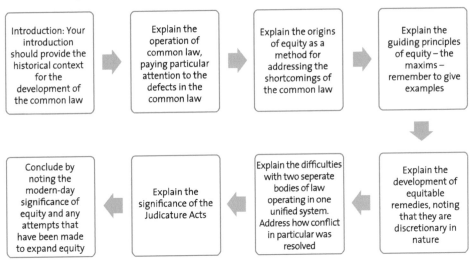

Introduction: Your introduction should provide the historical context for the development of the common law

Explain the operation of common law, paying particular attention to the defects in the common law

Explain the origins of equity as a method for addressing the shortcomings of the common law

Explain the guiding principles of equity – the maxims – remember to give examples

Explain the development of equitable remedies, noting that they are discretionary in nature

Explain the difficulties with two seperate bodies of law operating in one unified system. Address how conflict in particular was resolved

Explain the significance of the Judicature Acts

Conclude by noting the modern-day significance of equity and any attempts that have been made to expand equity

Outline answer

❖ This question calls for a historical narrative initially, one which explains the development of the common law.

❖ It is important to explain the defects that emerged in the common law and how the development of equity was a response to these defects and procedural injustice. A poor student will tend to over-focus on the descriptive narrative here and ignore the issues arising.

❖ It is important to explain the qualities of equity or the equitable maxims. It is not necessary to attempt to provide a definitive list. It is much better to cherry-pick a number of maxims and ensure that you are able to clearly articulate them and offer case illustrations of the maxims in operation.

❖ Make sure that you remember to include discussion in relation to remedies.

❖ In particular, you should note that equitable remedies are discretionary in nature. Contrast this with common law remedies, which are of course available as of right.

❖ You should next shift your focus to deal with the issues that arose as a result of two bodies of rules operating in different courts. In particular make sure that you discuss the issue of conflict resolution and *The Earl of Oxford's Case*.

❖ You will need to discuss the impact of the Judicature Acts 1873–75. Critically you should note that the Judicature Acts did not fuse together the common law and equity. They still exist as two distinct systems of law. The Judicature Acts merely brought together the administration of these systems – providing that the rules of equity and its remedies together with common law provisions should be available in all courts, not simply the Courts of Equity.

❖ It is at this juncture that you want to impress the examiner by demonstrating that you have conducted independent legal research. Explain the significance of equity in a modern context. Remember that in order to attain a very high mark you must demonstrate a detailed understanding of the subject; and that means supporting your arguments by reference to academic readings.

Key cases – equity

Case name	Area of law
D&C Builders v Rees [1996] 2 QB 617	Illustration of the equitable maxim 'He who comes to equity must come with clean hands'.
Burrough v Philcox (1840) 5 Myl & Cr	Illustration of the equitable maxim 'Equity is equality'.
Norris v Chambres (1861) 3 De GF & J 583	Illustration of the equitable maxim 'Equity acts *in personam*'.
Parkin v Thorold (1852) 16 Beav 59	Illustration of the equitable maxim 'Equity looks at the substance rather than the form'.
The Earl of Oxford's Case (1615) 21 ER 485	When there is conflict between equity and the common law, equity will prevail.

The doctrine of binding judicial precedent

Understand the law
- Do you understand the meaning of the term *stare decisis*?
- Are you able to explain the general principle upon which the doctrine of precedent operates?
- Do you understand the difference between *ratio decidendi* and *obiter dicta*?

Remember the details

- Can you explain the operation of precedent in each court, including the self-binding rule?

Reflect critically on areas of debate

- Can you reflect critically on the advantages and the disadvantages of the doctrine of precedent?
- Can you reflect critically on how conflicting decisions of the Supreme Court/House of Lords and the Privy Council have been addressed.

Contextualise

- Can you explain what impact our membership of the EU has had on the docrine of precedent?
- Can you explain the significance that the enactment of the Human Rights Act 1998 has had on the operation of precedent?

Apply your skills and knowledge

- Can you apply your knowledge using relevant authorities to support your work to the 'Putting it into practice' question at the start of this section?

Precedent

Topic Map

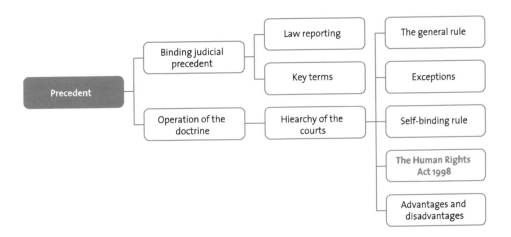

Putting it into practice – example essay question

'Analyse the extent to which the doctrine of *stare decisis* creates flexibility and certainty in the law.'

An outline answer is available at the end of this chapter.

Introduction

The doctrine of binding judicial precedent is also referred to as *stare decisis*. This Latin term means 'to stand by a decision'. Put simply, the doctrine of binding judicial precedent stipulates that the decisions of higher courts bind courts lower in the hierarchy.

This is however, a general rule, and law students need to know the limitations of and exceptions to general rules. In particular, if you are answering a question on the doctrine of binding judicial precedent you will need to know:

❖ Which courts are bound by their own previous decisions?
❖ When and under what circumstances can a court depart from a decision made by a higher court?
❖ What mechanisms, if any, exist for avoiding precedents?

You will find it helpful to refer to the diagrams of the court structure in Chapter 1 when reading this section.

Binding judicial precedent

In practice, precedent operates in the following way. Judges when trying cases will look to see whether the legal issues in the case before them have been dealt with before. In particular, a judge will be looking for decisions by superior courts.

If a judge finds a precedent by a superior court, where the material facts of the cases are the same and which raises the same points of law, they will in most cases be bound to follow it.

Summary

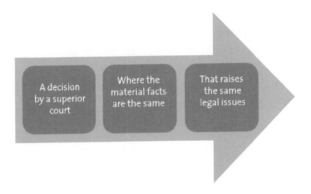

The doctrine of binding judicial precedent is preferable to allowing judges to decide cases on a case-by-case, or *ad hoc* basis. By following the decisions of the superior courts, in cases that raise the same legal issues, the law becomes more consistent and predictable. This means that lawyers can provide clients with clear advice as to how best to order their affairs.

Law reporting

The only way that a system of binding judicial precedent can work effectively is if the decisions of judges are meticulously recorded and if those decisions are accessible to judges in future cases. As such, we have an extensive law reporting process that operates in the English legal system. This system provides the legal profession with access to judgments, which allows the profession to identify relevant precedents with respect to cases that they are dealing with.

Aim Higher – revision tip

The first judgments that you read will be challenging and you will probably need to re-read some, or all, of the judgment. Reading judgments can be extremely time-consuming and challenging. The good news is that this is all perfectly normal!

The more judgments that you read, the more familiar you will become with the tone and vocabulary used by members of the judiciary. In the meantime a good-quality law dictionary will help with translation. Most examiners feel that this is something that students struggle with. The solution is not to avoid reading judgments.

At the conclusion of a case, the presiding judge/judges will issue a judgment or speech. The first thing that a new law student will notice about judgments is that they are usually very long! The second thing that you will notice is that the use of language is often technical and sometimes rather confusing.

It is important to remember that not everything in a judgment is binding. Only the *ratio decidendi* of a judgment is binding.

Key terms	
Ratio decidendi	This is Latin for 'the reason behind the decision'. The *ratio* of a case is the legal principle that was established by the court. This is the part of the judgment that is binding.
Obiter dicta	This means 'things said by the way'. *Obiter* are statements made by the judge/judges that are not central to the decision. This could include the following: 1. Statements made by the judge/judges that are general statements of law. 2. Illustrations, examples and hypothetical scenarios.
Persuasive precedents	These are precedents, which are not binding, but they may be of persuasive authority. For example, *obtier dicta* from the House of Lords/Supreme Court are of strong persuasive authority. Decisions of the Privy Council are also persuasive.

Aim Higher

It is of critical importance that you are able to show that you understand the meaning of these key terms and that you are able to offer illustrations and examples. You may find it helpful to visit the companion website and use the Flash Cards to test your understanding of these and other key legal terms.

Precedent and the courts

The doctrine of precedent operates on the basis of the hierarchy of the courts. In order to fully understand the operation of precedent, you will need to know the hierarchy of the courts and the individual rules that pertain to each court in relation to the operation of precedent.

The Supreme Court

In 2009 the Supreme Court replaced the Judicial Committee of the House of Lords. The Supreme Court sits at the top of the court structure in the English legal system. The decisions of the Supreme Court and its predecessor the House of Lords are binding on all lower courts.

For many years the House of Lords was bound by its own previous decisions, *London Tramways Co Ltd v London County Council* (1898). In **1966** the House of Lords issued a **Practice Statement** in which they stated that in future they would regard themselves as free to depart from their own previous decisions. **The 1966 Practice Statement** made it clear that this newly created power applied only to the House of Lords/Supreme Court.

Let us briefly consider why this creation of this new power was significant:

❖   The ability to depart from previous decisions is important in order to ensure that the law is able to continue to develop.
❖   It is essential to have a mechanism for the correction of mistakes and errors.
❖   The law must be able to respond to changing circumstances, if it is to retain its relevance.

> It is possible to have several different cases that illustrate the same point. Different textbooks and lecturers use different illustrations – it doesn't mean someone has got it wrong!

In the years that followed, the House of Lords used this new power very cautiously. Where the House of Lords departed from its own previous decision is the case of *Conway v Rimmer* (1968), where the House of Lords overruled their decision in *Duncan v Cammell Laird* (1942). There are several cases that you can use to illustrate this point. The case of *R v Shivpuri* (1986) is an example of the House of Lords using this power to correct a mistake that they had made interpreting the law in the case of *Anderton v Ryan* (1985).

Key points: the Supreme Court

❖   Decisions of the Supreme Court are binding on all courts beneath it.
❖   The Supreme Court is not bound by its own previous decisions
❖   With regard to matters of EU law the Supreme Court is bound by the decisions of the European Court of Justice, as are all courts in the English legal system.
❖   Following the implementation of the Human Rights Act 1998, decisions of the European Court of Human Rights bind the courts in the English legal system.

Aim Higher

It is really important that you learn, from the outset of your studies, to support your statements of law and arguments by reference to authority. This applies not only to your study of the English Legal System, but it applies to all substantive law subjects.

You can support your propositions of law in the following ways:

1. by citing a relevant case;
2. by referring to statutes and delegated legislation;
3. by referring to judicial opinion;
4. by referring to academic opinion.

Extra marks

Examiners frequently complain that students 'fail to support their arguments,' or that work 'lacks authority'. All that you have to do to avoid this criticism of your work is to support your work with a relevant authority listed above. This will enable the examiner to award more marks!

Remember!

When you cite an authority you must always provide a source, by this we mean:

❖ the case name and the case citation;
❖ the title of an Act and the relevant section number;
❖ when referring to academic opinion you should cite the name of the academic and the name of the publication.

Conflicting Supreme Court and Privy Council Decisions

Strictly speaking the Privy Council sits outside the court structure in the English legal system. As such decisions of the Supreme Court are binding and must be followed by the Privy Council: *Tai Hing Ltd v Liu Chong Hing Bank* (1986). You do, however, need to remember that Privy Council decisions are of strong persuasive authority.

This strict view of the operation of the doctrine of precedent was unsettled by a series of cases that related to the operation of the defence of Provocation under s 3 of the Homicide Act 1957. In this string of cases the Court of Appeal in *R v James and Karimi* (2006) was faced with conflicting decisions of the House of Lords in *R v Smith (Morgan)* (2001) and the Privy Council in *Attorney General for Jersey v Holley* (2005).

The Court of Appeal in *R v James and Karimi* (2006) decided to follow the decision of the Privy Council in *Attorney General for Jersey v Holley* (2005) and as such it established that in exceptional circumstances it is possible to follow a Privy Council decision in preference to a decision of the Supreme Court/House of Lords.

The Court of Appeal Civil Division

The first general rule in relation to the Court of Appeal Civil Division is that, because it is positioned beneath the Supreme Court, it is bound by the decisions of the Supreme Court.

The next general rule is that the Court of Appeal is bound by its own previous decisions (this is known as the self-binding rule). There are however, a number of exceptions to this second general rule. These exceptions were explained in the key case of *Young v Bristol Aeroplane Co Ltd* (1944).

Case precedent – *Young v Bristol Aeroplane Co Ltd* (1944)

This case established three exceptions to the self-binding rule outlined above. The Court of Appeal may depart from its own previous decisions in the following situations:

1. Where a conflict exists between two previous decisions of the Court of Appeal the Court of Appeal can decide which decision to follow.
2. Where the Supreme Court has either expressly or impliedly overruled a Court of Appeal decision.
3. Where a decision by the Court of Appeal has been made *per incurium*.

Up for Debate

Several attempts were made by Lord Denning to expand the constraints placed on the Court of Appeal by the doctrine of binding judicial precedent.
His attempts were unsuccessful with the Supreme Court reasserting that:

❖ Decisions of the Supreme Court/House of Lords are binding on the Court of Appeal: *Miliangos v George Frank (Textiles) Ltd* (1976).
❖ In *Gallie v Lee* (1971), the Supreme Court reaffirmed that the Court of Appeal is bound by its own previous decisions, save for the exceptions outlined in *Young v Bristol Aeroplane Co Ltd* (1944).

Given that the Court of Appeal is in many cases the final court of appeal, do you think they should have greater flexibility in relation to the operation of the doctrine of binding judicial precedent?

As a consequence of s 3 of the European Communities Act 1972 the Court of Appeal may also disregard one of its own previous decisions if it is inconsistent with EU law.

The Court of Appeal Criminal Division

The general rule in the Criminal Division of the Court of Appeal is that the doctrine of binding judicial precedent operates as follows:

1. The Criminal Division of the Court of Appeal is bound by decisions of the Supreme Court.
2. It is also bound by its own previous decision unless the exceptions in *Young v Bristol Aeroplane Co Ltd* (1944) apply (self-binding rule).

However, it is accepted that the Criminal Division of the Court of Appeal has greater flexibility with regard to the self-binding rule.

1. The Criminal Division of the Court of Appeal can also depart from its own previous decisions where it believes that the previous decision was the result of a misunderstanding or misapplication of the law: *R v Taylor* (1950)

Aim Higher – thinking point

What is the justification for the Court of Appeal Criminal Division having greater flexibility than the Civil Division of the Court of Appeal?

The Divisional Courts

The general rules are as follow in the Divisional Courts:

❖ They are bound by decisions of the Supreme Court.
❖ They are also bound by the decisions of the Court of Appeal.
❖ They are generally bound by their own previous decisions, but may avail themselves of the exceptions laid down in *Young v Bristol Aeroplane* in civil cases. In criminal appeals the QBD may refuse to follow its own previous decisions where it feels the original decision was decided incorrectly (*DPP v Butterworth* (1994)).

The High Court

The rules that govern the doctrine of binding judicial precedent in the High Court can be articulated as follows:

❖ They are bound by the decisions of all superior courts.
❖ The decisions of the High Court are binding on all inferior courts.
❖ The decisions of the High Court are not self-binding but they are persuasive and normally followed in practice.

Inferior courts

The position of the Crown Court, the Magistrates' Court and the County Court can be summarised as follows:

❖ The inferior courts are bound by the decisions of the superior courts.
❖ These courts do not create precedents.
❖ These courts do not therefore bind themselves.

Diagram: the doctrine of binding judicial precedent

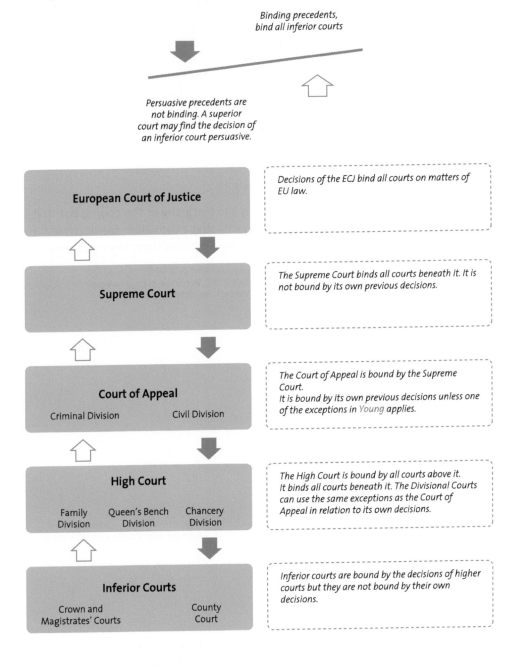

*Binding precedents,
bind all inferior courts*

*Persuasive precedents are
not binding. A superior
court may find the decision of
an inferior court persuasive.*

European Court of Justice

*Decisions of the ECJ bind all courts on matters of
EU law.*

Supreme Court

*The Supreme Court binds all courts beneath it. It is
not bound by its own previous decisions.*

Court of Appeal

Criminal Division   Civil Division

*The Court of Appeal is bound by the Supreme
Court.
It is bound by its own previous decisions unless one
of the exceptions in Young applies.*

High Court

Family
Division   Queen's Bench
Division   Chancery
Division

*The High Court is bound by all courts above it.
It binds all courts beneath it. The Divisional Courts
can use the same exceptions as the Court of
Appeal in relation to its own decisions.*

Inferior Courts

Crown and
Magistrates' Courts   County
Court

*Inferior courts are bound by the decisions of higher
courts but they are not bound by their own
decisions.*

The Human Rights Act 1998

The Human Rights Act 1998 requires all courts in the hierarchy to take account of
decisions of the European Court of Human Rights. Thus any precedent that is in
conflict with a decision of the European Court of Human Rights is now invalid.

Common Pitfall

Examiners often comment that students answering questions on precedent fail to acknowledge the significance of the **HRA 1998** and our membership of the EU. Why not use a subheading for each of these points to make sure that the examiner is aware at first glance that you haven't made the same error! You should always check with your lecturer whether they are happy for you to use subheadings and bullet points in assessments.

The operation of the doctrine

It is important that you understand not only the hierarchy of the courts, but that you are able to explain the different mechanisms that exist within the doctrine for avoiding binding precedents. The diagram below illustrates these key mechanisms:

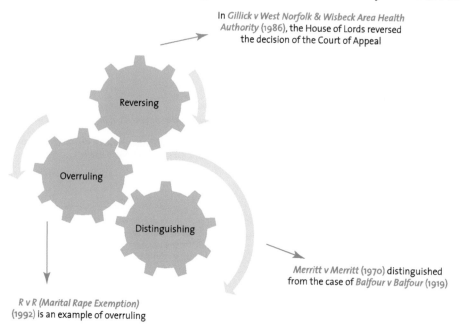

In *Gillick v West Norfolk & Wisbeck Area Health Authority* (1986), the House of Lords reversed the decision of the Court of Appeal

Reversing

Overruling

Distinguishing

Merritt v Merritt (1970) distinguished from the case of *Balfour v Balfour* (1919)

R v R (Marital Rape Exemption) (1992) is an example of overruling

Distinguishing

Distinguishing is an important tool that can be used to avoid a precedent. The *ratio* of any case is formulated on the basis of the material facts of the case. Thus a judge can seek to distinguish the facts of the case that they are hearing, from the material facts of a case establishing a precedent. Sometimes this is relatively easy to do, as the material facts will be significantly and substantively different. In other cases however, the distinction between cases can be much harder to determine, and some academics have suggested that judges have 'sought to distinguish the indistinguishable'. A good example of distinguishing can be seen in the case of *Merritt v Merritt* (1970), in which the material facts were distinguished from the case of *Balfour v Balfour* (1919).

Overruling

Overruling occurs when a superior court departs from a previously established legal ruling. An example of overruling can be seen in the House of Lords decision in *R v R (Marital Rape Exemption)* (1992) where the House of Lords overruled the long-standing marital rape exemption.

Reversing

This occurs when a superior court reverses the decision of an inferior court in the same case. An example of reversing can be seen in the case of *Gillick v West Norfolk and Wisbeck Area Health Authority* (1986), where the House of Lords, on appeal, overruled an earlier decision of the Court of Appeal in the same case.

Common Pitfall

Many students when answering a question on precedent will fail to address some of the critical issues that arise as a result of the doctrine. A good student will demonstrate that they understand that the question as to whether judges make law is controversial. Acknowledging the Declaratory Theory of Law as a starting position is one way of starting this discussion.

Other points that could be considered are:

❖ that judges are not democratically accountable – they are not elected;
❖ that the doctrine of precedent is not the only area in which scope of judicial law making exists (see Chapter 3 on Statutory Interpretation in particular).

The advantages and disadvantages of precedent

It is important to demonstrate to the examiner that you understand the advantages and disadvantages of the doctrine of binding judicial precedent in addition to the way in which it operates.

Advantages	Disadvantages
Consistency: the doctrine of precedent creates consistency. Cases are not decided on an *ad hoc* basis – this provides certainty.	**Volume and clarity:** the volume of decided cases can make it challenging for lawyers and judges to locate all relevant judgments. When a relevant judgment is identified the *ratio* of the case may not be clear.

Advantages	Disadvantages
Efficiency: the operation of precedent means that the same points of law do not need to be argued over and over again. This saves the courts, lawyers and clients time and money.	**Constitutional role of the judiciary:** the Declaratory Theory of Law stipulates that the role of the judge is to state the law and to apply it. The doctrine of precedent clearly allows for a degree of judicial flexibility and creativity.
Certainty: consistency in the law means that lawyers can advise their clients as to how best to order their affairs on the basis of previously decided cases.	**Lack of certainty:** mechanisms such as distinguishing introduce an element of uncertainty into the doctrine
Flexibility: the doctrine allows members of the judiciary to develop the law slowly and incrementally. The ability to distinguish, reverse and overrule enables flexibility and allows the doctrine to work effectively.	**Inflexible:** society and attitudes can change very quickly. From time to time precedents may become out of line with changes that have taken place in society. The doctrine relies on individual cases making their way up through the hierarchal structure and as such, changes to the law that are reliant on the doctrine of precedent can sometimes be very slow to materialise.

Aim Higher

Students new to the study of law are frequently daunted by the sheer quantity of information that they need to absorb. If in the exam you think that remembering all the relevant advantages and disadvantages of the doctrine of precedent is going to be difficult – all you need do is remember that the strengths of the system are also cited as weaknesses! For example:

❖ Precedent is flexible – Precedent is inflexible
❖ Precedent is consistent – Precedent can be inconsistent.

Other sources of law

The focus of this chapter thus far has been on equity and the doctrine of binding judicial precedent. In the interests of completeness it is important to briefly consider some minor sources of law in the English legal system. In this context we will consider:

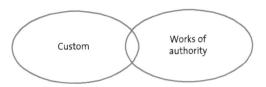

Custom

Custom is a minor source of law in the English legal system. Custom was defined in the *Tanistry Case* (1608) as 'such usage as has obtained the force of law'. There are a number of criteria that must be satisfied if a custom is to confer the force of law. Slapper and Kelly (2013) identify the following seven prerequisites:

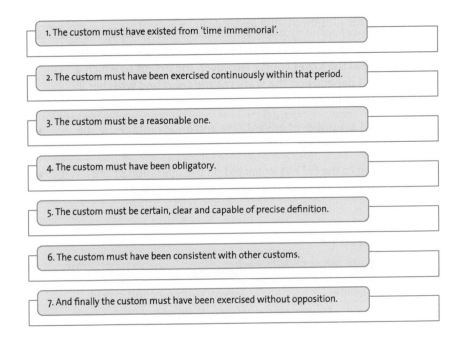

1. The custom must have existed from 'time immemorial'.

2. The custom must have been exercised continuously within that period.

3. The custom must be a reasonable one.

4. The custom must have been obligatory.

5. The custom must be certain, clear and capable of precise definition.

6. The custom must have been consistent with other customs.

7. And finally the custom must have been exercised without opposition.

It is worth noting that the burden of proof rests with the person claiming the existence of the custom.

Works of authority

Books of authority (sometimes referred to as books of antiquity) are also a minor source of law. The authors of these books were senior members of the judiciary and as the title 'antiquity' suggests, they were written many years ago. **Glanvill** is one such example of a book of antiquity.

It is important to distinguish books of antiquity from the writing of modern academics in journals and textbooks. Whilst it is certainly the case that the work of academics is cited in support of particular legal arguments, such works have persuasive authority only – they are not a source of law in their own right.

Core issues checklist

❖ The doctrine of binding judicial precedent is a significant source of law in the English legal system.	✔
❖ The operation of precedent is dependent upon a system of law reporting. A judgment can be divided into *ratio decidendi* (this is the binding part of the judgment) and *obiter dicta*.	✔
❖ The system relies on the court hierarchy; the general rule is that the higher courts bind the lower courts. However, the extent to which a court binds itself depends on the status of the court and whether it has civil or criminal jurisdiction.	✔
❖ The doctrine has a number of advantages and disadvantages, some of which are corresponding.	✔
❖ Our membership to the EU has impacted on the operation of the doctrine, as has the passing of the Human Rights Act 1998.	✔

Useful websites

Topic	Website
Supreme Court Website	www.supremecourt.gov.uk
British and Irish Legal Information Institute	www.bailii.org

Putting it into practice – example essay question

'Analyse the extent to which the doctrine of *stare decisis* creates flexibility and certainty in the law.'

Answer plan

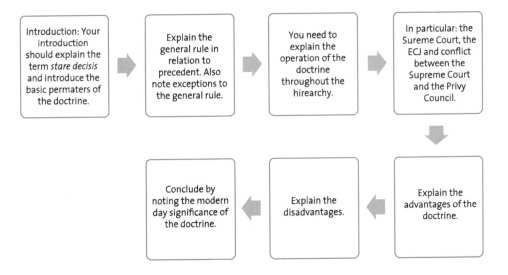

Introduction: Your introduction should explain the term *stare decisis* and introduce the basic permaters of the doctrine.	Explain the general rule in relation to precedent. Also note exceptions to the general rule.	You need to explain the operation of the doctrine throughout the hirearchy.	In particular: the Sureme Court, the ECJ and conflict between the Supreme Court and the Privy Council.

Conclude by noting the modern day significance of the doctrine.	Explain the disadvantages.	Explain the advantages of the doctrine.

Outline answer

❖ This question is asking you to consider some of the advantages of the doctrine of precedent. Sometimes examiners will use the Latin term, so it is important to ensure that you recognise that this is a question about precedent!

❖ You will need to introduce the doctrine. There is no need here to explain the development of the common law, but make sure that you have covered the following issues: *ratio decidendi*, *obiter dicta*, the significance of law reporting.

❖ A common pitfall is that students fail to explore the operation of the doctrine in individual courts. It is vitally important to explore the superior courts in detail.

❖ You will need to address the following:

1. Who is the court bound by?
2. Does it bind itself?
3. Which courts are bound by the decisions of this court?

❖ A good way to earn additional marks is to make sure that you address the European Court of Justice, the situation regarding the Privy Council and the significance of the Human Rights Act 1998. Many students will forget these critical issues and will loose valuable marks.

❖ Once you have explained the operation of the doctrine in the superior courts it is worth noting the position regarding the inferior courts. Again this is something frequently overlooked by students.

❖ You now need to explore the advantages of the doctrine – this question is giving particular focus to two advantages – but you can note that there are other advantages!

❖ This coverage needs to be balanced by recognising some of the corresponding disadvantages.

❖ Your conclusion should not seek to introduce new material or new key points but it should round the essay up. A good place to finish your response is to offer comment regarding the significance of the doctrine in the modern English legal system.

Aim Higher

Process words: analyse

When you are faced with an essay question that is asking you to 'analyse' a particular case or, as is the case here, the operation of a particular doctrine, you are being asked to break an issue/concept/case into its constituent parts. The examiner wants you to look in depth at each part using supporting authorities. You are being invited to consider arguments for and against the operation of the doctrine of binding judicial precedent. Significantly, you are also being asked to consider how the different elements of the doctrine interrelate with each other and other sources of law. For example, in the event of conflict between the common law and legislation which will prevail . . . and why?

Table of key cases referred to in this chapter

Case name	Area of law	Principle
Gillick v West Norfolk & Wisbeck Area Health Authority [1985] 3 All ER 402 (HL)	Illustration of reversing.	
Merritt v Merritt [1970] 1 WLR 1211, *Balfour v Balfour* [1919] 2 KB 571	Illustration of distinguishing.	
Miliangos v George Frank (Textiles) Ltd [1976] AC 443	This case examines the relationship between the Supreme Court/House of Lords and the Court of Appeal.	Decisions of the House of Lords/Supreme Court are binding on the Court of Appeal.

R v James and Karimi [2006] EWCA Crim 14	This case is concerned with the relationship between the Court of Appeal, the Privy Council and the Supreme Court.	Illustration of the Court of Appeal following a Privy Council Decision in preference to a decision of the House of Lords/ Supreme Court.
R v R (Marital Rape Exemption) [1992] 1 AC 599	Illustration of overruling.	
R v Taylor [1950] 2 All ER 170	This case considers the doctrine of binding judicial precedent in the criminal division of the Court of Appeal	The Criminal Division of the Court of Appeal follows the doctrine of precedent less rigidly.
Tai Hing Ltd v Liu Chong Hing Bank [1986] AC 80	This case relates to the operation of the doctrine of precedent. In particular the relationship between the Supreme Court and the Privy Council.	The Privy Council is bound to follow decisions of the Supreme Court/House of Lords.
Young v Bristol Aeroplane Co Ltd [1944] KB 718	This case is concerned with the operation of the doctrine of precedent in the Court of Appeal.	Lays down the circumstances in which the Court of Appeal can depart from its own previous decisions.

@ **Visit the book's companion website to test your knowledge**

❖ Resources include a subject map, revision tip podcasts, downloadable diagrams, MCQ quizzes for each chapter, and a flashcard glossary
❖ www.routledge.com/cw/optimizelawrevision

Revision objectives

Understand the law

- Do you understand the purpose and outcome of the Woolf Inquiry?

Remember the details

- Can you remember the key Civil Procedure Rules?
- Do you understand how the Rules are laid out?

Reflect critically on areas of debate

- Have you completed the additional reading outlined in the 'Aim Higher' boxes?

Contextualise

- Can you understand how the Civil Procedure Rules operate to achieve the overriding objective?

Apply your skills and knowledge

- Are you confident in answering the 'Putting it into practice' question?

Chapter Map

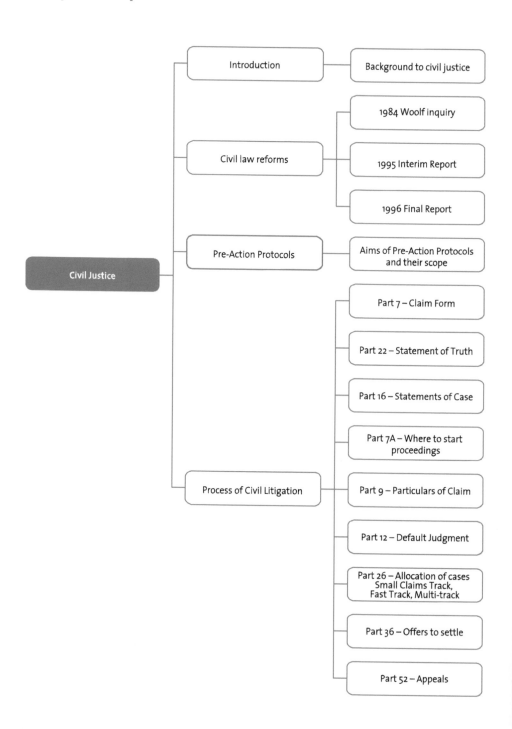

Putting it into practice – example essay question

Pauline works as a secretary for a large manufacturing company. She trips and falls on a loose stair carpet suffering some personal injury.

She has been informed that the stair carpet should have been repaired some months ago and she should receive compensation in the region of £800 for her injuries.

Advise Pauline
An outline answer to this question is available at the end of this chapter.

Introduction

The process of solving civil disputes has been through some dramatic changes in the last 20 years. Reform is ongoing with the most recent set of developments being implemented in July 2013. These amendments have been made in an effort to ensure that the civil courts run smoothly and efficiently.

For your assessments you will need to ensure you have some knowledge of the background to the changes, how the Civil Procedure Rules (CPR) operate, and, essentially, the different tracks that are available.

Ask yourself at the end of this chapter:

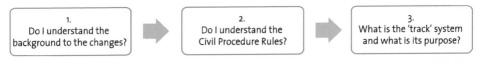

| 1. Do I understand the background to the changes? | 2. Do I understand the Civil Procedure Rules? | 3. What is the 'track' system and what is its purpose? |

Aim Higher

Although most assessments in this area will concentrate on the operation of the (up to date) rules, you will be expected to know a little of the background of civil litigation reforms (see below).

Check your module outline to see how much weight is given to this area.

We will start by looking (briefly) at the background to the reforms.

Civil law reforms

The major reforms began in March 1994 when the Lord Chancellor set up the Woolf Inquiry. The role of the inquiry was to undertake a review of the civil justice system.

In the 1995 **Interim Report**, it was stated that the system was in a **state of crisis**. The main problems were summarised as relating to **cost, delay** and **complexity**. This was coupled with **a lack of clear judicial responsibility for managing individual cases** *and* **for the overall administration of the courts**.

The spiralling costs of civil litigation also contributed towards the capping and cuts we are now seeing in the legal aid fund (see the chapter on 'Funding of Legal Services').

The **Final Report** (*Access to Justice: Final Report to the Lord Chancellor on the civil justice system in England and Wales*, also known as the 'Woolf Report') was published in July 1996.

The Civil Procedure Act 1997 was passed reflecting the recommendations in the Woolf Report. One of these was the creation of the Civil Procedure Rules 1998. The Rules lay down the practice and procedure that should be followed in the civil courts. The **overriding aim** of the rules is to ensure the civil justice system is **accessible, fair** and **efficient**.

These Rules are subject to constant review. The 66th update came into force in October 2013.

For your assessments you should show that you understand how the CPR are organised. They are divided into parts; each one deals with a separate topic and each part is divided into sub-rules. Many of the parts are followed by '**Practice Directions**' which explain how the Parts and Rules should be implemented.

To help you understand the rules you should familiarise yourself with the relevant website.

The current set of CPR can be found at: www.justice.gov.uk/courts/procedure-rules/civil/rules.

You should also be aware of the **Pre-Action Protocols** (more on these later). Their main aim is to encourage the parties to settle at an early stage, avoiding going to court.

Summary of the reforms

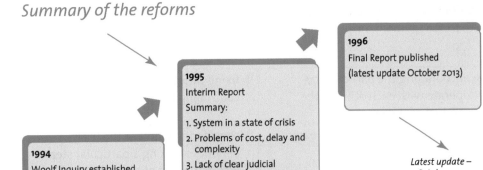

1994
Woolf Inquiry established

1995
Interim Report
Summary:
1. System in a state of crisis
2. Problems of cost, delay and complexity
3. Lack of clear judicial reponsibility for managing individual cases and for overall administration of the courts

1996
Final Report published
(latest update October 2013)

Latest update –
October 2013

The Civil Procedure Rules

When answering any questions on the CPR always begin by stating the '**overriding objective**', which is contained in Part 1.

Reiterate that the rules are designed to deal with cases '**justly**' and at '**proportionate cost**'.

Next, use the chart below to illustrate how the rules accomplish the overriding objective.

So the rules are designed to:

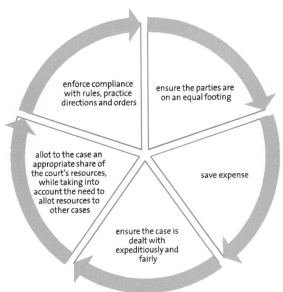

enforce compliance with rules, practice directions and orders

ensure the parties are on an equal footing

allot to the case an appropriate share of the court's resources, while taking into account the need to allot resources to other cases

save expense

ensure the case is dealt with expeditiously and fairly

The Court's duty to **manage cases** (Part 3) is also one of the overriding objectives. Active management includes:

❖ encouraging the parties to co-operate with each other in the conduct of the proceedings	❖ fixing timetables or otherwise controlling the progress of the case
❖ identifying the issues at an early stage	❖ considering whether the likely benefits of taking a particular step justify the cost of taking it
❖ deciding promptly which issues need full investigation and trial and accordingly disposing summarily of the others	❖ dealing with as many aspects of the case as it can on the same occasion
❖ deciding the order in which issues are to be resolved	❖ dealing with the case without the parties needing to attend at court
❖ encouraging the parties to use an Alternative Dispute Resolution (ADR) procedure if the court considers that appropriate and facilitating the use of such procedure	❖ making use of technology
❖ helping the parties to settle the whole or part of the case	❖ giving directions to ensure that the trial of a case proceeds quickly and efficiently

This means that the days of stronger parties stretching out court proceedings in an effort to force the weaker party to settle are over.

Aim Higher

You do not need to remember all of the 'active management' objectives given above, but to use one or two in your answer will show greater understanding of the court's duties.

The court's overriding objective is to deal with cases

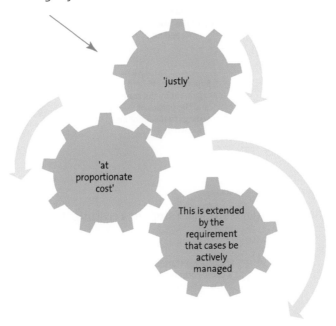

'justly'

'at proportionate cost'

This is extended by the requirement that cases be actively managed

Pre-Action Protocols (PAPs)

The rules for Pre-Action Protocols can be found here: www.justice.gov.uk/courts/procedure-rules/civil/protocol

You will see when you access the website that there are a set number of protocols covering different situations, for example those relating to defamation or personal injury. Not all actions are subject to pre-action protocols.

The Practice Direction governing Pre-Action Protocols states the aims of the PAP. It is not very long (see below) and you should familiarise yourself with it, along with the areas covered by PAPs.

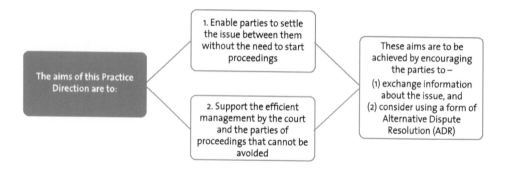

The process of civil litigation

The following diagram outlines the main steps in a civil litigation action.

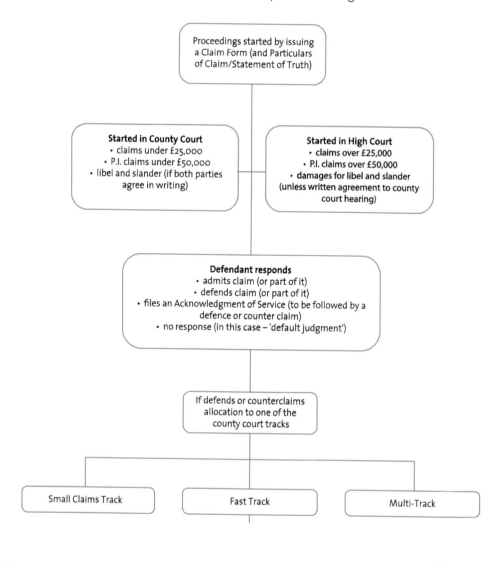

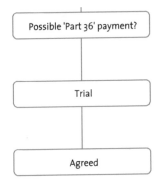

How to start proceedings – the Claim Form – Part 7

Proceedings start when the court issues a claim form at the claimant's (formally 'plaintiff's') request.

Part 16 sets out what the claim form must include (see later).

In addition, a 'particulars of claim' form must be served with the claim form or within 14 days of service of the claim form.

Statement of Truth – Part 22

The claim form should be verified by a 'statement of truth'.

The statement of truth is simply a statement that the person signing the claim form believes the facts in the document are true.

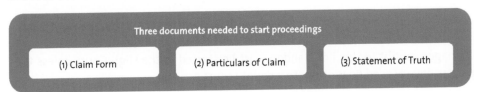

Three documents needed to start proceedings

(1) Claim Form   (2) Particulars of Claim   (3) Statement of Truth

Statements of Case (formally 'Pleadings') – Part 16

This Part deals with the contents of the **claim form, statement of value, particulars of claim** and **defence.**

The diagram below gives a list of items included in each form.

Claim Form

- (a) contains a concise statement of the nature of the claim;
- (a) contains a concise statement of the nature of the claim;
- (b) specifies the remedy which the claimant seeks;
- (c) where the claimant is making a claim for money, contains a statement of value in accordance with rule 16.3;
- (cc) where the claimant's only claim is for a specified sum, contains a statement of the interest accrued on that sum; and
- (d) contains such other matters as may be set out in a practice direction.

Statement of Value

- If the claimant is making a claim for money he must state:
- the amount of money claimed and that he expects to recover either:
  - (a) not more than £10,000;
  - (b) more than £10,000 but not more than £25,000;
  - (c) more than £25,000; or
  - (d) that he is unsure of how much he is likely to recover.

Particulars of Claim

- (a) a concise statement of the facts on which the claimant relies;
- (b) if the claimant is seeking interest, a statement to that effect;
- (c) if the claimant is seeking aggravated damages or exemplary damages, a statement to that effect and his grounds for claiming them;
- (d) if the claimant is seeking provisional damages, a statement to that effect and his grounds for claiming them; and
- (e) such other matters as may be set out in a practice direction.

Defence

- (a) which of the allegations in the particulars of claim he denies;
- (b) which allegations he is unable to admit or deny, but which he requires the claimant to prove; and
- (c) which allegations he admits.
- (e) such other matters as may be set out in a practice direction.

Where to start proceedings – Part 7A

Under Part 7A proceedings can be started in either the High Court or the County Court, although proceedings may not be started in the High Court unless the value of the claim is more than £25,000.

Personal injury claims must be in excess of £50,000 to be started in the High Court.

Damages sought for libel or slander must be started in the High Court unless the parties have agreed (in writing) to a county court hearing.

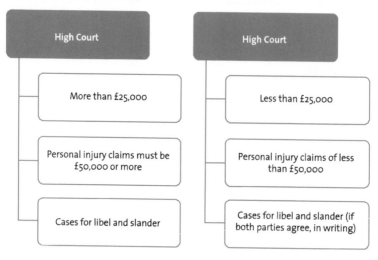

Responding to Particulars of Claim – General – Part 9

This part sets out how a defendant may respond to particulars of claim.

The defendant is given several options.

1. Admit the claim, or part of it (in accordance with Part 14).
2. File a defence, in full or in part – he may admit part of the claim (in accordance with Part 15).
3. File an acknowledgment of service (in accordance with Part 10); for instance, if he wishes to have more time to file a defence.

Default Judgment – Part 12

This means judgment given without a trial where a defendant has either failed to file an Acknowledgement of Service or has failed to file a defence.

Default judgments are not available for certain actions, such as a claim for delivery of goods subject to an agreement regulated by the Consumer Credit Act 1974.

Allocation – Part 26

The Part deals with the allocation of defended cases to case management tracks.

If a defendant files a defence a court officer will decide (on a provisional basis) which track appears to be most suitable for the claim.

A 'notice of proposed allocation' is then served on the each party.

This form will specify any matter that the parties must comply with and asks them to complete a 'directions questionnaire'.

A party can request that the proceedings be 'stayed' (for one month) while the parties try to settle the case by Alternative Dispute Resolution or other means.

There are three tracks:

    (a) the **small claims track**;
    (b) the **fast track**; and
    (c) the **multi-track**.

Scope of each track

The **small claims track** is the normal track for–

(a) any claim for personal injuries where –

    (i) the value of the claim is not more than £10,000; and
    (ii) the value of any claim for damages for personal injuries is not more than £1,000;
(b) any claim which includes a claim by a tenant of residential premises against a landlord where –

    (i) the tenant is seeking an order requiring the landlord to carry out repairs or other work to the premises (whether or not the tenant is also seeking some other remedy);
    (ii) the cost of the repairs or other work to the premises is estimated to be not more than £1,000; and
    (iii) the value of any other claim for damages is not more than £1,000.

The small claims track is the normal track for any claim which has a value of not more than £10,000.

The **fast track** is the normal track for any claim –

(a) for which the small claims track is not the normal track; and
(b) which has a value –

    (i) for proceedings issued on or after 6 April 2009, of not more than £25,000; and
    (ii) for proceedings issued before 6 April 2009, of not more than £15,000.

The **fast track** is the normal track for the claims above only if the court considers that –

(a) the trial is likely to last for no longer than one day; and
(b) oral expert evidence at trial will be limited to–

    (i) one expert per party in relation to any expert field; and
    (ii) expert evidence in two expert fields.

The **multi-track** is the normal track for any claim for which the small claims track or the fast track is not the normal track.

In summary,

Small Claims Track	Fast Track	Multi-Track
• Value of claim less than £10,000 • PI claim of not more than £1,000 • Landlord problems of less than £1,000 value • Normally claims below £10,000	• For claims where the small claims track is not the normal track • Not more than £25,000 in value (if started after 6 April 2009)	• Claims where the small claims and fast track are not the normal tracks

The court will take into account several factors when deciding which track is appropriate; these are set out below.

❖ the financial value, if any, of the claim;
❖ the nature of the remedy sought;
❖ the likely complexity of the facts, law or evidence;
❖ the number of parties or likely parties;
❖ the value of any counterclaim or other Part 20 claim and the complexity of any matters relating to it;
❖ the amount of oral evidence which may be required;
❖ the importance of the claim to persons who are not parties to the proceedings;
❖ the views expressed by the parties; and
❖ the circumstances of the parties.

Aim Higher – revision tip

Try to use one or two of these factors in your assessments, as it will show you have greater understanding of the reasoning behind the track used.

Offers to Settle – Part 36

This Part deals with offers to settle and the consequences of an offer being made.

An offer to settle is known as a 'Part 36' offer.

A Part 36 offer can be made at any time, including before the commencement of proceedings.

If a Part 36 offer is accepted, the claim will be stayed (in whole or in part).

The consequences of not accepting a Part 36 payment are important when considering allocation of costs.

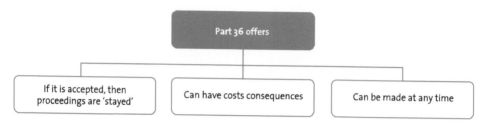

Appeals – Part 52

The rules in this Part apply to appeals to –

(a) the civil division of the Court of Appeal;
(b) the High Court; and
(c) a county court.

An appeal is not an automatic right, so permission to appeal needs to be granted

Core issues checklist

This area has been through major reforms and the reforms are set to continue	✔
The reform process began with the Woolf Report. The Interim Report stated the system was in a state of crisis due to costs, delays and the complexity of the system, as well as a lack of judicial responsibility for managing cases.	✔
The Civil Procedure Rules 1998 were created, reflecting the outcomes of the Woolf Report.	✔
Pre-Action Protocols exist for some types of disputes; the aim of these is to encourage early settlement, thereby avoiding court action.	✔
Claims will fall into one of the 'court tracks'. Three tracks exist: Small Claims Track, Fast Track and Multi-Track.	✔
The CPR are designed to deal with cases 'justly' and at 'proportionate cost'.	✔

Useful websites

Topic	Website
66th update of the Civil Procedure Rules	www.justice.gov.uk/courts/procedure-rules/civil

Putting it into practice – example essay question

Pauline works as a secretary for a large manufacturing company. She trips and falls on a loose stair carpet suffering some personal injury.

She has been informed that the stair carpet should have been repaired some months ago and she should receive compensation in the region of £800 for her injuries.

Advise Pauline.

Answer Plan

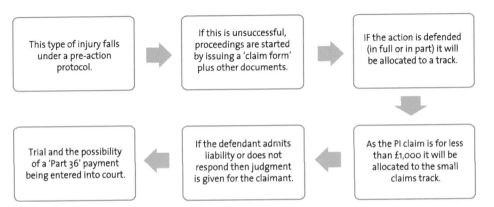

This type of injury falls under a pre-action protocol.

→ If this is unsuccessful, proceedings are started by issuing a 'claim form' plus other documents.

→ IF the action is defended (in full or in part) it will be allocated to a track.

↓

As the PI claim is for less than £1,000 it will be allocated to the small claims track.

← If the defendant admits liability or does not respond then judgment is given for the claimant.

← Trial and the possibility of a 'Part 36' payment being entered into court.

Outline Answer

* There is a Pre-Action Protocol for Personal Injury Claims, so in the first instance this should be followed.
* This is an attempt to settle the issue without the need to start proceedings.
* Parties may be encouraged to use an alternative method of dispute resolution.
* If this fails, then proceedings may be started under Part 7 by the issue of 'claim form' in the County Court. This should be accompanied by a 'particulars of claim' and a 'statement of truth'.
* If the action is defended then it will be allocated to one of the tracks.
* As the amount is less than £1,000 it will be allocated to the small claims track.
* If the action is admitted then judgment is given to the claimant.
* If the defendant does not respond then 'default judgment' is entered for the claimant.
* Other than this the matter will proceed to trial. The defendant may offer a 'Part 36' payment.

@ **Visit the book's companion website to test your knowledge**

❖ Resources include a subject map, revision tip podcasts, downloadable diagrams, MCQ quizzes for each chapter, and a flashcard glossary

❖ www.routledge.com/cw/optimizelawrevision

6

Alternative Dispute Resolution

Revision objectives

Understand the law
- Do you understand what is meant by Alternative Dispute Resolution?
- Are you able to explain the different types of resolution available?

Remember the details
- Can you remember how each resolution works?
- Can you remember which type of dispute is relevant to which type of resolution?

Reflect critically on areas of debate
- Can you outline the advantages and disadvantages of ADR?
- Are you able to critically assess the case law in this area?

Contextualise
- Can you see how this topic fits in with your topics on the court system?

Apply your skills and knowledge
- Can you complete the 'Putting it into practice' question?

Chapter Map

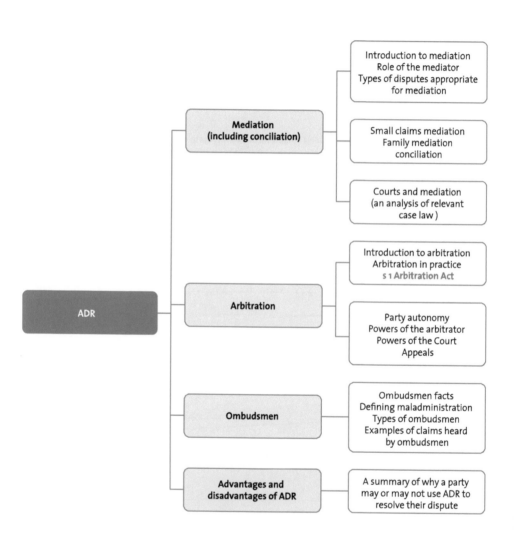

Putting it into practice – example essay question

'The courts have been promoting the use of alternative dispute resolution in civil litigation for a number of years. Critically assess why this is so and if mediation is now seen as compulsory following the cases of *Dunnett v Railtrack Plc* (2002) and *Halsey v Milton Keynes NHS Trust* (2004).'

You will find an outline answer to this question at the end of the chapter.

Introduction – Alternative Dispute Resolution (ADR)

In this chapter we will discuss the various forms of solving **civil** disputes that fall *outside* the court system.

Aim Higher

To do well in a question on ADR you need to understand the background to ADR, how it has developed, the types of ADR, how the judges have treated parties when they refuse to enter into ADR and the human rights issues surrounding the compelling of parties to use ADR. The key to success is showing you are well read and you have read the case law. It is this that will turn your essay from a descriptive one into an analytical one.

So, make sure you:

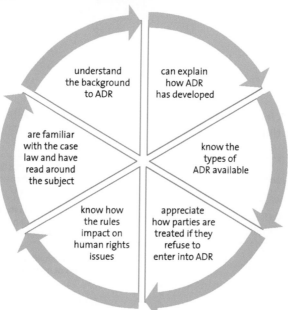

understand the background to ADR

can explain how ADR has developed

are familiar with the case law and have read around the subject

know the types of ADR available

know how the rules impact on human rights issues

appreciate how parties are treated if they refuse to enter into ADR

Note: you should be aware that Alternative Dispute Resolution is an umbrella term to describe the various options that parties can use to solve disputes, if they do not wish to, or it would be inappropriate, to go through the formal court system.

ADR has become more important due to the following:

* The Ministry of Justice (the body responsible for developing policies on ADR) stated that the courts should be the last resort for people involved in civil or family disputes.
* The use of ADR was encouraged in the Woolf Report (see your notes on Civil Litigation).
* You will see that by the Civil Procedure Rules of 1999 a judge can stop court proceedings and encourage the parties to try ADR.

Thus, the three bodies below have worked together in increasing the profile of ADR.

The various forms, as outlined in the 1999 Consultation Paper 'Alternative Dispute Resolution' are outlined below.

Arbitration	The parties agree that a third party will decide the outcome of the dispute
Mediation (including conciliation)	A mediator will help the parties to arrive at a decision between themselves
Ombudsmen	An Ombudsman will decide on matters of maladministration
Early neutral evaluation	The likely outcome of the case, should it go to court, is given

Expert determination	An independent third party expert will resolve the dispute. His decision is binding
Med-Arb	A comination of mediation and arbitration. Parties will use arbitration if mediation fails
Neutral fact finding	Each party's case is independently assessed. The findings are not binding
Utility regulators	Oversee the privatised utility providers, e.g. gas and electricity

When ADR is offered as a method of solving a dispute, it is normally *either* **arbitration, mediation** or the **ombudsman scheme** that is being considered. It is these three that we will concentrate on in this chapter.

So, remember the following:

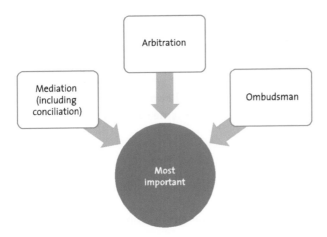

We will look at these three in more detail.

Mediation (and conciliation)

Mediation in general

Mediation is seen as an **informal** method of dispute resolution.

The parties are **assisted** in solving their dispute, rather than the dispute being settled through adjudication by a third party.

It is seen as arriving at a **'win–win'** situation rather than a 'win–lose', which is the outcome of a court hearing.

The parties **share the cost** of mediation.

Remember these key words:

What happens in mediation?

Mediation takes place by agreement; a party cannot be forced to have their dispute resolved by mediation.

Mediation can work in one of two ways.

❖ *In the first* the parties are in separate rooms. The mediator (an independent third party) goes between the parties in the hope of finding common ground and a solution. This would be appropriate where the relationship between the parties has broken down to such an extent that being in the same room would be detrimental to the proceedings, or where one of the parties is uneasy about communicating directly with the other party.

❖ *In the second* the parties are in the same room. Here the mediator's role is much the same as before.

The role of the mediator

He **does not** suggest a solution or give his opinion

He **facilitates** communication so the parties come to an agreement that they are both happy with.

Types of disputes suitable for mediation

Mediation is not suitable for solving all disputes.

The diagram below will give you an idea of the types of disputes suitable for a mediation hearing.

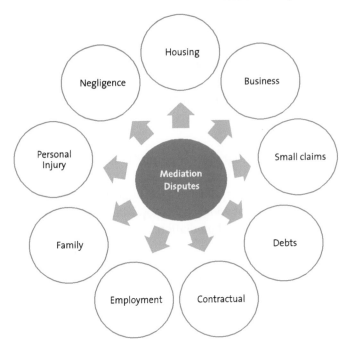

Next, we will consider how mediation works in practice

We will do this by considering (a) the small claims mediation service, (b) mediation in family cases, and (c) a note about conciliation.

Small Claims Mediation Service

* A dedicated system, offered as an alternative to the court system.
* Covers claims of less than £5,000 that are already going through the courts.
* If the parties agree, the matter can be dealt with by telephone.
* Face-to-face mediation is also available.
* The parties can always go to court if mediation fails. The judge will be unaware of the failed mediation attempt.

Mediation in family cases

* Particularly beneficial in the area of family disputes as it is hoped mediation will result in a more positive relationship in the future. This is desirable where children are involved.
* The traditional court system does little to help parties in this area, and it is seen as beneficial that parties feel they have come to an agreement between themselves, rather than having a decision imposed on them.

❖ The Family Law Act 1996 emphasised the use of mediation in this area, but you will gain marks if you show awareness of some of the pitfalls, in particular that the freedom to negotiate **may not** be exercised freely if the parties suffer from unequal bargaining power, i.e. a stronger party may be able to influence a weaker party despite the mediation process.

A note about Conciliation

❖ Similar to mediation, although the conciliator's role is more interventionist.
❖ The conciliator will go one step further and suggest possible solutions.
❖ The term 'conciliation' is **not** widely used nowadays and conciliation is now generally regarded as a form of mediation.

Mediation and the Courts

You should by now have an overall picture of mediation, and an idea of how it works, what it is trying to achieve, and that mediation is becoming increasingly important in dispute resolution.

You will need to show an understanding of the differences between the various types of mediation, but to help you gain the best mark in an exam we need to look in more depth at the law surrounding mediation and the role that the courts and legislation play.

Our **starting point** is to look at the court's duties under the **Civil Procedure Rules**.

Under Part 1.4, the 'Court's duty to manage cases', it is stated that active management includes:

> **'encouraging the parties to use an alternative dispute resolution procedure if the court considers that appropriate and facilitating the use of such procedure'.**

Other important rules include

❖ 26.4 – here the parties (or court) can request that the matter is dealt with by ADR.
❖ 44.3(5) – here parties can be penalised on costs if a party insisted on a court hearing where a settlement by ADR would have been more appropriate.

Consequences of not following the court's advice

Read the following case to see how the courts can penalise parties on costs.

Case precedent – *Dunnett v Railtrack Plc* (2002)

Facts: on an appeal hearing Railtrack refused to accept Miss Dunnett's request for arbitration.

Principle: cost implications for not engaging in ADR.

Application: although Railtrack won the appeal they were penalised on costs.

The important part of this case was the judgment by Brooks LJ:

> 'Skilled mediators are now able to achieve results satisfactory to both parties in many cases which are quite beyond the power of lawyers and courts to achieve. This court has knowledge of cases where intense feelings have arisen, for instance in relation to clinical negligence claims. But when the parties are brought together on neutral soil with a skilled mediator to help them resolve their differences, it may very well be that the mediator is able to achieve a result by which the parties shake hands at the end and feel that they have gone away having settled the dispute on terms with which they are happy to live. A mediator may be able to provide solutions which are beyond the powers of the court to provide'.

Q: Does this mean that if a party refuses mediation they will always be penalised on costs?
A: No, an objective test is used to decide whether a costs penalty should be awarded.

Read the following case where an objective test was applied.

Case precedent – *Hurst v Leeming* (2002)

Facts: Mr Hurst (a solicitor) sued Mr Leeming (a barrister) for professional negligence.

The claim failed and Mr Hurst argued that Mr Leeming should not be awarded costs as Mr Leeming had failed to agree to mediation.

Principle: costs will not always be applied if ADR is refused.

Application: the claim was unsuccessful. Leeming successfully proved to the court that mediation would not have worked due to Hurst's obsessive personality traits. The court took into account that Mr Hurst was a man convinced that he had been subject to an injustice, and would not have been able, or willing, to adopt the right attitude required for mediation to be successful.

Can a party be compelled to use ADR?
Read the case of *Halsey* below.

Case precedent – *Halsey v Milton Keynes General NHS Trust* (2004)

Facts: Mrs Halsey brought a claim against the Trust for medical negligence. She alleged a nasal drip had been incorrectly fitted, causing fluid to enter her husband's lungs.

The Trust won their case and Mrs Halsey's solicitors asks for costs not to be awarded under *Dunnett*, as the Trust had failed to agree to mediate.

Principle: cannot compel a party to use ADR.

Application: the original trial judge had awarded costs. This was upheld on appeal as Mrs Halsey had refused to show the Trust had acted **unreasonably** in refusing mediation.

Lord Justice Dyson's judgment is important.

'It is one thing to encourage the parties to agree to mediation, even to encourage them in the strongest terms. It is another to order them to do so. It seems to us that to oblige truly unwilling parties to refer their disputes to mediation would be to impose an unacceptable obstruction on their right of access to the court.

'If a judge takes the view that the case is suitable for ADR, then he or she is not, of course, obliged to take at face value the expressed opposition of the parties. In such a case, the judge should explore the reasons for any resistance to ADR. But if the parties (or at least one of them) remain intransigently opposed to ADR, then it would be wrong for the court to compel them to embrace it'.

So, clearly, Lord Dyson felt it was *wrong* to insist that unwilling parties mediate.

He continued to express the view that to do so would be a breach of the right of access to the courts under the European Convention on Human Rights (ECHR).

See the extract below:

'it seems to us likely that compulsion of ADR would be regarded as an unacceptable constraint on the right of access to the court and, therefore, a violation of Article 6. Even if (contrary to our view) the court does have jurisdiction to order unwilling parties to refer their disputes to mediation, we find it difficult to conceive of circumstances in which it would be appropriate to exercise it'.

Consider the following:

The last case to consider on this point is:

Case precedent – *Burchell v Bullard* (2005) citation

Facts: Mr Burchell (a builder) agreed to extend the home of Mr and Mrs Bullard. Mr and Mrs Bullard thought the work was sub-standard and refused to pay the bill, amounting to around £18,000.

Mr Burchell's solicitors suggested, to avoid litigation, the matter be referred to mediation.

The Bullards' building surveyor advised against this, stating that the matter was not suitable for mediation due to its technical and complex nature.

The matter went to court with Mr Burchell claiming around £18,000 and Mr and Mrs Bullard counterclaiming £100,000.

Principle: The costs implications of **not** using ADR.

Application: Mr Burchell was awarded nearly all of his £18,000 and Mr and Mrs Bullard were awarded just over £14,000, making it in effect a less than £5,000 dispute.

What is interesting is that the judge decided that as a general rule costs follow the event, which meant that Mr Burchell ended up with a costs order of around £136,000 and the Bullards were, in addition to the £5,000 awarded, a further £26,000 out of pocket. Add to that the costs of appeal – £13,500 for the appellants and £9,000 for the respondents – and it all comes to a staggering figure of just under £185,000.

Not surprisingly, Mr Burchell appealed against this costs order.

On the matter of the defendants' refusal to mediate Lord Justice Ward said:

> 'The offer to refer the matter for mediation was made in May 2001, long before the action started and long before the crippling costs had been incurred. The issue which arises is whether the defendants acted unreasonably in refusing ADR.'

In *Halsey v The Milton Keynes General NHS Trust* this court gave some guidance as to how that question should be answered. Among the relevant matters to take into account here are (a) the nature of the dispute; (b) the merits of the case; (c) whether the costs of the ADR would be disproportionately high; and (d) whether the ADR had a reasonable prospect of success.

Dealing with those in turn, it seems to me, first, that a small building dispute is par excellence the kind of dispute which, as the recorder found, lends itself to ADR.

Secondly, the merits of the case favoured mediation. The defendants behaved unreasonably in believing, if they did, that their case was so watertight that they need not engage in attempts to settle. They were counterclaiming almost as much to remedy some defective work as they had contracted to pay for the whole of the stipulated work. There was clearly room for give and take. The stated reason for refusing mediation that the matter was too complex for mediation is plain nonsense.

Thirdly, the costs of ADR would have been a drop in the ocean compared with the fortune that has been spent on this litigation.

Finally, the way in which the claimant modestly presented his claim and readily admitted many of the defects, allied with the finding that he was transparently honest and more than ready to admit where he was wrong and to shoulder responsibility for it augured well for mediation. The claimant has satisfied me that mediation would have had a reasonable prospect of success. The defendants cannot rely on their own obstinacy to assert that mediation had no reasonable prospect of success.

It seems to me, therefore, that the *Halsey* factors are established in this case and that the court should mark its disapproval of the defendants' conduct by imposing some costs sanction. Yet I draw back from doing so. This offer was made in May 2001. The defendants rejected the offer on the advice of their surveyor, not of their solicitor.'

Aim Higher

It may take a while to read the above quote but you should make the effort to do so. Showing evidence of reading judgments will help you gain a higher mark in the exam. A summary is provided below.

Providing an analysis of the above cases is a popular exam question.

To gain a good mark you need to show understanding of how the law has developed and how the judges have treated cases where ADR may be relevant. An exam question in this area would normally be an essay question asking you to analyse the judgments.

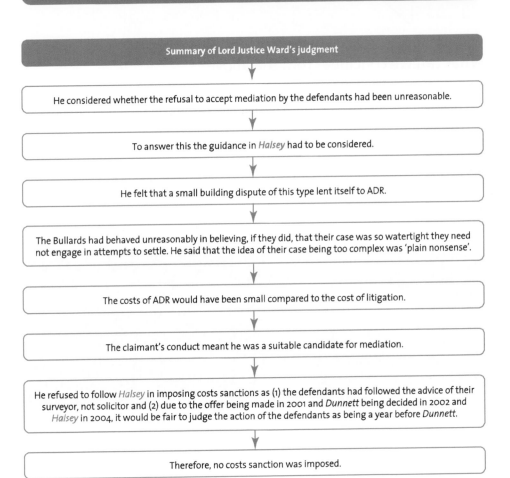

Summary of Lord Justice Ward's judgment

He considered whether the refusal to accept mediation by the defendants had been unreasonable.

To answer this the guidance in *Halsey* had to be considered.

He felt that a small building dispute of this type lent itself to ADR.

The Bullards had behaved unreasonably in believing, if they did, that their case was so watertight they need not engage in attempts to settle. He said that the idea of their case being too complex was 'plain nonsense'.

The costs of ADR would have been small compared to the cost of litigation.

The claimant's conduct meant he was a suitable candidate for mediation.

He refused to follow *Halsey* in imposing costs sanctions as (1) the defendants had followed the advice of their surveyor, not solicitor and (2) due to the offer being made in 2001 and *Dunnett* being decided in 2002 and *Halsey* in 2004, it would be fair to judge the action of the defendants as being a year before *Dunnett*.

Therefore, no costs sanction was imposed.

He did provide some guidance for the future.

> 'The profession must, however, take no comfort from this conclusion. Halsey has made plain not only the high rate of a successful outcome being achieved by mediation but also its established importance as a track to a just result running parallel with that of the court system. Both have a proper part to play in the administration of justice. The court has given its stamp of approval to mediation and it is now the legal profession which must become fully aware of and acknowledge its value. The profession can no longer with impunity shrug aside reasonable requests to mediate. The parties cannot ignore a proper request to mediate simply because it was made before the claim was issued. With court fees escalating it may be folly to do so. I draw attention, moreover, to paragraph 5.4 of the pre--action protocol for Construction and Engineering Disputes – which I doubt was at the forefront of the parties' minds – which expressly requires the parties to consider at a pre--action meeting whether some form of alternative dispute resolution procedure would be more suitable than litigation. These defendants have escaped the imposition of a costs sanction in this case but defendants in a like position in the future can expect little sympathy if they blithely battle on regardless of the alternatives.'

What can we conclude from the above?

❖ That this decision is **unlikely** to be followed.
❖ That *Halsey* has now established mediation as an important tool in dispute resolution.
❖ That the legal profession should take seriously a reasonable request for mediation.
❖ That pre-action protocols (see the Civil Justice chapter) should be adhered to.

Aim Higher – revision tip

As we discussed earlier, one of the challenges with your ELS exam is to show the examiner evidence of analysis. It is much easier to analyse the law in your other subjects.

The key to gaining good marks in your ELS exam is to show good understanding of the case law and that you have undertaken wider reading. Evidence of reading articles will be expected at degree level.

Arbitration
Arbitration facts

❖ It is the oldest (and most formal) form of Alternative Dispute Resolution.

❖ Arbitration is commonly used by those in a commercial relationship. It is now common to find an arbitration clause inserted into contracts.

❖ Proceedings are held in private, which is an advantage to those parties wishing to resolve their disputes confidentially.

❖ Although it is the most formal of the ADR systems, it is quicker and more informal than litigation. This is mainly due to the lack of formal rules for evidence.

❖ The procedure of arbitration is deemed to be more inquisitorial than adversarial.

❖ In common with other ADR options it is seen as quicker and cheaper than the traditional court system.

❖ The parties can be legally represented.

❖ The parties are more likely to continue their commercial relationship having gone through arbitration.

Remember these key points:

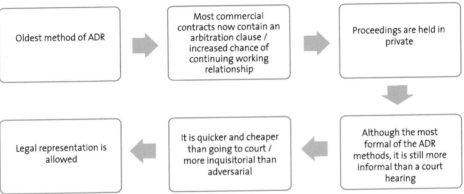

Arbitration in practice

❖ The parties to a dispute agree that a third party (the arbitrator) will resolve the dispute for them.

❖ The arbitrator may be an expert in his field or he can be a lawyer.

❖ The arbitrator's decision is legally binding on both parties; it is, therefore, the most court-like procedure.

❖ An arbitrator will sit alone or in a panel.

Arbitration is based upon certain principles. These are contained in s 1 Arbitration Act 1996.

Section 1 Arbitration Act 1996
• (a) the object of arbitration is to obtain the fair resolution of disputes by an impartial tribunal without necessary delay or expense;
• (b) the parties should be free to agree how their disputes are resolved, subject only to such safeguards as are necessary in the public interest;
• (c) in matters governed by the part of the Act, the court should not intervene except as provided by this part.

We will now consider the 1996 Act in more detail under the following headings:

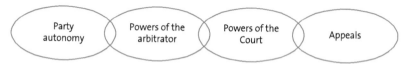

Party autonomy

Parties are free to tailor the process to their own needs. This is enshrined in s 1(b) of the 1996 Act (see above). From *Jivraj v Hashwani* (2011) we can see that arbitrators are not 'employees' and therefore, in their selection process, nationality and religion cannot be taken into account. This means that arbitrators can be selected from a particular religious group without contravening current laws.

The powers of the arbitrator

There are several sections of the Act to consider here.

On powers over jurisdiction see ss 30 and 32

Section 30 is important as it gives the arbitrator power to rule on matters relating to jurisdiction.

So, in the absence of agreement between the parties, he can rule on the following:

❖ whether there is a valid arbitration agreement;
❖ whether the arbitration tribunal is properly constituted;
❖ what matters have been submitted to arbitration in accordance with the agreement.

Section 32 allows the arbitrator to rule on substantive jurisdiction. The parties have limited grounds to raise objections, and can do so only with agreement of the parties, permission of the arbitration tribunal or agreement of the court.

On matters of arbitrator immunity see s 29

Section 29 provides immunity for the arbitrator. He is not liable or anything done or omitted in his function as an arbitrator unless he can be shown to have acted in bad faith.

On general duties of the tribunal see s 33

Section 33 creates a duty on the tribunal to act fairly and impartially, giving each side an opportunity to state its case. To assist this, the tribunal has the power to adopt procedures that avoid unnecessary expense and delay.

The Powers of the Court

There are several sections of the Act to consider here too

Section 9 covers the situation where one party has ignored a valid arbitration agreement; a party can request the court to stay the litigation in favour of the arbitration agreement.

Section 43 gives the court the power to compel a witness to attend a tribunal and to produce documentary evidence.

Section 24 gives the court power to remove an arbitrator.

An arbitrator can be removed for the following reasons

❖ He has not acted impartially.
❖ He does not possess the necessary qualifications.
❖ He lacks the required mental or physical capacity.
❖ He has refused or failed to properly conduct proceedings.

Appeals

There are limited grounds for appeal.

Section 67 allows an appeal challenging any award of the arbitral tribunal as to its substantive jurisdiction

Section 68 allows an appeal on procedural grounds (there has been a serious irregularity).

a. The Act sets out nine kinds of irregularity (four are reproduced below)
b. failure by the tribunal to comply with s 33 (general duty of tribunal);
c. the tribunal exceeding its powers (otherwise than by exceeding its substantive jurisdiction: see s 67);
d. failure by the tribunal to conduct the proceedings in accordance with the procedure agreed by the parties;
e. failure by the tribunal to deal with all the issues that were put to it.

Aim Higher – revision tip

In the exam you would be expected to show knowledge of the **1996 Arbitration Act**, its sections and what those sections state.

Ombudsman

The role of the Ombudsman

The Ombudsman's role is to investigate complaints of **maladministration**.

Ombudsman facts

❖ The first Ombudsman was appointed under the Parliamentary Commissioner Act 1967.

❖ His role was to investigate complaints of injustice resulting from **maladministration** by *government departments*. This was then expanded to cover any injustice or hardship caused by the National Health Service. Since then a number of other ombudsmen have appeared (see below).

❖ Ombudsmen are free of charge and independent of the organisation they are investigating.

❖ A person seeking the help of an Ombudsman will normally have to complain to the organisation first, before making a claim to the Ombudsman.

❖ Complaints are usually made on an application form to the relevant Ombudsman.

❖ If an Ombudsman upholds a complaint, he will recommend a course of action to the organisation concerned, and the organisation will normally follow the recommendation.

Defining maladministration	❖ Maladministration occurs where a person has suffered a personal injustice, hardship or financial loss due to the action (or lack of action) of an organisation. ❖ They are interested in the **way** an organisation has dealt with a situation or reached their decision, **rather** than the decision itself.

The 1967 Act does not define maladministration, but while the Bill was being debated, the Government spokesman, Richard Crossman, cited **'bias, neglect, inattention, delay, incompetence, ineptitude, arbitrariness'** as falling within the meaning of maladministration.

In 1993, the Ombudsman, Sir William Reid, expanded on Crossman's list, adding the following examples of maladministration.

❖ rudeness (though that is a matter of degree)

❖ unwillingness to treat the complainant as a person with rights

❖ refusing to answer reasonable questions
❖ neglecting to inform a complainant on request of his or her rights or entitlement
❖ knowingly giving advice which is misleading or inadequate
❖ ignoring valid advice or overruling considerations which would produce an uncomfortable result for the overruler
❖ offering no redress or manifestly disproportionate redress
❖ showing bias whether because of colour, sex or any other ground
❖ failing to follow proper procedures.

See below for types of ombudsmen and the areas of complaint that they cover:

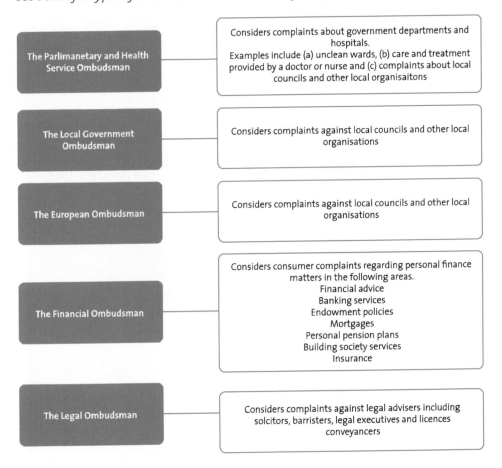

The Parlimanetary and Health Service Ombudsman — Considers complaints about government departments and hospitals.
Examples include (a) unclean wards, (b) care and treatment provided by a doctor or nurse and (c) complaints about local councils and other local organisaitons

The Local Government Ombudsman — Considers complaints against local councils and other local organisations

The European Ombudsman — Considers complaints against local councils and other local organisations

The Financial Ombudsman — Considers consumer complaints regarding personal finance matters in the following areas.
Financial advice
Banking services
Endowment policies
Mortgages
Personal pension plans
Building society services
Insurance

The Legal Ombudsman — Considers complaints against legal advisers including solcitors, barristers, legal executives and licences conveyancers

Advantages and disadvantages of ADR

Our last section concerns why people think using ADR is a good (or bad) idea. We will do this by considering the **advantages** and **disadvantages** of using ADR.

Advantages of using ADR

* Flexibility
* Informality
* Speed
* Cost-effective
* Confidential (no one outside of the process will be aware of the proceedings)
* The complexity of law and legal procedures can be avoided
* Avoids the intimidating atmosphere of court

* *In Mediation*
* Reach an agreement between themselves, more likely to stick and honour the outcome
* Individuals have greater control and responsibility, therefore it empowers individuals, they control the length, and what is discussed and the outcome
* More likely to have a continuing relationship
* If mediation fails, the parties can go to court to have their dispute settled

* *In Arbitration*
* An expert arbitrator can be used

 Disadvantages of using ADR

* *In Mediation*
* Imbalance of power
* Lack of legal expertise
* Enforcement problems
* Sometimes the success of the process can depend on the quality of the mediator

* *In Arbitration*
* No precedent
* May not necessarily be cheaper than a court action
* Informality may not suit everyone
* Limited avenues for appeal

Core issues checklist

ADR covers dispute resolution that falls outside the court system.	✔
Although there are several methods of ADR, the three most important are: mediation, arbitration and resolution by the Ombudsman.	✔
In Mediation a Mediator will talk to the parties, facilitating communication in the hope of helping the parties to arrive at an agreement. He does not suggest a solution.	✔
Mediation is not appropriate for all disputes. Problems relating to family, housing or debts issues may be solved this way if the parties agree.	✔
Arbitration is the oldest and most 'court-like' ADR method.	✔
Parties can be legally represented and it is common to find arbitration agreements in most commercial contracts.	✔
The Ombudsman will investigate complaints of 'maladministration'. This is where a party has suffered a personal injustice, hardship or financial loss due to the action of an organisation.	✔

Useful websites

Topic	Website
British and Irish Ombudsman Association	http://bioa.org.uk/
Centre for Effective Dispute Resolution	www.cedr.co.uk
Chartered Institute of Arbitrators	www.ciarb.org.uk

Putting it into practice – example essay question

'The courts have been promoting the use of Alternative Dispute Resolution in civil litigation for a number of years. Critically assess why this is so and if mediation is now seen as compulsory following the cases of *Dunnett v Railtrack Plc* (2002) and *Halsey v Milton Keynes NHS Trust* (2004).'

Aim Higher

To gain good marks at degree level you will be expected to provide some critical analysis.

It is unlikely you will be asked a question that requires a descriptive answer, although you would be expected to state why people use arbitration (advantages) and its downfalls (disadvantages).

A typical exam question is given below. This is asking you to critique the case law in this area.

Answer plan

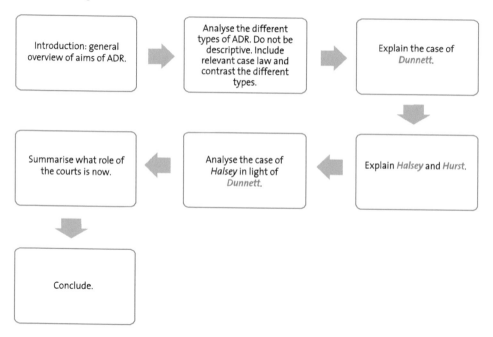

Outline answer

❖ Students should discuss the general aims of ADR, its purpose and why it is sometimes more suitable than court action.

❖ A more detailed analysis of each type of ADR (arbitration and mediation) and how it compares to the court system would help to explain the case law in this area. Emphasis should be drawn between the imposing of judgments (litigation), resolution of dispute by a third party (arbitration) and the negotiation of an outcome (mediation). The advantages and disadvantages of each would be discussed here. Instead of writing a list, it may be useful to compare each form of ADR with another when stating the advantages/disadvantages.

- ❖ You should now discuss the judgment in *Dunnett* where it was outlined there would be costs implications for those who failed to enter mediation.
- ❖ You should then discuss *Halsey*, where it was decided that only if mediation was 'unreasonably refused' would an order for costs be imposed. You could use the case of *Hurst* to illustrate your argument.
- ❖ Students should assess whether the judge in *Halsey* was correct in clarifying the judgment in *Dunnett*. Consider here whether it is contrary to the spirit of mediation to force a party to mediate.
- ❖ Conclude that in light of the human rights aspect highlighted in *Halsey*, it is probably incorrect to insist parties resolve their dispute through mediation, although, due to its several advantages, it is correct for judges to assess whether the dispute might be best settled by mediation.

Aim Higher

Read the case of *Leicester Circuits v Coates Brothers* [2003] EWCA Civ 474

Note: the court applied *Dunnett* in this case. Although judgment was awarded it did not award **full** costs, due to a failure to enter into mediation.

In particular note Lord Justice Judge at paragraph 27:

'It seems to us that the unexplained withdrawal from an agreed mediation process was of significance to the continuation of this litigation. We do not for one moment assume that the mediation process would have succeeded, but certainly there is a prospect that it would have done if it had been allowed to proceed. That therefore bears on the issue of costs'.

Aim Higher – putting it into practice

Can you answer the following questions without referring to your chapter notes?

1. What types of ADR are there?
2. When are they used?
3. Can the courts impose ADR?
4. State the relevant case law
5. Why might a party choose ADR?

Table of key cases referred to in this chapter

Case name	Area of law	Principle
Burchell v Bullard [2005] EWCA Civ 358	Refusal to mediate	To decide whether a party had been unreasonable in refusing to mediate, the guidance in *Halsey* must be considered.

Case name	Area of law	Principle
Dunnett v Railtrack Plc [2002] EWCA Civ 303	Costs penalties	A party may be penalised on costs if they unreasonably refuse ADR.
Halsey v Milton Keynes General NHS Trust [2004] EWCA Civ 576	Compel a party to ADR?	Although a party can be encouraged to use ADR they cannot be compelled to do so.
Hurst v Leeming [2002] EWCA Civ 1173	Objectives test applied to decide costs penalties	An objective test will be used to decide whether a party was unreasonable in refusing to use ADR.
Jivraj v Hashwani [2011] UKSC 40	Are arbitrators employees?	They are not employees, so can be appointed from a religious group

---

@ **Visit the book's companion website to test your knowledge**

❖ Resources include a subject map, revision tip podcasts, downloadable diagrams, MCQ quizzes for each chapter, and a flashcard glossary

❖ www.routledge.com/cw/optimizelawrevision

7

Criminal Justice

Revision objectives

Understand the law
- Do you understand the powers that police have to stop, search, arrest and detain?
- Do you understand the factors that may give rise to a miscarriage of justice?

Remember the details
- Can you remember the key provisions that deal with police powers and bail?

Reflect critically on the law
- Are you able to reflect critically on the potential causes of miscarriages of justice?
- Are you able to reflect critically on the measures that have been adopted in an effort to reduce the frequency of these miscarriages of justice?

Contextualise the law
- Are you able to contextualise the political/policy dimensions in relation to the criminal justice system?
- Do you understand the context in which decisions to prosecute are made?

Apply your skills and knowledge
- Are you able to apply your knowledge, using relevant cases and authorities, to the 'Putting it into practice' question at the end of this chapter?

Chapter Map

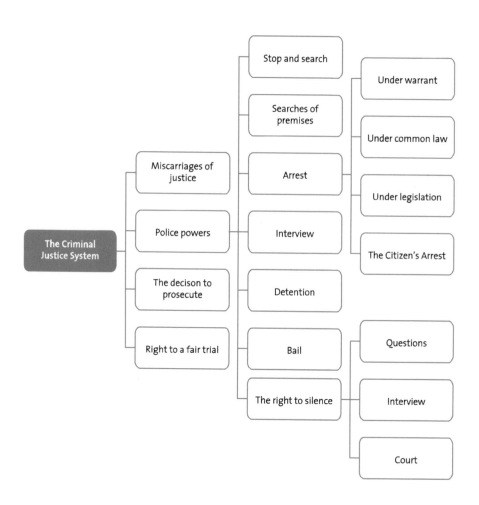

Putting it into practice – example essay question

'Consider critically what safeguards exist to guard against a miscarriage of justice within the English legal system.'

An outline answer is available at the end of this chapter.

Introduction

In this chapter we are going to consider several different aspects of the criminal justice system. The criminal justice system is a vast and complex area of any English legal system course. As a result we have taken the decision to focus our attention on areas which we believe are the most popular assessment areas. This means that certain aspects of the criminal justice system such as court procedure are not covered in this revision guide. You should check your course syllabus and speak with your lecturer regarding the scope and focus of **YOUR** course. Remember that there can be significant variations between courses in terms of content and focus.

A common theme in this chapter will be the balancing of competing interests. We start our examination of the criminal justice system by considering the purpose of the system. The aims of the criminal justice system can be articulated as follows:

❖ to deliver justice for all, by convicting and punishing the guilty;
❖ to help and support offenders to stop offending;
❖ to protect the innocent.

This chapter is divided into the following sections:

Miscarriages of justice • Police powers • The decision to prosecute • The right to a fair trial

Miscarriages of justice

It is important to note from the outset that criminal justice is a highly politicised area. As such, successive governments have sought to win votes and gain credibility through their policies on crime and criminal justice. This has frequently led to inconsistent, competing policies and objectives.

Key term: miscarriage of justice	❖ A broad meaning of this term refers to a situation in which there has been a failure of justice. ❖ A narrower meaning (perhaps a more common meaning) relates to a situation where an innocent person has been convicted of a criminal offence. It is this meaning that we will use in this chapter.

There are a number of reasons why a miscarriage of justice may occur. They can be the result of:

❖ poor legal representation;
❖ the adversarial process;
❖ where a witness identifies the wrong person;
❖ errors or misconduct in the investigation process;
❖ errors or misconduct in the prosecution process;
❖ incorrect/compromised forensic evidence;
❖ false confessions and false evidence;
❖ incorrect expert evidence;
❖ poor summing-up by the judge.

Miscarriage of justice cases

When answering a question on miscarriages of justice it is important that you are able to illustrate your answer by reference to relevant cases. Unfortunately, there are far too many to choose from. The most important thing to remember here is that it is not necessary to list as many cases as you can recall. It is much better to select a few cases which will ideally demonstrate some of the different causes (outlined above) of failures in justice.

	The Birmingham Six	Stefan Kiszko	Angela Cannings
Conviction	**Convicted of murder:** conviction obtained on the basis of confessions and forensic evidence.	**Convicted of murder and rape:** conviction obtained on the basis of confession, forensic evidence and witness accounts.	**Convicted of murdering her own children:** convicted on the basis of expert evidence.

Causes of the miscarriage of justice	The defendants claimed that they had been beaten and threatened by the police.	Kiszko had no legal representation at the police station. He confessed after oppressive questioning. Mistakes were made by the defence.	Cannings was convicted on the basis that three of her children had died in their infancy. An expert witness testified that the only plausible explanation was that Cannings had killed her children.
Outcome	Sixteen years later new forensic evidence indicated that the police had altered confessions.	Witnesses later admitted their statements were false. Forensic evidence also demonstrated that he could not be the perpetrator.	The expert witness in the case was later discredited and Cannings was released.

Miscarriages of justice undermine public confidence in the criminal justice system. Following a succession of high-profile miscarriages of justice, the Police and Criminal Evidence Act 1984 (PACE) was introduced as a means of protecting suspects' rights at the investigation stage of the criminal justice process. It should be clear from the foregoing that while errors or misconduct at the investigation stage can lead to miscarriages of justice, there are a number of other potential causes.

The Criminal Cases Review Commission

In 1997 the Criminal Cases Review Commission (CCRC) was set up by the Criminal Appeal Act 1995. The CCRC is an independent public body which reviews criminal cases where there has been an alleged miscarriage of justice. The CCRC consists of eleven Commissioners, appointed in accordance with the Office for the Commissioner for Public Appointments' Code of Practice. At least one third of the commissioners must be legally qualified.

It is particularly important for you to note that:

❖ The CCRC cannot overturn convictions or sentences.
❖ It can refer the following cases to the Court of Appeal:
    (a) convictions for indictable offences
    (b) verdicts of not guilty by reason of insanity

(c) a finding that a person was under a disability at the commission of the offence

(d) cases in respect of sentence.

❖ The CCRC can also refer convictions and sentences from the Magistrates' Court to the Crown Court.

❖ In most circumstances an application to the CCRC can only be made where the applicant has already appealed and failed.

❖ In order to refer a case, the CCRC will need to be satisfied that 'there is a real possibility that the conviction, verdict, finding or sentence would not be upheld if a reference were made'.

Case load*

Total number of applications for review	16,458
Cases waiting	608
Cases currently under review	545
Number of cases completed	15,305 (incl. ineligible), 530 referrals
Number of cases heard by the Court of Appeal	498 (of which 341 convictions were quashed, 145 convictions were upheld, and 2 reserved)

* Figures taken from the CCRC website in June 2013. Up to date figures can be obtained by going to: www.justice. gov.uk/about/criminal-cases-review-commission

Aim Higher

The CCRC has been the subject of significant criticism in recent years. A good student will demonstrate an understanding of these criticisms in addition to engagement with academic literature in the area.

Criticisms include:

❖ In order to conduct investigations into alleged miscarriages of justice, the CCRC frequently has to rely on the police for certain tasks; there is a concern that in cases where there are allegations of police misconduct or incompetence the police are not impartial.

❖ The process is lengthy and the CCRC has a significant backlog.

❖ The CCRC has focused time and resources on historic cases where the convicted person has long since died. This has deflected resources from living potential victims of miscarriages of justice.

❖ The CCRC Commissioners are appointed by the Government: this raises concerns about impartiality.

Common Pitfall

One of the most common mistakes that students will make when answering a question on miscarriages of justice is that they will provide a descriptive narrative of a number of high-profile cases without considering existing safeguards. You need to resist the temptation to 'tell a story' and remember that the focus of any law assignment is . . . the law!

Make sure that you consider a full range of safeguards against miscarriages of justice and the variety of causes.

POLICE POWERS

Aim Higher – revision tip

Police powers is an area in which examiners are likely to ask two types of question:

1. An essay question; or
2. A problem question.

Problem questions are a daunting prospect for many students, although problem questions quickly become the preferred question style for most law students. There are a few general points that we can make in relation to approaching problem questions that will help you improve your technique (and hopefully your marks)!

❖ Read the question carefully; every line in a problem question is there for a reason. Use a highlighter or underline the issues that you feel are important.
❖ Do not be tempted to repeat the facts of the question (no matter how eloquently) in your answer. This attracts no marks and wastes your valuable time and words.
❖ Deal with issues under subheadings in the order in which they appear in the question (chronological order).
❖ If you have several parties, use subheadings to make it clear to the examiner that you have addressed each party. Do not jump back and forth between issues/parties.
❖ Using legal authorities to support your statements of law is equally important in the context of a problem question. No law – no pass!
❖ Remember **IDAA**: **Identify** the relevant law, **Define** the law, **Apply** the law to the situation you are dealing with and provide **Authority** . . . Remember **IDAA**!

Topic Map

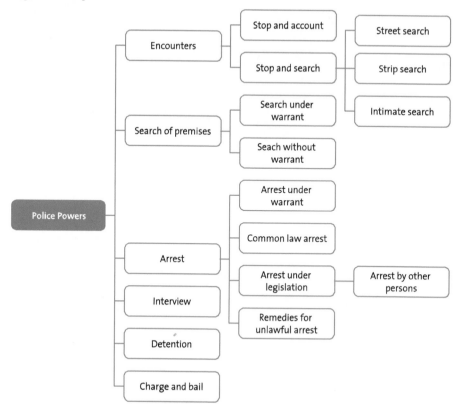

The Police and Criminal Evidence Act 1984 (PACE) was introduced as a response to a number of high-profile miscarriages of justice. The Act replaced a complex array of common law and legislative provisions. It establishes a code of police powers in relation to:

❖ stop and search
❖ arrest
❖ detention
❖ interrogation.

PACE also establishes the rights of suspects in relation to the above. The key statutes that you will need to be aware of in relation to police powers are:

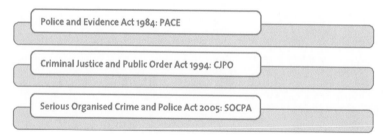

Police and Evidence Act 1984: PACE

Criminal Justice and Public Order Act 1994: CJPO

Serious Organised Crime and Police Act 2005: SOCPA

There are also a number of **Codes of Practice** which are drawn up by the Home Office under s **66** of **PACE**.

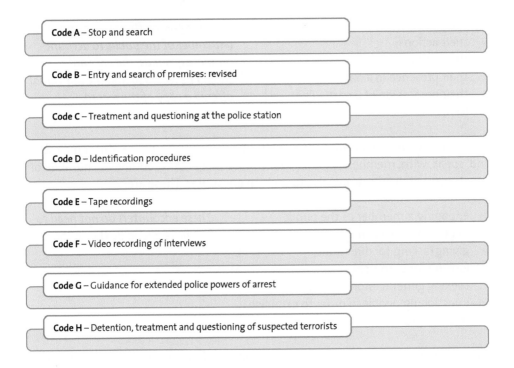

Code A – Stop and search

Code B – Entry and search of premises: revised

Code C – Treatment and questioning at the police station

Code D – Identification procedures

Code E – Tape recordings

Code F – Video recording of interviews

Code G – Guidance for extended police powers of arrest

Code H – Detention, treatment and questioning of suspected terrorists

The **Codes of Practice** provide additional detail on the legislative framework. In the event that the **Codes of Practice** are breached by the police:

❖ evidence obtained in breach of the **Codes of Practice** may be excluded at trial;
❖ disciplinary action may be taken against individuals who have breached the **Codes of Practice**.

Section 11 of the Criminal Justice Act 2003 made changes to the way in which the **Codes of Practice** are established and amended, making the process less bureaucratic.

Aim Higher

Although it is unlikely that you will need a detailed understanding of the Codes of Practice, you can find current, revised copies of the different codes by going to the following website: www.gov.uk/police-and-criminal-evidence-act-1984-pace-codes-of-practice.

Stop and account

Primary Code of Practice Code A *of* PACE

Stop and Account occurs when a police officer stops a member of the public and asks them to account for any of the following:

* themselves;
* their actions;
* their behaviour;
* their presence in a particular place;
* their possession of a particular item or items.

Where a police officer stops and asks a member of the public to account on these grounds, the encounter should be recorded and the individual offered a copy of the record.

There are of course, a number of other situations in which a police officer may stop and speak with members of the public. Code A of PACE outlines a number of situations that give may give rise to such an encounter. These are:

* engaging a member of the public in general conversation;
* giving/asking for directions;
* looking for witnesses;
* seeking general information;
* questioning people in order to establish the background to events.

These encounters do not need to be recorded by the police.

As has frequently been the case in this revision guide we will start by considering a general rule. The general rule is that individuals stopped and asked questions by the police are not under a legal obligation to answer questions. The authority for this is the case of *Rice v Connolly* (1966). There are, however, some qualifications to this general rule that you need to be aware of. While there is no requirement in law to answer questions when stopped by the police, refusing to do so in a rude and/or aggressive manner may constitute obstruction of the police, which is an arrestable offence: *Rickets v Cox* (1982).

A further qualification to the general rule is created by s 50 of the Police Reform Act 2002. This provides that a police officer can require an individual behaving in an antisocial manner to give their name and address. Refusing to do so, or misleading a police officer as to identity and address, is grounds for arrest under s 25 of PACE.

Members of the public are not under a legal obligation to attend at a police station unless they are under arrest. An individual who does attend a police station voluntarily is entitled to leave at any time, unless subsequently placed under arrest. Code C of PACE provides detail on the information that individuals attending voluntarily should be given.

Physical contact to stop

It is settled law that the police do not have the power to detain individuals short of arresting them for the purposes of assisting the police with their enquiries: *R v Lemsatef* (1977). If a police officer takes hold of a person in order to prevent them from leaving in order to compel them to answer questions this could constitute an unlawful detention and/or common assault: *Kenlin v Gardiner* (1967). It is worth noting that a *de minimus* interference (this is simply a Latin expression for minimal things), such as a police officer tapping a person on the shoulder, is unlikely to constitute an unlawful detention or common assault. The authority for this principle of law is the case of *Donnelly v Jackman* (1970).

Stop and search

Stop and search, like arrest, is a police power that most people are aware of. It is also a police power that has attracted much media and political controversy. Code A governs the exercise of police powers, without first making an arrest. Section 1 of PACE provides that a police officer may search a person or vehicle in a public place for stolen or prohibited items. The list of prohibited items includes:

❖ offensive weapons;
❖ items used for the purposes of committing a burglary or related crimes;
❖ professional fireworks;
❖ articles intended to cause criminal damage (added under the CJA 2003).

This power can be exercised only where the police have 'reasonable grounds for suspecting that they will find stolen or prohibited items'. What this means is that searches of this nature should never be random in nature. The police are entitled to seize any 'prohibited items' found during the search.

You will notice that controlled substances (drugs) are not contained within this list. The power to search a suspect for a controlled substance derives not from s 1 of PACE but from s 23 of the Misuse of Drugs Act 1971. As with a search under s 1 of PACE the police officer in question must have a reasonable suspicion that the suspect is in possession of a controlled substance.

As we have just seen PACE is not the only legislation which confers powers upon the police to stop and search individuals other legislation conferring stop and search powers includes:

- ❖ Section 7(2) of the Sporting Events (Control of Alcohol) Alcohol Act 1985. This Act provides that a police officer can search a person if they have reasonable grounds to suspect that the individual is in possession of alcohol at certain sporting events.
- ❖ Under s 43 of the Terrorism Act 2000, the police can search any person they reasonably suspect to be a terrorist in order to determine whether they have in their possession anything which may constitute evidence that they are a terrorist.
- ❖ Section 60 of the Criminal Justice and Public Order Act 1994 permits a police officer of the rank of inspector or above to authorise searches searches for dangerous instruments or weapons, in circumstances where there is a reasonable belief that serious violence may take place within an area.
- ❖ Under s 44 of the Terrorism Act 2000 the Home Secretary was able to authorise the police to conduct stop and searches at random in a designated area for a period of 28 days.
- ❖ The case of *Gillan and Quinton v United Kingdom - 4158/05* [2010] ECHR 2 held that searches undertaken under s 44 of the Terrorism Act 2000 were unlawful as they were not based on reasonable suspicion. As such they were incompatible with Article 8 of the ECHR.
- ❖ Section 44 of the Terrorism Act 2000 has been repealed by the Protection of Freedoms Act 2012.

> Note: Searches under s 60 of the Criminal Justice and Public Order Act (CJPO) 1994 and s 44 of the Terrorism Act 2000 before it was repealed permitted searches at random. In short 'reasonable suspicion' was not required.

Reasonable grounds

The power to stop and search must be exercised fairly and with respect for the person being searched. The Equality Act 2010 makes it unlawful for police officers to discriminate against or harass any person on the grounds of the 'protected characteristics' of age, disability, gender, race, religion or belief, sex and sexual orientation, marriage and civil partnership, pregnancy and maternity when using their powers.

Reasonable grounds for suspicion can be established in a number of different ways but it will most likely be the result of:

- ❖ a suspect's behaviour; or
- ❖ accurate intelligence or information.

Procedure for a stop and search

Aim Higher – revision tip

A problem-style question may outline a scenario in which there have been both breaches of procedure and breaches of law. In this situation the examiner is asking you to distinguish between the two and explain what remedies may be available for a breach of procedure versus a breach of law.

Before a search can take place the police officer must:

1. explain that the suspect is being detained for the purposes of a search;
2. give their (the officer's) name;
3. identify the station that they are based at;
4. provide the legal search power that is being exercised, e.g. s 1 PACE or s 23 Misuse of Drugs Act 1971;
5. provide a clear explanation of the object of the search in terms of the article or articles for which there is a power to search.
6. Suspects searched are entitled to a record of the search.

Where can a search take place?

Section 1(1) of PACE stipulates that a search can take place in any place to which the public, or any section of the public, has access either on payment or otherwise, by virtue of express or implied permission. For example this includes:

❖ roads and pavements;
❖ places that individuals have express permission to enter such as cinemas, theatres and nightclubs;
❖ places where individuals have implied permission to enter such as gardens, places of business, shops and restaurants.

The powers under s 1 of PACE cannot be used to search:

❖ a person in a dwelling;
❖ a person in the garden of a dwelling, if that person has permission from the owner to be there, or permission from anyone else living in the dwelling;
❖ a vehicle located on land attached to a dwelling, if the person who lives in the dwelling has given permission for the vehicle to be located on that land.

Key points: searches

❖ The police are entitled to use reasonable force in order to conduct a stop and search under s 117 PACE. This should however, be used only as a last resort and never on a detainee who is compliant.
❖ The police can only ask a detainee to remove certain items of clothing: s 2(9) of PACE. You can use the acronym J.O.G to help you remember which items of clothing a police officer conducting a search can request be removed: Jacket, Outer Coat and Gloves.
❖ In circumstances where authorisation has been given under s 60 of the Criminal Justice and Public Order Act 1994 (CJPO) it is provided (s 60AA) that police officers can additionally request the removal of disguises such as masks.
❖ A police officer can conduct a more detailed search requiring removal of a T-shirt, footwear or headgear but this must take place out of public view. It should be conducted by a police officer of the same sex as the suspect.
❖ The length of time a person is detained for a search must be reasonable: Code A.

Strip searches and intimate searches

The police can carry out strip searches but only at a nearby police station or other location, which is out of public view. An officer of the same sex as the suspect must carry out a strip search.

Section 55 of PACE allows the police to conduct an intimate search of a suspect (this is sometimes referred to as an internal body cavity search). This type of search must be authorised by a superintendent, who must have grounds for believing that a weapon or drug is concealed in a body orifice. The search itself must be conducted by a health care professional.

Following an amendment by the CJPO 1994 a search of the mouth is not classified as an intimate search.

Aim Higher – revision tip

It is important to draw a distinction between 'stop and search' powers and police powers to conduct 'other searches'.

In this context stop and search can be taken to mean:

❖ searches undertaken under s 1 of PACE;
❖ searches undertaken under s 23 of the Misuse of Drugs Act 1971;
❖ searches undertaken under s 60 of the Criminal Justice and Public Order Act 1994.

In July 2013 the Government launched a public consultation into police powers to stop and search in relation to some of legislation outlined above. A copy of the consultation paper can be found at: www.gov.uk/government/uploads/system/uploads/attachment_data/file/212014/Stop_and_Search_consultation_Revised_WEB_v2.pdf

The consultation process closed in September 2013.

Search after arrest

Following arrest, police officers need to search suspects for evidence or anything that may be used to cause harm. Section 32 of PACE allows a police officer to search a person under arrest at a place other than a police station and s 54 of PACE allows the police to search an arrested person on arrival at the police station. The police can seize items which they reasonably suspect might be evidence, or items which may be used to injure anyone, or used to escape.

Search of premises

Primary Code of Practice **Code B** of **PACE**
We are now going to continue our consideration of searches but in the context of the search of premises.

Search of premises after arrest
Section 18 of PACE allows the police to search the premises of a person under arrest for an indictable offence. In this context the police are searching for evidence of the offence in question, or a similar offence. Section 18(3) limits the power to search to the extent that is reasonably required for the purpose of discovering such evidence.

Code B allows the police to use reasonable and proportionate force to gain entry to premises if the occupier has refused entry, or if it is not possible to communicate with the occupier.

What constitutes premises?
The term premises includes the following: any place in the open air; any place under occupation or ownership. It is important to note that the premises in question must be occupied or controlled by the suspect. Searches should be made at a reasonable hour. This is not always practical however, particularly if the results of the search are likely to be prejudiced.

Procedure for a search of premises

Before starting the search a police officer should identify themselves to any person present at the premises. They should also explain the grounds for the search. The police can seize and retain evidence obtained in the search. We are now moving on to consider the search of premises under warrant.

Search of premises under warrant

Key term: warrant

❖ A warrant is a formal document of authority issued by a magistrate or a judge. It instructs the person to whom it is addressed to carry out a specific action on behalf of the court. The most common warrants are:
❖ a search warrant;
❖ a warrant of arrest.

Under s 8 of PACE the police can apply to a magistrate for a search warrant. This is an additional and distinct power from a s 18 search as outlined above. It allows the police to search the premises of individuals in order to search for evidence.

Section 8 of PACE states that a warrant may be granted where there are reasonable grounds for believing:

(a) that an indictable offence has been committed; and
(b) that there is material on the premises ... which is likely to be of substantial value ... to the investigation of the offence; and
(c) the material is likely to be relevant evidence; and
(d) that it does not consist of or include items subject to legal privilege, excluded material or special procedure material.

In addition at least one of the following criteria must apply:

It is not practicable to communicate with any person entitled to grant entry to the premises; or

it is practicable to communicate with a person entitled to grant entry to the premises but that person is not entitled to grant access to all of the evidence; or

entry to the premises will not be granted unless a warrant is produced; or

the purpose of the search may be frustrated or seriously prejudiced unless the police can secure immediate entry.

It is helpful to note that there are two types of search warrant:

* **Specific premises warrants** – this type of warrant applies only to the premises specified in the application for a warrant.
* **All premises warrants** – this type of warrant applies to all premises occupied or controlled by the suspect.

We are now moving on to consider the search of premises without warrant. A s 18 search under PACE falls under this heading, although we have already dealt with this in some detail earlier on in the chapter.

Search of premises without warrant

The police have a range of powers under PACE to search premises without a warrant.

Section 17 of PACE allows the police to enter and search premises in order to:

* execute a warrant of arrest;
* arrest without warrant;
* capture someone unlawfully at large;
* protect people from serious injury;
* protect property from serious damage.

Other searches of premises without warrant that can be conducted under PACE include:

* A search under s 18 of PACE allows the police to search the premises of a person under arrest for an indictable offence (discussed in more detail above).
* Section 32 of PACE provides that following arrest for an indictable offence the police may search for evidence relating to the arrest at premises that the suspect was at, when arrested, or was at immediately before arrest.

Having considered the powers that the police have to stop and search, we are now going to move on to consider arrest.

Arrest

Primary Codes of Practice **Code C** and **Code G** of **PACE**

We will consider each of these in turn, before considering the remedies available for unlawful arrest.

Aim Higher – revision tip

Police powers and civil liberties is a topic that is examinable in a number of different law courses. For example:

❖ It features in most courses on the English legal system.
❖ It also features as a topic in many public law/constitutional and administrative law courses.
❖ It is also a feature of some criminal law courses and courses on criminal litigation.

As such, it is a topic that you can get an awful lot of mileage out of! You will find coverage of this topic in many textbooks on the topics mentioned above. So if you are finding it a difficult area to gel with, you may find that borrowing a textbook from the library in an area of law with a different focus does the trick!

Remember

In the early stages of your course you are still learning about your own learning style and what resources and methods work best for you. Different authors have different writing styles and sometimes doing something as simple as trying a different textbook can make all the difference to your knowledge, understanding and confidence in a subject. Once you know more about your learning preferences you can look out for textbook series that focus on your preferences. For example, Angela prefers books which have a heavy text focus; I, on the other hand, prefer textbooks with lots of charts, diagrams and interactive websites. We choose and tend to recommend what works best for us!

Under warrant

A warrant of arrest authorises the police to arrest the person named on the warrant. Warrants of arrest can be used in the following circumstances:

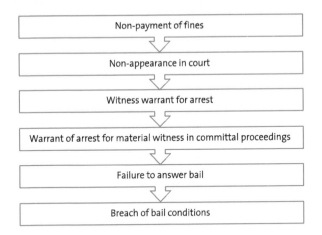

Non-payment of fines
Non-appearance in court
Witness warrant for arrest
Warrant of arrest for material witness in committal proceedings
Failure to answer bail
Breach of bail conditions

Common law arrest

A common law power of arrest exists in the case of a breach of the peace.

Key term: breach of the peace definition: *R v Howell* (1981)

❖ A breach of the peach can take place in a public place or on private premises. It occurs where:
❖ actual harm is done or is likely to be done, to a person;
❖ harm is actually done or likely to be done to a person's property in their presence; or
❖ a person is genuinely in fear of harm to himself or his property in his presence as a result of an assault, affray, riot or other disturbance.

A breach of the peace is a term that you may have heard before. It describes a situation that is more than a mere disturbance. Shouting and swearing, for example, are insufficient to constitute a breach of the peace, although this sort of behaviour may constitute an offence under s 5 of the Public Order Act 1986.

The common law provides that a police officer can arrest and detain a person until such time as the likelihood of a breach of the peace his passed.

We are now moving on to consider arrest under legislation.

Arrest under legislation

The police have the power to arrest without warrant. This general power of arrest exits under s 24 of PACE as amended by s 110 of the Serious Organised Crime and

Police Act 2005. The following conditions must be met in order for an arrest without warrant to be lawful. These are:

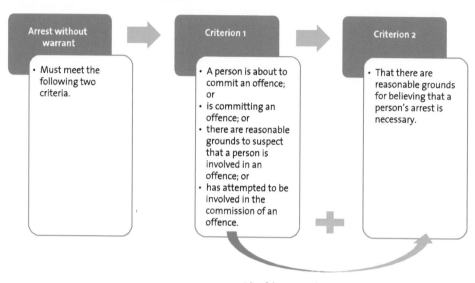

Arrest without warrant	Criterion 1	Criterion 2
• Must meet the following two criteria.	• A person is about to commit an offence; or • is committing an offence; or • there are reasonable grounds to suspect that a person is involved in an offence; or • has attempted to be involved in the commission of an offence.	• That there are reasonable grounds for believing that a person's arrest is necessary.

A lawful arrest without warrant requires both criterion 1 and criterion 2 to be met.

You can find more detail on why an arrest may be necessary in s 24(5) of PACE, Code G. A brief summary is provided here.

An arrest is deemed necessary if it is:
❖ in order to obtain a person's name
❖ in order to obtain a person's address
❖ to prevent injury to the suspect or any other person, or to prevent damage, indecency or obstruction
❖ to protect a vulnerable individual
❖ to ensure prompt investigation
❖ to prevent a suspect from disappearing

Procedure upon arrest

Section 28 of PACE stipulates that in order for an arrest to be lawful:

1. The suspect must be informed at the time of the arrest, or as soon as is reasonably practicable that they are under arrest.
2. The suspect must be informed that they are under arrest even if it is obvious from the circumstances.
3. The suspect must be informed of the grounds for arrest.

Reasonable force may be used in order to carry out an arrest: s 3(1) of the Criminal Law Act 1967 and s 117 of PACE.

Cautions

A person, whom the police suspect of committing an offence, must be cautioned. Code C of PACE provides that a caution must be given to a suspect at various stages in an investigation.

The police caution is as follows:

> 'You do not have to say anything, but it may harm your defence if you do not mention (now or when questioned) something you later rely on in court. Anything you do say may be given in evidence'.

Arrest without warrant other persons: citizen's arrest

In this section we are considering the circumstances in which someone other than a police officer can carry out an arrest. Section 24A of PACE provides powers of arrest to persons other than a police officer. This is often referred to as a 'citizen's arrest'.

These powers can be used only:

1. where there is no police officer present to carry out the arrest; and
2. where the offence concerned is an indictable offence; and
3. where the arrest is necessary in order to prevent:

   ❖ injury to the suspect;
   ❖ injury to another person;
   ❖ damage to property;
   ❖ the suspect escaping before the police can carry out an arrest.

A person other than a police officer can also arrest without warrant if they see:

1. anyone in the act of committing an indictable offence: s 24A(1) PACE; or
2. anyone whom a person has reasonable grounds for suspecting to be committing an indictable offence: s 24A(1) PACE; or
3. an indictable offence has been committed: s 24A(2) PACE.

Remedies for unlawful arrest

There are a number of remedies for unlawful arrest, broadly speaking they can be catagorised as follows:

> To bring a writ of *habeas corpus*: the burden of proof here rests with the detainer (the police), to establish that the detention is lawful. If successful the detainee will be released.

> To argue that the unlawful detention and any subsequent prosecution should fail.

To bring an action for damages for false imprisonment.

To bring an action for damages for false imprisonment.

Detention, the right to silence, interview, detention and evidence

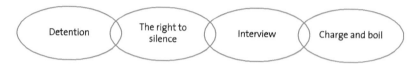

Detention | The right to silence | Interview | Charge and boil

Right to silence and interview

We are now moving on to consider the right to silence before moving on to consider interview. The right to silence is another popular assessment area. We will consider the right to silence in the following different contexts:

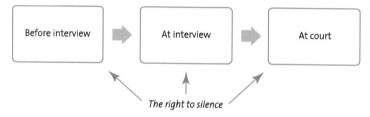

Before interview ➡ At interview ➡ At court

The right to silence

The right to silence: before interview

Individuals accused of a criminal offence have traditionally afforded a right to silence. This is sometimes referred to as the 'privilege against self incrimination.' Although not explicit in Article 6 of the ECHR, the privilege against self incrimination is implicit in Article 6 of the ECHR *Murrary v UK* (1996) 22 EHRR 29.

Earlier in the chapter we discussed a general rule in English law in relation to answering police questions. That general rule being that there is no legal obligation to answer police questions: *Rice v Connolly* (1966). We also discussed some exceptions to a general rule including:

❖ Section 50 of the Police Reform Act 2002, where a person acting in an antisocial manner can be asked by a police officer for their name and address. A failure to provide this information or attempts to mislead a police officer with regards to this information, perhaps by someone giving their name as 'Mickey Mouse' and their address as 'Disneyland', is an arrestable offence.

Note that this only applies where an individual is behaving in an antisocial manner.

Other notable exceptions to this rule include circumstances where a police officer has reasonable grounds for suspecting that a vehicle has been involved in an accident. In this situation there is a duty for the driver to give their details to the police officer.

The diagram below details other statutes which create a legal obligation to provide information.

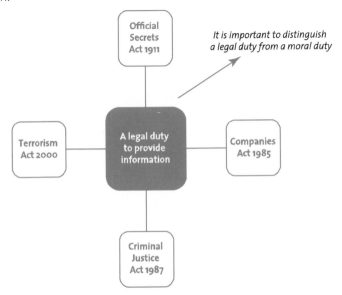

Examples of statutes which create a legal duty to provide information.

The right to silence at interview and in court

Prior to the Criminal Justice and Public Order Act (CJPOA) 1994, the position at common law, was that those accused of a criminal offence had a right to remain silent. This was supplemented by an additional right not to have adverse inferences drawn from the exercise of this right.

This was changed by CJPOA and ss 34–37 of the Act have limited the right to silence. Naturally, nothing can be done to physically compel a suspect to answer questions. However, a judge and the prosecution are now able to make comment in certain situations on the silence of the defendant, thus allowing a court 'to draw such inferences as appear proper' from the silence of the accused.

Aim Higher

For more marks consider the rationale or justifications for limiting the right to silence under the **CJPOA**. You may also want to consider research conducted by Zander that suggests that only a limited number of suspects actually made use of the right to silence. See M Zander, 'Abolition of the Right to Silence, 1972–1994' in *Suspicion and Silence: The Right to Silence in Criminal Investigations*, edited by D Morgan and GM Stephenson, Blackstone Press Ltd 1994.

Even when the delay of legal advice has been lawful it may deprive the accused of a fair trial under Article 6 of the ECHR. Section 34(2A) of the CJPO 1994 was added by s 58 of Youth Justice Criminal Evidence Act 1999 and addresses this issue specifically.

No adverse inferences should be drawn if the accused has been denied legal advice at the police station. A jury should be directed that a failure to answer questions or give evidence is not in itself proof of guilt. The jury/magistrates must still be satisfied that the prosecution has established its case beyond a reasonable doubt.

In what circumstances can an adverse inference be drawn from a defendant's silence?

The jury are entitled to draw adverse inferences from a defendant's silence, where the defendant has failed to mention something when questioned that they later attempt to rely on in their defence. However, they can do so only in circumstances where the defendant could have reasonably have been expected to provide this information and the defendant's silence can only be attributed to the accused having no sensible answer to the allegation: ss 34 to 37 of the CJPOA.

The cases of *Condron v UK* (2000) and *R v Beckles* (2004) consider the extent to which adverse inferences can be drawn from a defendant's silence, in circumstances where the defendant is acting on legal advice to remain silent. A defendant who discloses that they were advised to remain silent by their solicitor does not necessarily waive legal privilege: *R v Seaton* [2011] 1 All ER 932.

However, if the defendant does not wish the court to draw an adverse inference under the CJPOA 1994, it may be necessary for the accused to provide more detail and in doing so, the accused may well waive legal privilege.

Balancing the right to silence

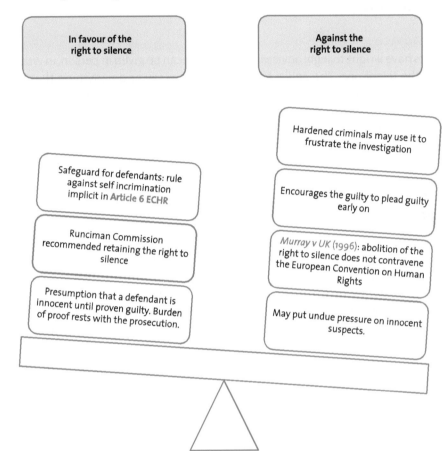

In favour of the right to silence

Against the right to silence

Hardened criminals may use it to frustrate the investigation

Safeguard for defendants: rule against self incrimination implicit in Article 6 ECHR

Encourages the guilty to plead guilty early on

Runciman Commission recommended retaining the right to silence

Murray v UK (1996): abolition of the right to silence does not contravene the European Convention on Human Rights

Presumption that a defendant is innocent until proven guilty. Burden of proof rests with the prosecution.

May put undue pressure on innocent suspects.

Interview

Primary Code of Practice **Code C** and **Code E** of **PACE**

In the case of indictable offences all interviews with suspects are tape recorded on time-coded tapes. In reality the use of tape recording is widespread in relation to other offences. Before an interview commences a suspect should be reminded of their entitlement to legal advice. They should be cautioned again: Code C PACE.

Code C of PACE stipulates that police officers are not allowed to use oppressive questioning methods in order to elicit information from the suspect.

Legal advice and detention

In this section we are going to consider the right of a suspect accused of a criminal offence to legal advice. We will then consider the detention timeline. A suspect has a right 'not to be held incommunicado'. What this means is that they are entitled to notify someone of their arrest, detention and location.

Legal advice

Suspects have a right to legal advice in private; this can be given in person, in writing or over the telephone. The police are not allowed to say or do anything that may dissuade or discourage a person from seeking legal advice. Once a suspect has requested legal advice they should not be interviewed until they have received such advice. There are some exceptions to this general rule and a superintendent can in certain cases authorise that questioning continues.

Detention

Code C of PACE stipulates that all persons in custody must be dealt with expeditiously, and released as soon as the need for detention no longer applies. Suspects who have been arrested can be detained:

❖ under s 41 of PACE a suspect can be detained for 24 hours without charge;
❖ under s 42 of PACE a police officer of the rank of Superintendent or above can authorise detention without charge for a further 12 hours;
❖ under s 43 of PACE a warrant for detention beyond 36 hours can be obtained from magistrates. Magistrates can authorise detention for anything up to a further 60 hours.

Detention timeline (non-terrorist offences)

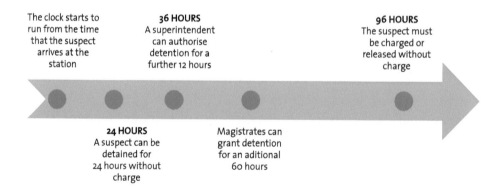

The clock starts to run from the time that the suspect arrives at the station

36 HOURS
A superintendent can authorise detention for a further 12 hours

96 HOURS
The suspect must be charged or released without charge

24 HOURS
A suspect can be detained for 24 hours without charge

Magistrates can grant detention for an aditional 60 hours

Release and bail

In this section we are considering the next stage in the criminal justice process, which is release and bail.

Bail

> The term 'bail' refers to the temporary release of a suspect from custody. This release is pending the trial of the suspect. Bail can be granted by:
> * the police;
> * a Magistrates Court;
> * the Crown Court.
>
> Bail can be granted with or without conditions. Typical conditions include:
> * reporting conditions;
> * curfew conditions;
> * the condition not to contact certain persons;
> * the surrender of the suspect's passport;
> * that 'surety' be offered in case the suspect absconds. Surety simply means money; If the suspect then fails to attend bail, the surety will be lost.

Key terms:
bail

Once a defendant has been charged they will either be released on bail or remanded in custody. There is a presumption in favour of granting bail to a suspect. Remember that a suspect in English law is innocent until proven guilty.

The key legislation in this area is the Bail Act 1971 which created a statutory presumption in favour of bail.

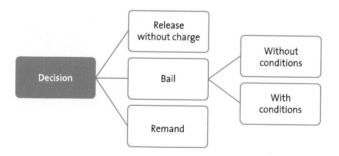

It is important to note that the criminal justice system must strike a balance between protecting the rights of the suspect (and honouring the presumption of innocence) and the interests of the community. Blatantly there will always be situations in which an individual should not be released from custody pending trial.

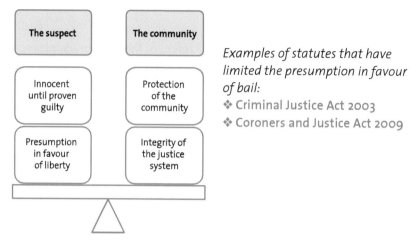

Examples of statutes that have limited the presumption in favour of bail:

❖ Criminal Justice Act 2003
❖ Coroners and Justice Act 2009

Balancing the interests of the suspect with the interests of the community.

Bail may be denied:

❖ in the case of certain offences;
❖ where there is a history of committing a particular offence;
❖ where there is a danger that the suspect may abscond or has absconded previously; or
❖ where the suspect has committed offences on bail previously.

Up for Debate

In recent years there has been growing concern regarding the number of suspects who re-offend whilst on bail. This has led to the gradual erosion of the presumption in favour of liberty, particularly with regards to serious offences.

Do you think that it is right that a person denied bail who is subsequently found not guilty should receive compensation for having been wrongly deprived of their liberty?

The decision to prosecute

In this penultimate section we are going to consider who brings prosecutions in the English legal system before moving on to consider the criteria on which the decision to prosecute is made.

The key prosecuting authorities in the English legal system are:

❖ the Crown Prosecution Service (CPS)
❖ the Police

- ❖ the Attorney General
- ❖ the Director of Public Prosecutions
- ❖ Government departments may also have powers to bring prosecutions, e.g. the Health and Safety Executive.

Although it is not commonplace, it is worth noting that it is possible for individuals to bring a private prosecution.

The Crown Prosecution Service

In deciding whether or not to prosecute the CPS is guided by the **Crown Prosecutors Code**. This code requires prosecutors to apply a two-stage test:

The Evidential Test	• There must be sufficient evidence to bring a posecution • There must be a realistic prospect of securing a conviction	*All prosecutions must pass the Evidential Test*
The Public Interest Test	• The severity of the offence in question • The circumstances of the offence • The circumstances of the victim • The circumstances of the accused	*A prosecution can be discontinued if it is not in the public interest, even if the evidential threshold is met*

The full Code Test.

Aim Higher

The Code for Crown Prosecutors is a public document and you can obtain a copy of the code in a range of different languages by going to the following website: www.cps.gov.uk/publications/code_for_crown_prosecutors

The right to a fair trial

At the start of this chapter we considered miscarriages of justice. In this final section we have almost travelled a full circle. As we are now going to consider what safeguards are in place to protect a person accused of a criminal offence from a miscarriage of justice.

The right to a fair trial is another popular assessment area for examiners. It can occur as a stand-alone question, focused only on the right to a fair trial, or, as is the case in our 'Putting it into practice' question, the issue may be raised in the context of a more general question on miscarriages of justice.

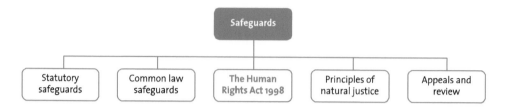

Statutory safeguards

There are a number of statutory safeguards in place, which protect the rights of individuals accused of a criminal offence. The most obvious example of legislative safeguarding is PACE, which limits police powers and provides rights for suspects in relation to stop, search, arrest, detention and interview.

Admissibility of evidence

Section 76 of PACE renders inadmissible confessions that are obtained as a result of oppressive police questioning. Confessions that are considered 'unreliable' are also inadmissible. Section 78(1) of PACE enables the court to disregard or exclude evidence that may have been obtained in breach of PACE.

Other examples of legislation which can be said to safeguard the rights of individuals includes:

❖ Criminal Procedure and Investigations Act 1996;
❖ Criminal Procedure Rules 2005.

Common law safeguards

The burden of proof in criminal trials rests with the prosecution (the CPS): this means that the Crown must prove their case. It is not for the accused to prove that they are innocent. There is a presumption that the accused is 'innocent until proven guilty' in English law.

The standard of proof in criminal prosecutions is also very high: 'beyond a reasonable doubt'. Thus the prosecution must prove, beyond a reasonable doubt, that the accused committed the crime alleged.

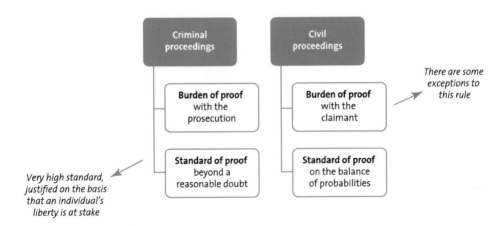

The European Convention on Human Rights

In addition to the above safeguards the European Convention on Human Rights incorporated into domestic law by the Human Rights Act 1998 provides additional protection. You can find more detail on this in Chapter 2 of this revision guide.

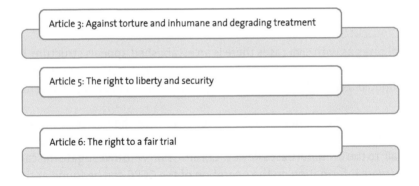

Article 3: Against torture and inhumane and degrading treatment

Article 5: The right to liberty and security

Article 6: The right to a fair trial

Rules of natural justice

The rules of natural justice are enshrined in common law. We have categorised them here separately, to help you remember that these principles should be discussed in more detail when dealing with an assessment question when dealing with an assessment question on the right to a fair trial.

Rules of natural justice are concerned with procedural justice. They are designed to ensure that decisions are made fairly and in an objective manner. The rules stipulate that:

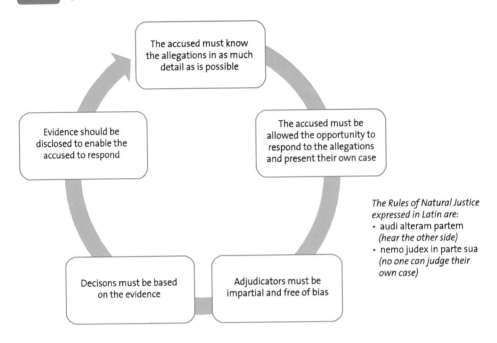

The accused must know the allegations in as much detail as is possible

The accused must be allowed the opportunity to respond to the allegations and present their own case

Evidence should be disclosed to enable the accused to respond

The Rules of Natural Justice expressed in Latin are:
- audi alteram partem
  (hear the other side)
- nemo judex in parte sua
  (no one can judge their own case)

Decisons must be based on the evidence

Adjudicators must be impartial and free of bias

Appeals and review

In criminal cases as with civil cases there is an established appeals structure, but the routes and grounds for appeal vary. Appeal courts can quash a conviction, order a retrial or uphold a conviction. There is also provision for appeals against sentences.

In circumstances where a defendant believes that he or she has been the victim of a miscarriage of justice it is possible for them to apply, or for someone to apply on their behalf, to the Criminal Cases Review Commission who investigate miscarriages of justice (more information on the operation of the CCRC can be found at the start of this chapter).

Core issues checklist

The criminal justice system is a highly politicised area that attracts much media attention.	✔
A miscarriage of justice can occur as a result of a number of different factors. High-profile miscarriages of justice have led to significant reforms, particularly in relation to the investigation of criminal offences.	✔
The police have a number of powers to stop, search, arrest, interview and detain individuals whom they suspect of committing or being party to a criminal offence. These powers should be exercised in compliance with the PACE Codes of Practice. Serious breaches of the Codes may lead to evidence being inadmissible in court, and or disciplinary procedures.	✔

The CPS is the primary prosecuting authority in the ELS. Crown prosecutors in determining whether or not to bring a prosecution use a two-part test: the evidential test and the public interest test.	✔
There are a number of safeguards in place, which are designed to ensure that a suspect receives a fair trial and that suspects' rights are protected.	✔

Useful websites

Topic	Website
This is the website for the criminal justice system	www.gov.uk/browse/justice
The Home Office	www.homeoffice.gov.uk
Ministry of Justice website	www.gov.uk/government/ organisations/ministry-of-justice

Putting it into practice – example essay question

'Consider critically what safeguards exist to guard against a miscarriage of justice within the English legal system.'

Answer plan

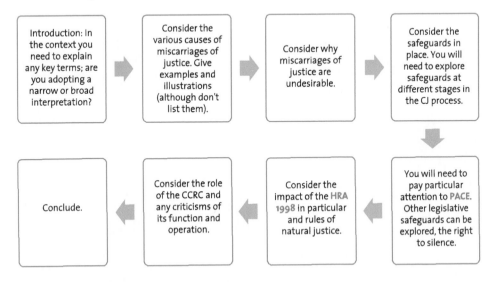

Introduction: In the context you need to explain any key terms; are you adopting a narrow or broad interpretation?

Consider the various causes of miscarriages of justice. Give examples and illustrations (although don't list them).

Consider why miscarriages of justice are undesirable.

Consider the safeguards in place. You will need to explore safeguards at different stages in the CJ process.

You will need to pay particular attention to PACE. Other legislative safeguards can be explored, the right to silence.

Consider the impact of the HRA 1998 in particular and rules of natural justice.

Consider the role of the CCRC and any criticisms of its function and operation.

Conclude.

Outline answer

❖ In this question you are being asked to consider 'critically' the safeguards that exist to reduce the likelihood of miscarriages of justice. The examiner is inviting you to formulate an opinion. This opinion can develop throughout your essay, but it should be clear by the end of your essay whether you believe the safeguards are sufficient in guarding against miscarriages of justice.

❖ The structure for this essay should be to explore miscarriages of justice, initially offering some well-articulated examples of miscarriages of justice. Examiners are generally impressed by evidence of independent research so it would be sensible to identify some of your own illustrations that go beyond the examples that your lecturer has used in class.

❖ You will need to consider the different factors that can cause a miscarriage of justice. You can link these causes back to the specific examples that you have offered.

❖ Next you will need to explore what safeguards exist: PACE, the right to silence, the burden and standard of proof, the presumption of innocence, other legislative safeguards, rules of natural justice, an appeals structure.

❖ You also need to consider the impact that the HRA 1998 has had on safeguarding suspects' rights.

❖ Your essay can conclude by considering the CCRC; in particular you will need to consider the criteria that need to be met in order for an individual who is claiming they are the victim of a miscarriage of justice to successfully apply. It would also be helpful to consider the 'types' of cases the CCRC will consider. This section of your essay can conclude by considering some of the recent criticisms that have been made regarding the CCRC – in particular the extent to which they are impartial and the backlog of cases.

❖ Your conclusion should indicate the extent to which the current safeguards protect against miscarriages of justice. What more if anything could be done?

Aim Higher

Process words: critically

Of all the process words, this is probably the one that causes students the most anxiety. It is also a process word that you will encounter with increasing frequency as your studies progress. When an examiner uses the word **critically** in an assessment they are asking you to formulate an argument. This might be in terms of whether a particular statement is accurate or whether you agree with a particular statement/argument. You are being asked to look at the pros and the cons in a given area, the relative strengths and weaknesses of a particular argument. You must remember that relevant authorities must support any arguments that you advance; any statements of law that you offer must also be supported. Ideally your essay should formulate a supported opinion. Hand pick arguments and academic opinion that support your opinion, rather than simply stating 'in my opinion'.

Remember that unless specifically asked to do so by your lecturer you should not write in the first person, e.g. I feel that ... I suggest that ... I think that. Instead you should write in the third person, e.g. It is submitted that ... It is argued that. This is a more objective and professional writing style.

Where you are being asked to consider or evaluate an issue, case or topical critically you need to ensure that your conclusion flows logically from the main body of your essay.

Table of key cases referred to in this chapter

Case name	Area of law	Principle
Rice v Connolly [1966] 2 All ER 649	This case establishes the general common law rule regarding an individual's legal obligation to answer police questions when stopped.	There is no legal obligation to answer police questions when stopped.
Rickets v Cox [1982] Crim LR 184	This case is concerned with qualifications to the general rule above.	A person who refuses to respond, or responds aggressively, or in an obstructive manner may commit an arrestable offence.
R v Lemsatef [1977] 1 WLR 812	This case is concerned with police powers to detain an individual in order to ask them questions.	A police officer who takes hold of a person in order to prevent them from leaving in an attempt to ask them questions may be unlawfully detaining the individual and or committing a common assault.
Donnelly v Jackman [1970] 1 WLR 562	This case follows on from the previous one and concerns minimal bodily contact by the police.	A *de minimus* interference is unlikely to constitute an unlawful detention or common assault.

@ Visit the book's companion website to test your knowledge

❖ Resources include a subject map, revision tip podcasts, downloadable diagrams, MCQ quizzes for each chapter, and a flashcard glossary

❖ www.routledge.com/cw/optimizelawrevision

8

The Judiciary

Revision objectives

Understand the law
- Do you understand the role that magistrates and judges play in the English legal system?

Remember the details
- Can you remember the qualification, selection and apointments procedures for magistrates and judges?
- Can you remember what reforms have taken place under the Courts and Legal Services Act 1990 and the Constututional Reform Act 2005?

Reflect critically on areas of debate
- Can you reflect critically on the importance of a representative magistracy and judiciary?

Contextualise
- What steps have been taken to address diversity in the magistracy and the judiciary. Have these steps been sucessful?
- What training is offered to magisitrates and judges?

Apply your skills and knolewdge
- Using authorities to support your answer, can you apply your knowledge to answer the 'Putting it into practice' question?

JUDGES

Chapter Map

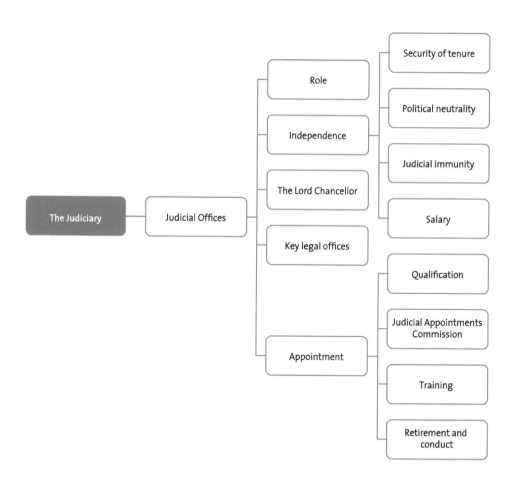

'Explain the selection and appointments process for the judiciary and the magistracy. To what extent do the judiciary and magistracy represent the communities that they serve?'

An outline answer is available at the end of this chapter.

Introduction

In the first part of this chapter we are going to consider the role, function and appointment of members of the judiciary. In this context we are only concerned with professional judges. We will consider lay magistrates in the second part of this chapter.

There have been a number of significant changes in recent years, both to judicial roles and to the way in which judges are appointed. This means that questions in relation to the role of the judiciary, their appointment and composition are likely to be popular with examiners.

Aim Higher – revision tip

Areas that have been subject to recent development, or have recently been subject to recommendations for reform, provide fertile ground for assessments.

You should get into the habit of reading a quality newspaper from the start of your studies, as this will help you keep up to date with legal developments. You can access the law section of the Guardian Newspaper online at www.guardian. co.uk/law

Issues that tend to arise in relation to the judiciary can be grouped together under the following common themes.

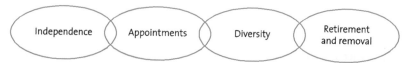

Independence   Appointments   Diversity   Retirement and removal

Aim Higher – revision tip

It is unlikely that you will be asked an assessment question that is inviting a general discussion 'about the judiciary'. You must therefore make sure that you tailor your response to the question that you have been asked.

A helpful technique is to make sure that you refer back to the question throughout your answer is to ask yourself 'how does this section of my work go some way to answering the question?' If the answer to the question is, it doesn't – then you probably don't need to include it!

Judicial offices

The table below outlines the various judicial offices within the English legal system. You will see that the table also indicates the gender balance (or lack of it) in different judicial offices. The final column on the right indicates representation of BME (Black and Minority Ethnic) officers in the judiciary. You will find it helpful to revisit some of these statistics a little later on in this section, when we consider the composition of the judiciary, and appointment in particular.

Senior Court Judges				
Judicial Office	Court	Number	% Female	% BME*
Justices of the Supreme Court	The Supreme Court	12	8.3% (one female Supreme Court Judge)	0%
Heads of Division	Lord Chief Justice Master of the Rolls President of the Queen's Bench Division President of the Family Division Chancellor of the High Court	5	0%	0%
Lord/Lady Justices of Appeal	The Court of Appeal	35	11.4%	0%
High Court Judge	High Court and Crown Court	108	16.7%	4.6%

Inferior Court Judges					
Circuit Judge	Crown Court and County Court	654	18.5%		2.3%
Recorder	Crown Court	1,198	17.4%		5.7
District Judge Deputy District Judge	County Court	447 764	27.4% 36.1%		6.1% 5.1%
District Judge Magistrates' Court Deputy District Judge Magistrates' Court	Magistrates' Court	142 145	28.9% 32.4%		2.8% 7.6%

* BME – Black and Minority Ethnic
Statistics drawn from the Judicial Database 2012–13

A judge's role

In Chapter 3 we explored the role that members of the judiciary play in the interpretation of statutes and in Chapter 4 we considered the important role that judges play in the development of the common law and the doctrine of binding judicial precedent. As such, it is clear that in addition to the central role judges play in criminal and civil litigation, members of the judiciary play an important role in the development of the law in the English legal system.

Judicial independence

According to the Rule of Law (considered earlier in Chapter 2), judges play an important constitutional role in the English legal system. This means that judges must act in an impartial and independent manner. They must be free from the influence of the executive; they must be politically neutral, unbiased and incorruptible. The Constitutional Reform Act 2005 now requires the Government to uphold the independence of the judiciary.

The doctrine of Parliamentary Supremacy dictates that a judge cannot declare an Act of Parliament invalid. They can, however, issue a declaration of incompatibility in relation to the Human Rights Act 1998. It is not unusual for members of the judiciary to find they are presiding in a case that is politically sensitive. This can put members of the judiciary in a position of potential conflict with the Government. If members of the judiciary are not independent – by which we mean:

* free from the exercise of political pressure;
* free of the fear that they may be dismissed;
* free from political or other bias

– then they will not be able to uphold the rule of law (see Chapter 2 for more detail on the Rule of Law).

There are a number of mechanisms in place that secure the independence of the judiciary in the English legal system. These are:

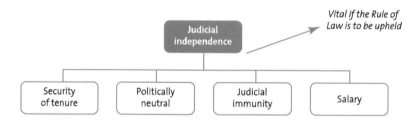

Let us now consider some of these mechanisms in more detail.

Security of tenure

Under the **Act of Settlement 1700**, judges have security of tenure. This means that senior judges remain in post 'during good behaviour', and they can be removed only following a petition from the House of Lords and the House of Commons.

This procedure has only been used once to remove a judge in Ireland in 1830!

Politically neutral

Judges are expected to be politically neutral, without bias, and as such senior judges are not permitted to become Members of Parliament.

Judicial immunity

In order to ensure judicial independence and integrity, judges cannot be sued for words said or things done in the performance of their role.

Salary

Members of the professional judiciary receive a generous salary, which is set at a level intended to reduce the temptation to accept bribes.

❖ In 2012 the Lord Chief Justice received a salary of £239,845.
❖ A District Judge Magistrates' Court received a salary of £102,921 in 2012.

Up for Debate

In *The Politics of the Judiciary* (5th edn, 1997) J A G Griffith argues that there are a number of cases that illustrate that members of the judiciary do exercise political bias (and as such lack impartiality, at least at a political level). This bias tends to be in favour of the establishment and the *status quo*

❖ *Bromley Borough Council v Greater London Council* (1983)
❖ *AG v Guardian Newspapers Ltd* (1987)
❖ *R v SS Home Office ex parte Brind* (1991)

Have a look at these cases and see whether you agree. Griffith suggests that these views are likely the result of the narrow socioeconomic group that the judiciary is normally drawn from.

The position of the Lord Chancellor

Montesquieu's theory of the Separation of Powers underscores the importance of judicial independence. Before the Constitutional Reform Act 2005 was introduced the position of the Lord Chancellor, in particular, was inconsistent with the principle of separation of powers (more information on the separation of powers can be found in Chapter 2).

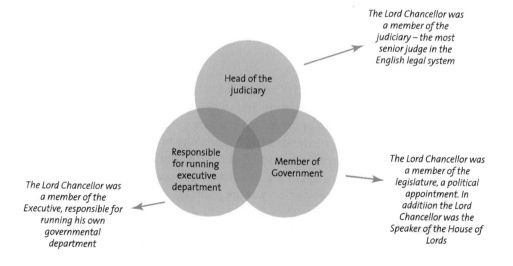

The Lord Chancellor was a member of the judiciary – the most senior judge in the English legal system

Head of the judiciary

Responsible for running executive department

Member of Government

The Lord Chancellor was a member of the Executive, responsible for running his own governmental department

The Lord Chancellor was a member of the legislature, a political appointment. In additiion the Lord Chancellor was the Speaker of the House of Lords

The party-political role of the Lord Chancellor was the subject of much controversy, largely because the position created a number of fundamental conflicts of interest. Following the case of *McGonnell v UK* (2000), the position was also arguably in conflict with Art 6 of the European Convention of Human Rights.

Under the Constitutional Reform Act 2005 the office of Lord Chancellor was retained in name, but the judicial functions were transferred to the President of the Courts of England and Wales.

Other key legal offices

We discussed the CPS in more detail in Chapter 7.

You will come across many cases involving the DPP when you study criminal law.

Legal Office	Notes
Attorney General	The Attorney General (AG) is a political appointment and acts as an advisor to the Government.
The Solicitor General	The Solicitor General is the AG's deputy.
The Director of Public Prosecutions	The Director of Public Prosecutions (DPP) is the head of the Crown Prosecution Service.

Appointment

There are a number of key issues that need to be addressed under this heading. They are:

Qualification | The Judicial Appointments Commission | Training | Retirement and removal | Criticisms

Qualification

Under the Courts and Legal Services Act 1990 (CLSA) significant changes were made to the eligibility criteria for judicial office. The CLSA 1990 expanded rights of audience throughout the court structure and in doing so created the opportunity for other legal professionals to apply for judicial office. The Tribunals, Courts and Enforcement Act 2007 further extended the opportunity to apply for judicial office by abolishing the requirement for 'rights of audience' and instead requiring that applicants must satisfy 'eligibility criteria'. It is therefore now possible for academics and legal executives to become members of the judiciary.

The Judicial Appointments Commission

The Constitutional Reform Act 2005 established the Judicial Appointments Commission (JAC). The JAC has responsibility for the appointment of all judges in the English legal system. The power to appoint magistrates is however, retained by the Lord Chancellor's Advisory Committee on Justices of the Peace.

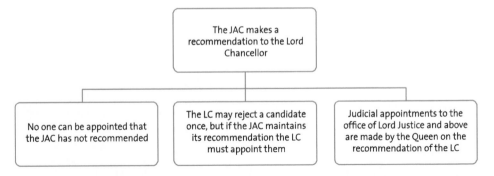

Composition of the Judicial Appointments Commission

The Constitutional Reform Act 2005 establishes the composition of the JAC. The Judicial Appointments Commission consists of 15 members:

- ❖ six members of the JAC must be lay members (the chair of the commission must be a lay member;
- ❖ five members of the JAC must be members of the judiciary;
- ❖ two members of the commission must be members of the legal profession;
- ❖ one member of the commission must be a magistrate;
- ❖ and finally one member of the commission must be a tribunal member.

Judicial qualities and abilities

The JAC has identified five core qualities and abilities that are required in order to hold judicial office. These are:

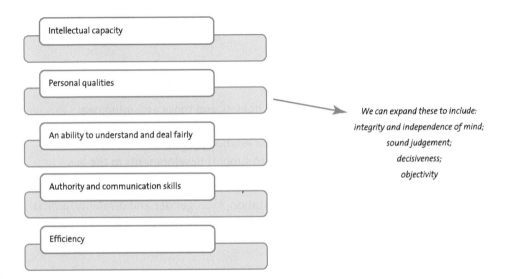

Judicial diversity

The JAC is committed to widening diversity, it encourages and welcomes applications from a broad range of constituencies. However, if we glance back to the table on pages 178 and 179, it is clear that white males overwhelmingly dominate the judiciary.

Up for Debate

The extent to which the JAC has been successful in its remit of broadening the diversity of the judiciary is debatable. In 2008 the JAC was criticised when it was publicised that all of the appointments it had made to the High Court were appointments of men.

In 2011 the House of Lords Constitution Committee announced an inquiry, 'Judicial Appointments'. One of the findings of the report was that a more diverse judiciary was essential if the public are to maintain their confidence in the justice system. The report also found that insufficient steps had been taken by the JAC to widen the diversity of the judiciary.

Later that year, the Ministry of Justice published a consultation document: *Appointments and Diversity: A Judiciary for the 21st Century*. You can download a copy of the responses to the consultation at: https://consult.justice.gov.uk/digital-communications/judicial-appointments-cp19-2011

Training

In 2011 the Judicial Studies Board (JSB) and the Tribunals Judicial Training Group were merged and became the Judicial College. The newly formed Judicial College assumes responsibility for providing training to judicial office holders. Prior to the establishment of the JSB the training received by judicial office holders in England and Wales was limited, at best.

The Judicial College now delivers training under the following headings:

❖ Initial training for new judicial office holders and those assuming new responsibilities;
❖ Continuing professional education for existing judges;
❖ Change and modernisation training to support developments in the law.

In response to allegations that certain members of the judiciary are insensitive with regard to matters involving sexual orientation, race, gender and disability, judicial office holders now receive equal opportunities training (you can link this to some of the criticisms of the judiciary later in this chapter).

Aim Higher

In August 2013 the Lord Chief Justice announced plans to draw up a list of judges who will receive specialist training on how to conduct serious cases involving offences of a sexual nature. It is envisaged that this specialist panel of approved and trained judges will hear:

❖ all cases of serious sexual offending, likely to last more than ten days;
❖ cases where one or more witnesses are deemed to be 'significantly vulnerable'.

The training will be delivered by the Judicial College.

Aim Higher

We have suggested a number of readings here that will help embellish your knowledge and understanding of the judiciary.

❖ Blom-Cooper, L (2009) 'Bias, Malfunction in "judicial decision-making"', [2009] *Public Law* 199
❖ Griffith, J A G (1997) *The Politics of the Judiciary*, London: Fontana
❖ Holland, L. and Spencer, L. (1992) *Without Prejudice? Sex Equality at the Bar and in the Judiciary*, London: Bar Council

Retirement and judicial conduct

The age of retirement for judges is 70 years of age. A judge may remain in office beyond this point at the discretion of the Lord Chief Justice with the Lord Chancellor's approval.

Judicial conduct

Section 108 of the Constitutional Reform Act 2005 established powers for the Lord Chief Justice to:

1. advise judicial office holders;
2. warn judicial office holders;
3. formally reprimand judicial office holders;
4. suspend a judge in limited circumstances.

It is still the case however, that for a judge of High Court level or above, the only means of removal is by way of resolutions in the House of Commons and the House of Lords (see security of tenure earlier in this chapter).

You can link this back to the principle of judicial independence in an assessment for more marks!

Judges beneath the High Court do not have the same degree of security of tenure as senior judges. They can be removed for 'misbehaviour' or on the grounds of 'incapacity'.

Criticisms of the judiciary

There are a number of significant criticisms of the judiciary. These can be broadly categorised under the following headings.

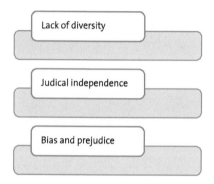

Lack of diversity

Judical independence

Bias and prejudice

Lack of diversity
We have touched on this point briefly already. If you revisit the key points table for the judiciary on pages 178 and 179 then you will see that the judiciary in England and Wales is predominantly white and male. In reality the demographic profile of the judiciary is even narrower than the table on pages 178 and 179 suggests.

❖ The average age of a member of the judiciary is 58 years old.
❖ The majority of judges in the middle-ranking and superior courts have an Oxbridge education.

| White | Male | Oxbridge educated | Most were barristers | Old! | = the dominant profile of the judiciary in England and Wales |

Judicial independence
Earlier in this chapter we considered the significance of the independence of the judiciary; particularly in relation to upholding the rule of law. It would be naive, however, to assume that the principle of judicial independence is itself unproblematic.

The doctrine of parliamentary supremacy dictates that Parliament is supreme. Members of the judiciary are subordinate to the will of Parliament. They cannot therefore hold an Act of Parliament invalid: *British Railways Board v Pickin* (1974).

To what extent do you think it would be desirable for senior members of the judiciary to be able to 'strike down' legislation? Remember that judges are not democratically elected in the English legal system and that means that they are not democratically accountable!

Remember that the courts can make a declaration of incompatibility with the Human Rights Act 1998 under s 4 HRA 1998.

The extent to which judges are 'impartial and independent' is also open to criticism, particularly when we consider their participation in chairing politically sensitive public inquires. Look again at the criticisms made by Professor Griffith earlier in this chapter.

Bias and prejudice

❖ Sadly, there are far too many public examples of members of the judiciary exhibiting bias and prejudice towards women, ethnic and religious minorities and individuals with disabilities.

❖ Professor Griffith argues that there are also many cases that illustrate that members of the judiciary exhibit 'right-wing bias'.

MAGISTRATES

Topic Map

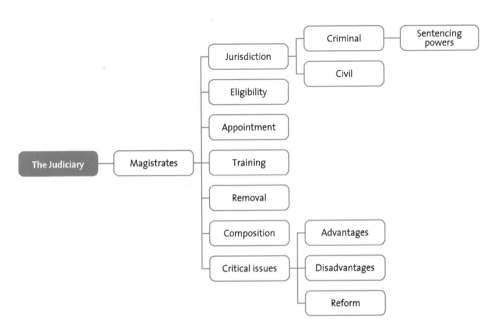

Introduction

In this section we are going to consider the role and function of magistrates in the English legal system. Magistrates are also known as Justices of the Peace, and they have a long history in the English legal system.

As of 1 April 2013 there were 23,244 unpaid lay magistrates in post. Lay magistrates should be distinguished from Stipendiary Magistrates (now called District Judges Magistrates' Courts). The former are unpaid and part-time lay people (normally without a legal qualification), while the latter are professionally qualified, salaried judges.

This section will focus primarily on lay magistrates. The table below identifies some of the key features for comparison between lay magistrates' and District Judges Magistrates' Courts.

Key points

	Lay Magistrates	District Judges Magistrates' Court (DJMCs)	Deputy District Judges Magistrates' Court (DDJMCs)
Role and jurisdiction		Civil and criminal jurisdiction. They are empowered to hear evidence and reach a verdict. In criminal cases they are also empowered to pass sentence.	
Legally qualified	Lay magistrates do not normally possess a legal qualification.	District Judges are legally qualified professional judges. They have seven years' post-qualification experience.	Deputy District Judges are part-time District Judges, frequently gaining experience in order to become a full-time District Judge.

Appointment and training	Appointed by the Lord Chancellor on behalf of the Queen, following consultation with Local Advisory Committees	Appointed by the Lord Chancellor.	Appointed by the Lord Chancellor.
	Upon appointment the Judicial College provides training. They must also attend training courses following initial training.	Upon appointment.	Upon appointment.
Sitting	Lay magistrates must sit at least 26 half-days per year. They usually sit in a panel of two or three.	Full-time post. DJMCs sit alone.	Part-time post. DDJMCs sit alone.
Advisor	Lay magistrates are advised by a professionally qualified Justices' Clerk.		
Salaried	Lay magistrates' are not paid. They are entitled to expenses and compensation for loss of earnings.	DJMCs receive a salary.	DDJMCs receive payment for sitting.
Powers	Limited to a 12-month custodial sentence for one offence and a £5,000 fine.		

Jurisdiction

Lay magistrates have criminal and civil jurisdiction. If you attempt a question on magistrates you should be prepared to address this dual jurisdiction, albeit that your focus will likely lean towards criminal jurisdiction.

Criminal

In terms of their criminal capacity, magistrates hear in the region of 95 to 98 per cent of all criminal cases. This represents over a million cases each year, and as such the significant contribution that they make to the administration of justice should not be understated.

❖ Magistrates deal with requests for search and arrest warrants.
❖ Magistrates exercise a number of pre-trial judicial powers.
❖ Magistrates hear applications for the grant of bail.
❖ Magistrates hear the evidence, reach a verdict and pass sentence, if a defendant is convicted.

Types of offences

Type of offence	Explanation	Example
Summary offence	Summary offences are the least serious offences. They are triable only in the Magistrates' Court.	Criminal Damage (under £5,000) Road Traffic Offences Common Assault/Battery
Either-way offence (hybrid)	Either-way offences as the name may suggest are triable in either the Magistrates' Court or the Crown Court.	Theft Stalking Assault Occasioning Actual Bodily Harm
Indictable offence	Indictable offences are the most serious offences. The trial will take place in the Crown Court.	Murder Rape Robbery

Magistrates hear only summary offences and some triable-either-way (hybrid) offences.

Their jurisdiction to hear a broader range of cases has been expanded considerably in recent years because:

❖ a number of triable-either-way offences have been made summary only offences;
❖ many new offences created by the legislature are summary only offences;
❖ the Crown Prosecution Service may charge with a lower offence in order to increase the probability of conviction.

Aim Higher

Recommendations to further expand the range of cases that magistrates' can hear have been proposed by the Government. The most controversial were calls to limit the right to trial by jury in small-value thefts.

These recommendations met with strong criticism and were never implemented. Part of the rationale for the right to trial by jury in these cases is that conviction for a dishonesty offence can have serious consequences for an individual's reputation and their career prospects.

In reality, most defendants accused of a low-value dishonesty offence will either plead guilty to the offence or elect to have their case heard in the Magistrates' Court.

Limited sentencing powers

Magistrates have limited sentencing powers, which include:

❖ sentences of up to 12 months in prison for one offence;
❖ up to a £5,000 fine;
❖ magistrates can commit a person to be sentenced at the Crown Court if they feel that their sentencing powers are insufficient.

Civil jurisdiction

Magistrates also have a considerable civil jurisdiction.

❖ Magistrates grant licences.
❖ Magistrates hear appeals from local authority decisions regarding a failure to grant a licence, in respect of the sale of alcohol, or a Hackney cab, or a betting/gaming licence.
❖ Magistrates also have power of recovery in respect of non-payment of council tax and non-payment of television licenses.
❖ Magistrates hear family proceedings under the Domestic Proceedings and Magistrates' Court Act 1978 and the Children Act 1989. This may include applications for residence, applications for contact orders and adoption proceedings.

Magistrates hearing family proceedings receive specialist training. When sitting in this capacity the court is referred to as a Family Proceedings Court. There is a requirement that each Family Proceedings Panel is comprised of at least one male and one female magistrate.

Eligibility criteria

There are a number of eligibility criteria to become a magistrate:

Eligibility criteria	Disqualified
❖ They must be over 18 and under 65 years of age ❖ They must live within 15 miles of the catchment area in which they will work ❖ They must be able to sit at least 26 half days per year	❖ Police officers ❖ Members of the armed forces ❖ Traffic wardens ❖ Individuals that have a close relative on the same bench ❖ People with certain criminal convictions ❖ Undischarged bankrupts ❖ People with a disability that would prevent them carrying out their duties as a magistrate

Appointment

The Lord Chancellor, on the advice of local advisory committees, appoints magistrates under the Justices of the Peace Act 1997, on behalf of the Monarch. Candidates may be nominated from local political parties, charitable organisations, trade unions and so forth. In 1998 the procedures for appointing magistrates were changed in order to make the appointment criteria more transparent. It is now possible to make a direct application to become a magistrate. The job description for a magistrate identifies six qualities:

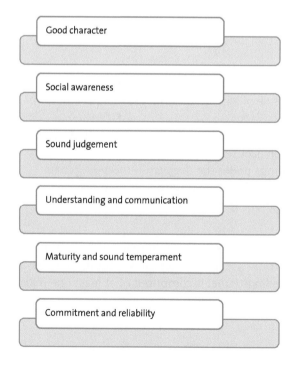

Good character

Social awareness

Sound judgement

Understanding and communication

Maturity and sound temperament

Commitment and reliability

Note: Vacancies for magistrates are now widely advertised in a range of media, in an attempt to attract greater diversity in applicants

Training

Upon appointment magistrates receive training for their forthcoming duties. This training is organised by the Judicial College and delivered by the Magistrates' Commission Committees. Magistrates are not expected to be legal experts and many will have little or no knowledge of the law prior to their training. The training that they receive is intended to provide them with knowledge and understanding of the following areas:

❖ Law and court procedure
❖ Function and powers of the magistrates' bench
❖ Sentencing
❖ Evidence.

New magistrates receive an induction and are appointed a mentor. Initially they will 'work shadow' another magistrate before sitting themselves. After a number of sittings a new magistrate will receive an appraisal, which will help to guide further development needs. While serving as a magistrate they will also have to engage with a process of continuous training, although this requirement is not particularly onerous.

Specialist training is required for the following areas:

1. Youth Court
2. Family Proceedings Court
3. Chairing the bench.

Justices' Clerk

As previously mentioned lay magistrates do not usually have legal qualifications. Nor is their training intended to make them legal experts. A legally qualified Justices' Clerk advises magistrates on the following:

❖ Law
❖ Procedure
❖ Practice.

Matters of fact are for the magistrate and not for the Justices' Clerk to determine.

Removal

The Lord Chancellor can remove a magistrate on the grounds of:

❖ misbehaviour or incapacity under s 11(2)(a) of the Courts Act 2003;
❖ incompetence under s 11(2)(b);
❖ declining or neglecting their duties as a magistrate under s 11(2)(c).

In reality the majority of magistrates removed are removed not for the reasons outlined above, but because they fail to meet the requirement to sit 26 half days per year.

A magistrate can also resign their position under s 11(1) of the Courts Act 2003.

Critical issues

If you are attempting a question on magistrates you must be able to demonstrate a critical understanding of this area.

Common Pitfall

Demonstrating a critical understanding of the English legal system is becoming a reoccurring theme in this revision guide. Many students will demonstrate an understanding of the advantages and disadvantages of the magistracy but few students will address recommendations for reforming the magistracy.

Swift and Sure Justice

One of the most recent recommendations to reform the role of magistrates in the English legal system has been made in the *Swift and Sure Justice* Government consultation paper. This paper recommends that a single magistrate could sit alone to deal with uncontested and low-level offences. This could lead to a significant efficiency gain in the Magistrates' Court.

In order to assist you in developing your critical understanding of the magistracy we have identified a number of key themes under the headings Advantages and Disadvantages. They can be broadly categorised as follows:

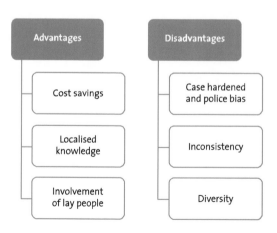

Advantages

Cost savings

Research carried out by Morgan and Russell in 2000 indicates that magistrates cost significantly less than DJMCs. The average cost of a lay magistrate is less than £500 per year; a District Judge is paid in excess of £90,000 per year.

Aim Higher

There are hidden costs associated with magistrates that should not be overlooked. Morgan and Russell suggest for example:

- ❖ Professional judges are able to deal with a much heavier case load than lay magistrates.
- ❖ Professional judges deal with cases much more quickly than a bench of lay magistrates.
- ❖ Lay magistrates require more support and make greater use of court facilities etc.
- ❖ These hidden costs may even out the cost differential between magistrates and DJMCs.
- ❖ Professionally qualified judges are more likely to impose a custodial sentence than lay magistrates. They are also more likely to remand a defendant.

You can read a copy of the research findings of Russell and Morgan by going to this website: www.civil-pi.com/Albert-docs/the_judiciary_in_the_magistartes_courts.pdf
(and yes, there is a spelling mistake in the URL!).

Localised knowledge

One of the eligibility criteria for a lay magistrate is that they must live within 15 miles of the area which they serve. This means that lay magistrates have local knowledge, enabling them to understand and respond to local concerns and priorities.

Involvement of lay people in the administration of justice

It is generally thought desirable to include lay people in the administration of justice. It introduces a democratic and humanising element into the trial process. It also upholds the principle of 'trial by one's own peers'. This is a theme that we will revisit when we consider the jury system in the next chapter.

Gender balance

Unlike many areas of the professional judiciary there is a fairly good gender balance in the magistracy, with women accounting for 52 per cent of the total number of serving magistrates.

Disadvantages

Police bias and case hardened

Magistrates, like professional judges, are expected to hear cases in a fair and impartial manner. However, one criticism frequently made of magistrates is that they exhibit bias in favour of the police. In *R v Bingham Justices ex parte Jowitt* (1974), a magistrate admitted in open court, that where there was conflicting evidence between a police officer and a defendant, he would accept the police officer's evidence as an accurate record of events. This clear bias led to a successful appeal and the defendant's conviction was quashed. It is also argued that the sheer volume of cases that magistrates hear can lead to them becoming case hardened (unlike a jury).

Inconsistency

Concerns have long existed regarding the consistency of decisions and sentences handed down by lay magistrates.

❖ In 1985 a Home Office Report entitled *Managing Criminal Justice* noted that there was little consistency in the sentences passed by benches in different areas of the country.

❖ Sixteen years later in 2001 a Government White Paper, *Justice for All*, highlighted significant inconsistency in the imposition of custodial sentences and the grant of bail between benches in different areas.

❖ In response to these criticisms the Government established the Sentencing Guidelines Council and enhanced training for magistrates in order to create greater consistency.

Diversity

The composition of the magistracy has been an area that has attracted particular criticism. The Auld Review in 2001 recommended that the magistracy should reflect the community that it serves; in particular, magistrates should be drawn from a wider variety of groups. The concern here was that middle-class, middle-aged conservatives dominate the magistracy. There have subsequently been a number of campaigns which have sought to widen the diversity of the magistracy.

Statistics appear to suggest that there is no longer an issue in terms of gender balance in the magistracy with 52 per cent of the bench being female. However, as of 1 April 2013 91 per cent of the magistracy was white and 55.5 per cent of the magistrates in post were 60 years of age or over. Only 3.2 per cent of magistrates were under the age of 40.

What concerns does an unrepresentative magistracy raise? Elliott and Quinn, *The English Legal System* (Longman, 2013) provides excellent coverage of these issues.

Unlike members of the judiciary, who are required to maintain political judicial independence, there is no such requirement for lay magistrates. Many magistrates are actively involved in local politics. There also appears to be an issue regarding political affiliation, with a strong Conservative bias. It is not clear, however, what impact this unrepresentative composition has on the decisions that magistrates make.

Research by Bond and Lemon in 1979, entitled 'Changes in Magistrates: Attitudes During the First Year on the Bench', suggested that magistrates with a Conservative affiliation take a 'harder line' with respect to sentencing, handing down harsher sentences. It is perhaps pertinent to note, however, that this research was carried out over 30 years ago.

It is certainly arguable that a magistracy that is unrepresentative of the community that it serves may have a negative impact on the public's perception of justice, weakening confidence in the criminal justice system.

Reforms

Magistrates v District Judges Magistrates' Court

We have already touched on this issue when we considered some of the cost advantages of lay magistrates. Replacing lay magistrates with professional judges could speed up the trial process significantly. Research by Morgan and Russell in 2000 suggested that DJMCs are also able to handle a heavier case load than their lay counterparts. There are a number of hidden costs associated with replacing lay magistrates with DJMCs. If, as Morgan and Russell estimate, one DJMC would be required for every 30 magistrates this would mean that around 775 new DJMCs would need to be appointed.

Composition and selection

If the magistracy is to reflect the community that it serves, then much more needs to be done to attract under-represented demographic groups. As it currently stands younger people are significantly under-represented on the bench. More needs to be done to encourage applications from younger people.

Auld recommendations

A key recommendation of the Auld Report was that the criminal courts in the English legal system be restructured. This would involve the creation of a new criminal court known as the District Division. The diagram below illustrates this proposal.

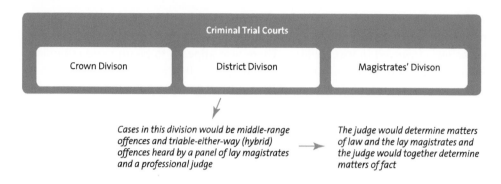

Cases in this division would be middle-range offences and triable-either-way (hybrid) offences heard by a panel of lay magistrates and a professional judge → The judge would determine matters of law and the lay magistrates and the judge would together determine matters of fact

Aim Higher

In 2000 Liberty published a report entitled *Magistrates' Courts and Public Confidence – a Proposal for Fair and Effective Reform in the Magistracy*, in which it criticised the Auld Report recommendations on reforming the magistracy on the basis that the creation of an intermediate court (The District Division), would constitute an unacceptable attack on jury trial – the cornerstone of the British justice system. (See Chapter 9 for more information on the jury.)

The report also argued that the Auld recommendations regarding the District Division Court were being used to obscure the real need and reasons for reform of the magistracy.

You can read the Liberty report by going to this website: www.liberty-human-rights.org.uk/policy/reports/magistrates-court-review-february-2003.pdf

Community Justice: Modernising the Magistracy in England and Wales

In 2001, Saunders conducted research into the skills and competencies required of lay and professional magistrates. In his report, entitled *Community Justice: Modernising the Magistracy in England and Wales*, he argues that a mixed bench composed of professional and lay magistrates is likely to provide the optimal skill and knowledge sets necessary in complex cases.

Core issues checklist

Independence of the judiciary is paramount	✔
The system of judicial appointments was reformed under the CLA 1990 and the CRA 2005.	✔

There are issues with regards to diversity for both judges and magistrates. There have been a number of attempts to create a more balanced bench.	✔
Magistrates deal with the vast majority of criminal cases – between 95 and 98 per cent of all criminal cases are dealt with in the Magistrates' Court. It is important to remember that magistrates have considerable civil jurisdiction too.	✔
There is a distinction that must be drawn between lay magistrates and the District Judges Magistrates' Court. Their qualification, selection and appointment differ.	✔
There are a number of advantages and disadvantages to the use of lay magistrates. Remember to link back to concepts that you have covered earlier in the book, such as the 'right to trial by one's own peers'.	✔
A number of suggestions have been made with regards to reforming the use of lay magistrates.	✔

Useful websites

Topic	Website
This is the website for the judiciary in England and Wales	www.judiciary.gov.uk
This is the website for the Supreme Court	www.supremecourt.gov.uk
This is the Ministry of Justice website	www.gov.uk/government/organisations/ministry-of-justice

Putting it into practice – example essay question

'Explain the selection and appointments process for the judiciary and the magistracy. To what extent do the judiciary and magistracy represent the communities they serve?'

Answer plan

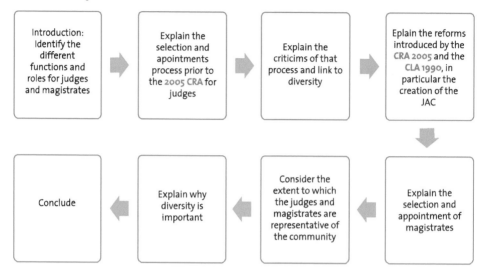

Outline answer

❖ This question is essentially a two-part question, which focuses on professional judges and the magistracy. It is important that you address both questions in relation to judges and magistrates. Make sure that there is equality here in terms of coverage. Giving too much coverage to one element of the question will limit the award of marks that the examiner can make.

❖ A brief explanation regarding the function and role of judges and magistrates is a good place to start. In particular you should remember that magistrates have a civil jurisdiction. You should also note that a judge's role differs in criminal and civil proceedings. Remember that juries are very rarely used in civil proceedings, and this means that judges are also the arbiters of fact in most civil cases.

❖ You may want to use sub-headings to segment your work, as this will help you structure your response.

❖ You will need to provide some historical context, particularly in relation to the selection and appointment of judges. Do not linger too long here, though; the core of the question is not past procedure and processes, but the current process. Some critical consideration here regarding lack of transparency and the 'old boys' network' will attract more marks.

❖ You should explain the changes that were made regarding judicial appointments under the CLA 1990 and the CRA 2005, in particular the creation of the JAC.

❖ Next you could explain the selection and appointment process for magistrates.

❖ You need to explain the extent to which the judiciary (including the magistracy) is representative of the community that they serve – there are several points you could make here: why is it desirable that the bench is representative? Is it representative? Is it improving? Does it matter?

Aim Higher

Process words: explain

Where an assessment question is asking you to 'explain' a particular issue or topic, you are being asked by the examiner to clarify a topic / issue / rule of law by giving a detailed account of the area. You will need to define any key terms. Your explanation of the topic should not be a 'simplistic overview'. You will need to ensure that your explanation has clarity, so that you are able to demonstrate to the examiner that you understand relevant, complex procedures, rules and policies. As with all legal essays you must support your work by reference to relevant authorities (see Chapter 4 for more information on what constitutes a relevant authority in a law assignment).

Table of key cases referred to in this chapter

Case name	Area of Law	Principle
AG v Guardian Newspapers Ltd (1987)	Judicial impartiality and independence	This is a case offered in illustration by Professor Griffith of suggested pro-establishment bias.
Bromley Borough Council v Greater London Council (1983)	Judicial impartiality and independence	This case can be used in an assessment as an illustration of suggested judicial bias.
McGonnell v UK (2000)	The role of the Lord Chancellor	Illustration of a lack of judicial impartiality/conflict of interest and contravention of Art 6 HRA
R v Bingham Justices ex parte Jowitt (1974)	Impartiality in the magistracy	This is an illustration of explicit bias of a magistrate. It can be used to demonstrate that open bias is grounds for appeal.
R v SS Home Office ex parte Brind (1991)	Judicial impartiality and independence	This case is an illustration of suggested political bias.

@ Visit the book's companion website to test your knowledge

❖ Resources include a subject map, revision tip podcasts, downloadable diagrams, MCQ quizzes for each chapter, and a flashcard glossary

❖ www.routledge.com/cw/optimizelawrevision

9 Juries

Revision objectives

Understand the law
- Can you identify the key legal provisions that apply to trial by jury in the English legal system?
- Can you identify the scope of proceedings in which trial by jury operates?
- Can you identify the key critical debates regarding trial by jury?

Remember the details
- Are you able to explain the symbolic significance of trial by jury in addition to the statistical significance of jury trials?
- Are you able to explain the rules that govern qualification, ineligibility, disqualification, excusal and deferrment of jury service?
- Are you able to explain the role of the jury in criminal and civil proceedings?
- Are you able to explain the role of that the jury play in Coroners' Courts?

Reflect critically on areas of debate
- Are you able to reflect critically on the key academic and political debates surrounding trial by jury?
- Are you able to reflect critically on the strengths and the weaknessess of trial by jury?
- Are you able to reflect critically on research conducted into the operation of the jury system?
- Are you able to reflect critically on the alternatives to trial by jury?

Apply your skills and knowledge
- Are you able to apply your knowledge giving appropriate authorities for your aruments?
- Are you able to apply your knowledge to an examination question ensurng that all statments of law are supported by reference to statutory provisons and or case law?

Chapter Map

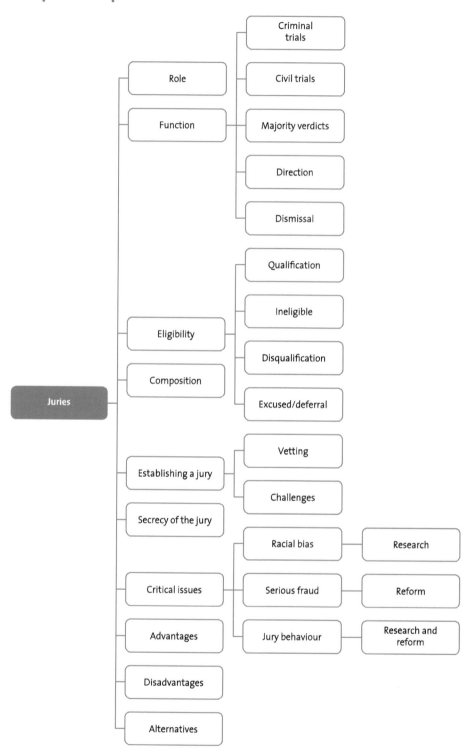

Introduction

In this chapter we will consider the use of juries in the civil and criminal justice system. The jury system is often referred to as a cornerstone of the English legal system. Its origins pre-date the **Magna Carta** of **1215**, in which the right to be tried by one's peers was recognised. **Lord Devlin** described the jury system as 'the lamp that shows freedom lives'.

The use of juries in the justice system has been the subject of political and academic criticism; and as a direct result, it is a popular examination topic as a stand-alone question. It is worth noting that a question on juries can also be presented as a question on 'laypeople', in which case you should consider not only the jury system but magistrates too.

Up For Debate

Notable supporters of the jury
❖ In *Trial by Jury* in 1956 Lord Devlin, a former Lord of Appeal in Ordinary, described the jury as the '**the lamp that shows freedom lives**'.
❖ E P Thompson in *Writing by Candlelight* said: 'A jury attends in judgment not only upon the accused but also upon the justice and humanity of the law'.

Notable critics of the jury
❖ P Darbyshire in 'The Lamp that Shows that Freedom Lives – is it Worth the Candle?' *Criminal Law Review*, 1991, p. 740

The jury: preliminary issues

Jury role → Jury function → Verdicts → Discharge

Defining the role of the jury

The judge and the jury perform different roles in the trial process. The function of the jury is to determine matters of fact; the judge determines matters of law. Jury members take an oath that they will 'try the defendant and give a true verdict according to the evidence'. It is contempt of court for a juror who has been sworn in to refuse to come to a decision.

The diagram below illustrates the distinct roles of the judge and jury. It is important to note that both the judge and jury perform subtly different roles in civil and criminal proceedings.

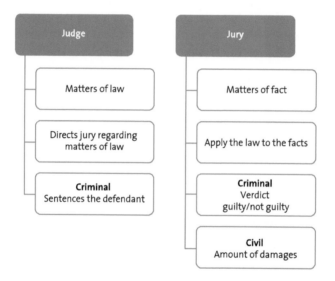

The function of the jury

Although the general focus of this chapter will be the operation of juries in the criminal justice system, it is important to remember that juries are still used in certain civil proceedings.

Civil Proceedings

Prior to 1854, a judge and jury decided all civil cases that came before the courts. In 1854 the Common Law Procedure Act made provision, where the parties agreed, for cases to be settled without a jury. From this point onwards the use of juries in civil proceedings has been gradually eroded and now under s 69 of the Senior Courts Act 1981, the right to a jury trial in civil cases is limited to only four specific areas.

Role of the jury in civil law

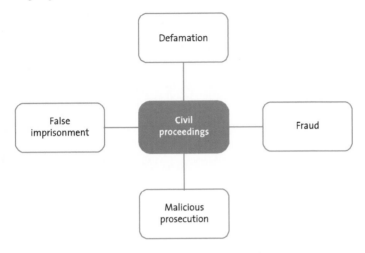

Critical issues with civil trials by jury

There has been significant academic and political criticism of the use of juries in civil proceedings. The table below outlines some of the key criticisms regarding jury trial in civil cases.

Juries in civil trials	Note	Case Illustration
❖ The right to trial by jury in defamation cases has been heavily criticised, particularly their ability to determine appropriate damages.	In 1975 **The Faulks Committee** expressed concerns with respect to the award of damages by juries in civil proceedings.	❖ *Sutcliffe v Pressdram Ltd* (1990)
❖ Section 8 of the Courts and Legal Services Act 1990 provides appeal courts with the power to alter the award of damages made by a jury.		❖ *Rantzen v Mirror Group Newspapers* (1993)
❖ Excessive damages awarded against the police in civil actions has also been heavily criticised.		❖ *Hill v Comissioner of Police for the Metropolis* (1998)

Juries in Coroners' Courts

An introduction: Coroners' Courts

The Coroners' Courts inquire into violent or unnatural deaths, sudden deaths where the cause is unknown, and deaths which have occurred in prison or police custody. A coroner is an independent judicial office holder who is either a lawyer or a doctor.

Most Coroners' Inquests are held without a jury, but there are particular circumstances in which a jury will be called. These include:

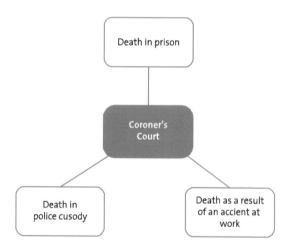

The role of the jury in the Coroners' Courts

In every jury inquest the coroner decides matters of law and procedure and the jury decides the facts of the case and reaches a verdict.

The jury cannot blame someone for the death at an inquest. If there is any blame, this can be established only through legal proceedings in the civil or criminal courts. However, a jury at an inquest can state facts which make it clear that the death was caused by a particular failure or by negligence.

The Coroners Rules 1984 provide for the following verdicts in relation to how a particular death has occurred:

Criminal trials

The remainder of this chapter will focus on the use of juries in the criminal justice system. The Magistrates' Court deals with over 95 per cent of all criminal cases. In reality trial by jury operates in fewer than 1 per cent of all criminal cases heard. A significant number of defendants appearing at the Crown Court plead guilty on all counts; in these cases a single judge determines the defendants' sentence.

In recent years different governments have attempted to reduce the use of juries throughout the justice system. For example, in 1973 the right to trial by jury was abolished for certain offences in Northern Ireland. This was in response to concerns regarding jury intimidation. In criminal proceedings associated with terrorism in Northern Ireland a Diplock Court (a court comprising of a judge sitting alone) will hear the case.

Directions from the judge to the jury

Juries hear only the more serious criminal offences, that is, triable-either-way offences and indictable offences.

In cases where there is insufficient evidence to convict the accused the judge has the power to direct the jury to acquit the accused. The judge does not, however, have a corresponding power to direct the jury to convict the accused: *DPP v Stonehouse* (1978). A judge must not put pressure the jury to reach a guilty verdict: *R v McKenna* (1960).

Members of the jury may seek the advice of the judge regarding their understanding and application of law. Responses to such inquiries by the jury must be given in open court, so as to avoid any allegation of misconduct: *R v Townsend* (1982).

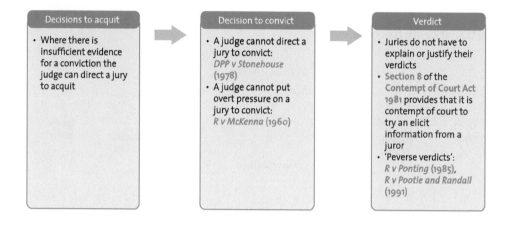

Jury verdicts

Juries do not have to explain or justify their verdicts. Section 8 of the Contempt of Court Act 1981 provides that it is contempt of court to try to elicit such information from a jury member. The fact that juries do not need to provide an explanation for their decision means that they can deliver 'perverse verdicts' such as *R v Ponting* (1985), *R v Pootle and Randall* (1991) and *R v Kronlid* (1996).

Key term	
Perverse verdict	Perverse verdicts occur when a jury simply refuses to convict a defendant in defiance of the law and evidence before them.

Majority verdicts

The Criminal Justice Act (CJA) 1967 removed the requirement for unanimous verdicts. A jury can therefore deliver a majority verdict where:

❖ there are not less than 11 jurors and 10 of them agree; or
❖ there are 10 jurors and 9 of them agree.

Where a jury has reached a guilty verdict on the basis of a majority decision, s 17(3) of the Juries Act 1974 requires the foreman of the jury to state in open court the number of jurors for the verdict and the number of jurors against: *R v Barry* (1975). There is no corresponding requirement for details of the voting to be declared in a majority verdict of not guilty.

Discharge of jury

In the event that irregularities occur in a trial, the judge can discharge the entire jury. This might happen, for example, where a defendant's previous convictions are revealed.

It may be necessary in certain circumstances for a judge to discharge individual jurors during a trial. This may be necessary where a juror becomes ill or where they are unable to continue for other reasons. Section 16(1) of the Juries Act 1974 permits a judge in these circumstances to discharge individual jurors. Where this happens the jury must not fall below nine members.

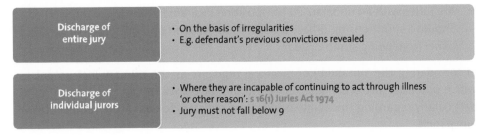

Discharge of entire jury	• On the basis of irregularities • E.g. defendant's previous convictions revealed
Discharge of individual jurors	• Where they are incapable of continuing to act through illness 'or other reason': s 16(1) Juries Act 1974 • Jury must not fall below 9

Appeals against jury decisions

There is no right of appeal against a jury verdict to acquit a defendant. Where a defendant has been acquitted s 36 of the Criminal Justice Act 1972 allows the Attorney General to refer a case to the Court of Appeal in order to seek advice on points of law raised. However, this will not change the outcome of the case for the defendant; it merely clarifies the law for future cases. An example of this procedure can be seen in *AG Reference (No 3 of 1998) (1999)*.

In civil cases a jury verdict can be overturned on appeal, if the verdict is perverse.

Jury selection

Jury service is considered a compulsory civic duty. If a person refuses to perform jury service they may face a fine.

There are a number of key statutes that you will need to be familiar with in relation to jury selection and qualification. These include the Juries Act 1974 as amended by the Criminal Justice Act 1988 and the Criminal Justice Act 2003.

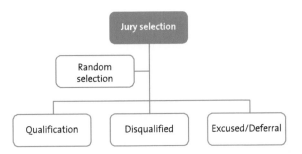

Random selection

Juries are selected at random from the electoral register. A jury that is selected at random may be all male, or all female; entirely composed of people from ethnic minorities or all white. As such, random selection can, and frequently does, produce unrepresentative jury panels. This is an issue that has received much criticism. In particular:

❖ Are juries with an unbalanced composition desirable?
❖ Should a summonsing officer take steps to avoid an unrepresentative jury panel from being summonsed?

In considering the suitability of electoral registers as the primary instrument by which potential jurors are selected, a number of points should be borne in mind, particularly regarding the ability of electoral registers to constitute representative jury panels.

Problems with electoral registers

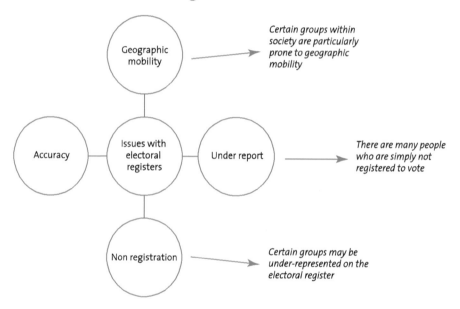

Qualification
Section 1 of the Juries Act 1974 stipulates that in order to serve as a juror individuals must meet the following criteria:

Ineligibility

Prior to the Criminal Justice Act 2003, there were a number of people deemed ineligible to serve on a jury, due to the nature of their employment. Those considered ineligible to serve were judges and magistrates; members of the legal profession; the police and probation officers; and members of the clergy.

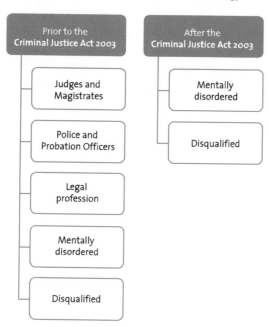

The Criminal Justice Act 2003 reduced the number of persons considered ineligible to serve on a jury. Paragraph 2 of Sched 33 of the Criminal Justice Act 2003 removed the following groups of persons as ineligible:

❖ the judiciary;
❖ others concerned with the administration of justice;
❖ the clergy.

This leaves only the mentally disordered and those disqualified as ineligible to serve.

The justification prior to the Criminal Justice Act 2003 for excluding certain groups on the basis of their vocation or employment was based on an assumption that the clergy and those involved in the administration of justice could unduly influence other members of the jury. The inclusion of these categories of persons previously excluded has not been without challenge.

> **Case precedent** – *R v (1) Abdroikov (2) Green (3) Williamson* (2005) citation
>
> **Facts:** the provisions in the Criminal Justice Act (CJA) 2003 with regards to eligibility to serve as a member of a jury were challenged as being contrary to Art 6 of the ECHR. In these separate cases the defendants appealed against their convictions on the grounds that the juries in their trials had contained jurors who were employed in the criminal justice system.
>
> **Principle:** the House of Lords recognised that there were situations where those involved in the administration of justice would meet the test of impartiality; however, that did not mean that they would do so automatically.
>
> **Application:** you can use these cases to demonstrate that although the CJA 2003 removed those involved with the administration of justice from the category of persons ineligible to serve on a jury this does not automatically mean that those involved in the administration are impartial in a particular case. If it is established that such a person is not impartial this could be grounds for appeal.

In the case of *R v Khan* (2008) Lord Phillips reiterated that although the Criminal Justice Act 2003 had abolished automatic ineligibility on the grounds of occupation this did not provide these individuals with immunity against claims of bias.

Disqualification
Certain categories of persons are disqualified from serving as jurors.

	Disqualified for life	Disqualified for 10 years	Other
1	Anyone who has been sentenced to a term of imprisonment or youth custody of five years or more.	Anyone who has served a term of imprisonment.	Anyone on bail.
2	Juveniles sentenced under s 91 of the Criminal Court Sentencing Act 2000 to life or five or more years.	Anyone who has received a suspended sentence.	
3	Anyone sentenced to imprisonment or detention for public protection under s 227 or s 228 of the Criminal Justice Act 2003.	Anyone who has received a community punishment as defined by s 177 of the Criminal Justice Act 2003.	
4	Anyone sentenced to an extended sentence.		

Excusal and deferment

Under s 9(1) of the Juries Act 1974 a range of persons were 'excused as of right' from jury service. Paragraph 3 of Sched 23 of the Criminal Justice Act 2003 repeals s 9(1) of the Juries Act 1974 and as such no one is entitled to 'excusal as of right' from jury service.

Section 9(2) of the Juries Act 1974 provides that if a person summonsed for jury service can show that there is 'good reason' why their summons should be deferred or excused they can make an application to the Jury Central Summonsing Bureau. Grounds for such excusal or deferral should only be made on the basis of 'good reason'. Examples of 'good reason' include:

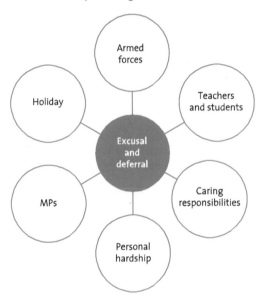

It is important to note that excusal from jury service is reserved only for those cases where the summonsing officer is satisfied that it would be unreasonable to require the person to serve at any time within the following 12 months. Deferral of service should be considered in the first instance.

Procedure for establishing a jury

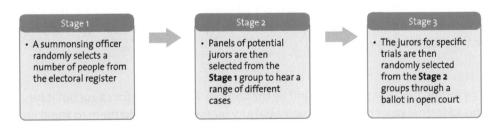

Stage 1	Stage 2	Stage 3
• A summonsing officer randomly selects a number of people from the electoral register	• Panels of potential jurors are then selected from the **Stage 1** group to hear a range of different cases	• The jurors for specific trials are then randomly selected from the **Stage 2** groups through a ballot in open court

Challenges to jury membership

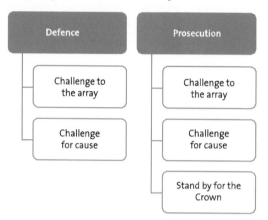

Prosecution and defence

Under s 12(6) of the Juries Act 1974, both prosecution and defence have a right to make a challenge to 'the array'.

Challenge to the array

The prosecution or the defence can challenge the whole jury on the basis that the summonsing officer has acted improperly in composing the jury panel. This form of challenge is rare; an attempt was made in *R v Danvers* (1982), where the defendant tried to challenge the racial composition of the jury.

Challenge by the defence

Until the Criminal Justice Act (CJA) 1988 there were two ways in which the defence could challenge potential jurors. However, the CJA 1988 abolished the right to peremptory challenge.

Challenge for cause

The defence can challenge any number of potential jurors for cause. Challenging for cause occurs where there is a significant reason why a particular juror should not serve in a specific case. This might occur where a potential jury member has had previous dealings with the defendant or where a potential juror has been involved in the case in some way.

Challenges by the prosecution

The prosecution has the same right as the defence to challenge for cause but it has the additional power to exclude potential jury members by asking them to stand by for the Crown.

Stand by for the Crown

In essence this is holding a juror in reserve. A juror who is asked to stand by for the Crown will only be called upon to serve if no other suitable jurors are available. It reality it is unlikely that there will be insufficient suitable jurors as the panel groups for juries are large. It is therefore unlikely that a juror asked to stand by for the Crown will be recalled.

The Crown should only exercise its power to 'stand by' potential jurors in the following circumstances:

1. To prevent the empowerment of a **manifestly unsuitable** juror with the agreement of the defence.
2. In circumstances where the Attorney General has approved **authorised checks** of the potential jury members and the results of those checks suggest that a potential jury member poses a security risk.

Jury vetting

Jury vetting is the process by which the Crown checks the background of potential jurors to assess their suitability. This process runs counter to the notion of random selection. It is, however, justified on the basis that it is crucial to ensure that jury members are not disqualified, and that any information revealed to them in a sensitive trial remains confidential. It is also used to ensure that people with extreme political views are not able to influence the outcome of a case.

Jury vetting is the process by which the Crown checks the background of potential jurors to assess their suitability

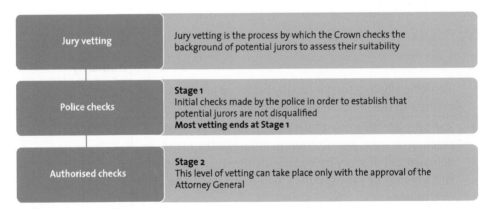

Vetting is a two-stage process. The Court of Appeal in *R v Mason* (1980) approved criminal record checks in order to establish whether potential jurors were disqualified from serving. In the vast majority of cases a check of police criminal records will be sufficient to reveal whether a further investigation by the security services is required. Any further investigation requires prior approval of the Attorney General.

Critical issues: the jury

There are a number of critical issues worthy of exploration in relation to the jury. It is possible that an assessment question will be focused on one or more of these critical issues. These critical issues can be identified under the following headings:

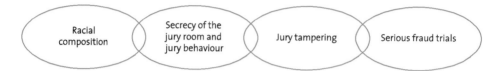

Racial composition   Secrecy of the jury room and jury behaviour   Jury tampering   Serious fraud trials

In this section we will focus on three of these critical themes. You will find detailed coverage of the remaining areas in Slapper and Kelly's *The English Legal System* (15th edition), published by Routledge.

1. The racial composition of the jury
2. Jury tampering
3. Secrecy of the jury room and jury behaviour.

The racial composition of the jury

We have already touched on the problematic issue of racial composition in relation to challenging jury membership. You will remember that in *R v Danvers* (1982) the defence unsuccessfully sought to challenge the array on the basis that a black defendant could not have complete confidence in the impartiality of an all-white jury. This is an issue that has vexed the courts on a number of occasions, as illustrated by the following cases.

Key Points

		Authority
1	To artificially construct a racially balanced jury runs counter to the principle of random selection.	*R v Ford* (1989)
2	Random selection must take place from the 'normal catchment area'. Any attempt to influence the racial composition of a jury by 'out of catchment selection' of the jury may be valid grounds for a conviction to be overturned.	*R v Tarrant* (1997)
3	A randomly selected all-white jury does not breach a defendant's rights under Art 6 of the HRA 1998.	*R v Smith* (2003)
4	The Runciman Commission recommended that the prosecution or the defence should be able to insist that up to three jury members be from ethnic minorities and that at least one of those should be from the same ethnic minority as the accused or victim.	Runciman Commission

| 5 | Empirical research suggests that racially balanced juries are not needed to ensure fair decision-making in jury trials with black and minority ethnic defendants. | *Professor Cheryl Thomas* (2010) |

Racial bias in jury decision-making

It is clear from the above cases that the law does not permit the artificial creation of ethnically balanced juries. However, it is important to consider whether there are adequate safeguards in place to address racially biased decision-making by juries. The most significant barrier to addressing allegations of racially prejudiced decision-making by juries is the operation of s 8 of the Contempt of Court Act 1981, which prevents investigation into what occurs in the privacy of the jury room.

Key cases: racially biased jury decisions

> *Miah* (1997)

Facts: a complaint arose after the jury had delivered their verdict regarding racist comments made by members of the jury.

> Held

Investigations into what had happened in the jury room were precluded.

The court will not investigate allegations relating to jury deliberations. The following are cases where this principle has been applied.
- *R v Qureshi* (2002)
- *R v Mirza* (2004)
- *R v Smith and Mercieca* (2005)

> *Gregory v UK* (1998)

Facts: the jury in this case asked that one member be excused on the basis of racial prejudice. The judge directed the whole jury to try the case on the evidence. The juror was not excused. The defendant was later convicted. He appealed to the European Court of Human Rights claiming that his rights under Art 6 of the ECHR had been infringed.

> Held

The European Court held that the judge's clear and carefully worded warning was sufficient to ensure that Gregory's rights under Art 6 were not infringed.

Where allegations regarding bias/prejudice are brought to the attention of the judge the jury should be given a clear direction that the jury should 'try the case on the evidence'. A carefully worded and clear direction will ensure that a defendant's rights under Art 6 ECHR are not infringed.

Compare the case of *Gregory* with the case of *Sander v UK* (2001). In this case a juror reported racist remarks made by other members of the jury to the judge. The judge separated the juror making the allegation from the other jurors while representations were made to the court. The juror making the allegations then re-joined the other jurors. The judge instructed the jury to put aside any prejudices and 'try the case on the evidence'.

The jury in *Sander* then wrote a letter to the judge which was signed by all members of the jury, including the original complainant, denying any allegations of racism. One member of the jury wrote to the judge separately apologising if any remarks he had made had caused offence. Sander was convicted, then appealed on the basis that his rights under Art 6 of the ECHR had been infringed.

The European Court of Human Rights held that the judge should have discharged the jury. The defendant's rights under Art 6 of the ECHR had been infringed. The European Court of Human Rights distinguished *Sander* from *Gregory* (see above) on the basis that in *Gregory* no juror had admitted responsibility for racist remarks. They also expressed concerns regarding the separation of the juror making the allegation and cast doubt on the validity of the letter refuting racism.

Aim Higher

P Robertshaw, in 'Responding to bias amongst Juries' (2002) 66(1) *Journal of Criminal Law* 84–95, provides detailed analysis of these cases.

Jury tampering

Jury tampering covers a range of circumstances in which the jury's independence and decision-making is compromised. Such a situation could come about because of:

❖ actual harm or threats of harm to jury members;
❖ possible intimidation;
❖ bribery of jury members;
❖ similar improper approaches to the juror's family or friends.

In response to concerns regarding jury tampering the Criminal Justice Act 2003 provides for trial on indictment to take place in the Crown Court without a jury.

Key provisions for jury tampering: the **Criminal Justice Act 2003**

Section	Provision	Comment
s 44	Provides for trial on indictment in the Crown Court to be conducted without a jury 'where there is a danger of jury tampering, or for a trial to continue without a jury where a jury has been discharged because of jury tampering'.	For an application to be granted, the court must be satisfied that there is evidence of a real and present danger that jury tampering would take place. In addition the court must be satisfied that the danger of jury tampering is substantial, and that steps cannot be taken to prevent tampering.
s 44(6)	Sets out examples of what might constitute evidence of a real and present danger of jury tampering which include:	1. a retrial where the previous jury was discharged because of jury tampering; 2. a case where jury tampering has taken place in previous criminal proceedings involving the defendant(s); 3. a case where there has been intimidation, or attempted intimidation, of any person who is likely to be a witness.
s 46	Deals with trials already under way, where jury tampering has taken place or appears to be taking place.	If the judge decides to discharge the jury, and is satisfied that tampering has occurred, the judge can make an order that the trial should continue without a jury if satisfied that this would be fair to the defendant.

Illustrations of the **Criminal Justice Act 2003** in action

R v Twomey (2010)	R v J, S, M (2010) & R v KS (2009)
Facts: this case concerned members of a gang that was alleged to have committed a £1.75 million armed raid on a warehouse near Heathrow Airport in February 2004. In this case there had been three previous failed trials in which there were allegations of jury tampering.	**Facts:** two unrelated cases in which there was a suggestion of jury tampering

Application under s 44 CJA 2003	Applications under s 44 and s. 6 of the CJA 2003
The prosecution made a sucessful application under the CJA 2003 for trial without a jury.	The Court of Appeal overturned orders for trial without a jury. It offered guidance on how ss 44 and 46 of the Criminal Justice Act should operate. The making of an order for non-jury trial should be the last resort; the statutory conditions of the Criminal Justice Act 2003 must be fulfilled.

Secrecy of the jury room and jury behaviour

Key Statute

Section 8 of the Contempt of Court Act 1981
It an offence to obtain, disclose or solicit any particulars of the statement made, opinion expressed, arguments advanced, or votes cast by members of the jury in the course of their deliberations in any legal proceedings.

❖ Section 8(1) applies not just to jurors, but also to any others who publish their revelations – *Attorney General v Associated Newspapers* (1994).
❖ In *Gregory v UK* (1998), the ECtHR approved protection of jury secrecy under UK law. Section 8 is not in conflict with Art 6 of the ECHR. See *Misra* (1987).

As a general rule the court will not investigate anything said in the course of a jury's deliberations. An exception to this rule is where an allegation is made which suggests that the jury decided not to reach a decision, but instead decided the case by other means such as tossing a coin or using a Ouija board: *R v Young (Stephen)* (1995).

Case precedent – *Attorney General v Scotcher* (2005)

Facts: the defendant had been a member of a jury that reached a guilty verdict. The day after the case, Scotcher wrote a letter to the mother of one of the convicted men detailing misconduct that he alleged had taken place in the jury room. Scotcher was charged with contempt of court under s 8 of the Contempt of Court Act 1981.

Principle: the key principle here is that the secrecy of the jury room is paramount. A juror wanting to raise concerns without risking prosecution can:

1. contact the clerk of the court or the jury bailiff, or
2. send a sealed letter to the court by an outside agency such as the Citizens Advice Bureau.

Application: the House of Lords upheld the principle that the secrecy of the jury room should be paramount. It also recognised the need to advise jurors as to what to do if they subsequently feel that they have participated in an unfair trial.

The use of the internet and other electronic means of communication

Members of a jury must rely on the evidence presented to them in court. They are not permitted to conduct their own research, nor are they allowed to rely on other outside sources of information in order to come to their decision. The growth and penetration of information technology in modern society has increased the possibility that jurors may be influenced by sources outside the courtroom. A number of cases illustrate the difficulties the courts have had to contend with regarding jury accessibility to 'outside' material.

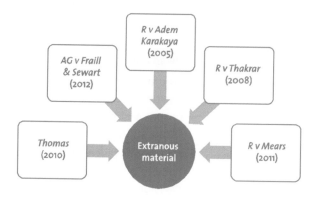

❖ In *R v Adem Karakaya* (2005) the Court of Appeal held that material downloaded from the internet and taken into a jury room by one of the members of the jury was contrary to the rule that the jury would not rely on privately obtained information or receive the information after it had retired.
❖ In *R v Thakrar* (2008) a member of the jury supplied fellow jury members with inaccurate information, obtained from the internet. On appeal against his conviction the Court of Appeal held that there should be a retrial.

- ❖ In *AG v Fraill & Sewart* (2012) it became apparent that a member of the jury had been in contact via Facebook with parties to the case. The juror and the person they were in contact with were found guilty of contempt of court.
- ❖ In *R v Mears* (2011) evidence emerged that a juror had exchanged text messages with a member of the public in the gallery during the trial. The Court of Appeal overturned the conviction because of the risk of prejudice.

Up For Debate

- ❖ In her report on the fairness of the jury, Professor Cheryl Thomas found that, in high-profile cases, almost three-quarters of members of the jury were aware of media coverage of that case.
- ❖ The report raised questions about use of the internet by jury members. Twelve per cent of jurors in high-profile cases admitted that they had looked for information on their case on the internet.

For more information on this leading research go to: www.justice.gov.uk/downloads/publications/research-and-analysis/moj-research/are-juries-fair-research.pdf

---

Advantages and disadvantages of juries

The table below outlines some of the main advantages and disadvantages of the use of juries.

Advantages	Disadvantages
Involvement of lay people: public participation in the justice system	**Trauma:** performing this civic duty can be a harrowing experience as jury members can be exposed to disturbing evidence throughout the trial.
Conscience: a jury is able to act according to their conscience.	**No reasons given:** the fact that juries do not need to provide an explanation for their decision means that they can deliver 'perverse verdicts'.
Random selection	**Competence:** there are some trials, particularly long and complex fraud trials, in which the competence of the jury has been questioned. Highly technical evidence can be extremely difficult for a jury to follow, particularly if it is a long case. If a jury does not understand the evidence it is hard to see that they will be able to come to the right decision, whatever that may be.

Less conviction minded and not case hardened: statistics on conviction rates in the Crown Court and Magistrates' Court suggest that juries are less prosecution minded than magistrates and professional judges.	**Prejudice and bias:** members of any jury panel may exhibit racial, gender, political and religious bias and prejudice.
Public opinion: they can be a gauge of public opinion	**Unrepresentative:** the notion of random selection does not ensure that a representative jury will be empaneled.
Bias and prejudice neutralised: it is argued that any prejudice and bias is overcome by having 12 members on a jury	**Jury tampering:** juries are susceptible to jury tampering. **Cost and time:** juries are expensive and slow as compared to lay magistrates and professional judges. **Excessive damages in civil trials:** juries have a reputation for awarding excessive damages in civil cases. **Jurors with disabilities:** there is limited provision for accommodating jurors who have physical disabilities. **Media influence:** jurors are exposed to media influences and as a result may try defendants not on the basis of the evidence before them but on the basis of 'outside' material.

Reform of the jury system

Suggested reform	Discussion	Progress towards reform
Triable-either-way offences (Hybrid offences)		
The Runciman Commission's Report suggested that defendants should not be able to choose their court trial on the basis that they think will get a fairer hearing at one level rather than another.	The Criminal Justice (Mode of Trial) Bill was introduced in the Parliamentary session 1999 to 2000. This sought to amend the Magistrate's Court Act 1980 by giving magistrates the power to decide in which court a case should be heard.	

Suggested reform	Discussion	Progress towards reform
Triable-either-way offences (Hybrid offences)		
The Auld Report also suggested that the defendant should no longer have an elected right to trial by judge and jury in either-way cases.	The Bill was defeated in the House of Lords in 2001.	
Auld Report		
1. The jury should be more widely representative of the national and local communities from which they are drawn. 2. No one in future should be eligible for, or excused as of right, from jury service. Those with criminal convictions and mental disorder should continue to be disqualified. The CJA 2003 removed all ineligible classes of person. Only those with qualifying criminal convictions and the mentally disordered are ineligible. 3. Provision should be made to enable ethnic minority representation on a jury where race is likely to be a relevant and important issue in the case. 4. Trial judges and all the Court of Appeal should be entitled to examine alleged impropriety in the jury room. 5. If a jury verdict appears to be perverse, the prosecution should be entitled to appeal.		
Serious fraud cases		
The Auld Report suggested that the trial judge should have the power to direct trial by himself with two lay members drawn from a panel established by the Lord Chancellor or if the defendant requests by sitting alone.	CJA 2003	

Alternatives to trial by jury

Trial by a single judge

Trial by a panel of laypeople and a professional judge

Panel of judges

Specially selected jury who are selected on the basis of specialist knowledge and expertise

Core issues checklist

Core issues	
❖ The jury has a long history in the English legal system. Trial by jury is considered a civic right.	✔
❖ The use of juries has been declining.	✔
❖ Juries are a feature primarily of the criminal justice system. They do however, have a limited role in civil law, where they can be used in defamation cases, malicious prosecution cases, fraud cases and false imprisonment cases. They are also used in certain cases in the Coroners' Courts.	✔
❖ Jurors are randomly selected from the electoral register. They must meet the eligibility criteria to serve on a jury. A number of individuals are disqualified from serving as a juror. The CJA 2003 reduced the number of individuals deemed ineligible to serve as a member of the jury. It is possible in certain circumstances to defer or be excused from jury duty.	✔
❖ Both the prosecution and the defence can challenge/object to the whole or individual jurors.	✔
❖ Section 8 of the Contempt of Court Act 1981 protects the secrecy of the jury room. This provision limits the nature and quality of research that can be conducted into jury decisions and reasoning.	✔
❖ There has been political and academic criticism of jury trials in relations to: jury competence in serious fraud cases; the racial composition of the jury; jury tampering; jury behaviour.	✔
❖ Over the years a range of reforms have been proposed, some of which have been adopted.	✔

Putting it into practice – example essay question

'Consider critically the operation of juries in the English Legal System.'

Answer plan

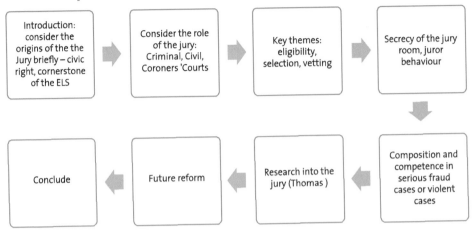

Outline answer

❖ The key process word in the essay title is 'critically' – this means that the examiner is looking for more than a descriptive account. You must demonstrate that you are able to engage with the critical themes concerning the jury if you want to attain a high mark.

❖ Your introduction should introduce the topic and set the context for your essay. It is always helpful to signpost the reader in terms of the structure of your essay too.

❖ After a brief introduction regarding the origins of the jury you can move on to consider the role that juries play in the English legal system. Many students will focus entirely on their function in the criminal justice system. A good student will recognise that they also have a function in certain civil trials and in the Coroners' Courts.

❖ It is important to demonstrate that you understand the role of the jury and how it is distinct from the role of the judge. It would also be helpful to demonstrate the different verdicts that can be delivered.

❖ The focus of the essay after this point is likely to lean towards their function in criminal trials. It would be helpful to explain their statistical significance (what percentage of cases are heard by a jury), in addition to their symbolic significance.

❖ You now need to focus on the key issues regarding jury trial. It would be sensible to block these, perhaps under subheadings dealing with each sub-topic in its entirety. It is not helpful to jump back and forth. You need to explain the eligibility criteria for jurors and deal with the issue of disqualification and excusal. You should note that significant changes were made to some of these criteria under the Criminal Justice Act 2003.

❖ You will need to deal with the issue of composition in particular. Under this heading you need to consider the significance of racial composition and why if at all this is significant.

❖ It is important to deal with the impact of the Contempt of Court Act 1981 in terms of jury secrecy and how this impacts on research into jury competence. Consider the research that has been undertaken in this area. How do we know that juries come to the right decisions, for example?

❖ You also need to deal with the issue of jury behaviour, in particular the impact of the media and social media. Look at the key research in this area to support your arguments.

❖ A good student will be able to explain the erosion of jury trial within the ELS and understand current proposals for reform (including proposals that have not been adopted). This could include brief consideration of the alternatives to trial by jury.

Aim Higher

Content and process words

Most essay questions contain two core elements: content words and process words.

For example: '**Consider critically the operation of the jury system in the English Legal System.**'

The **content words** tell you what the topic of the essay is, together with its specific focus. In this illustration the content words tell you that the topic is the jury system in the ELS.

Process words on the other hand tell you to do something particular. In the above example, you are being asked to consider the operation of the jury system in the ELS **critically**.

A good student will engage with both the content and the process words in the question and this will allow the examiner to award a higher mark. A weaker student will simply write all that they know about the jury system.

Remember!
To score a high mark in an essay-style question you must demonstrate not only accuracy of knowledge, but engagement with the process words in the question. Many students fail to engage with the process words and as a result they limit the award of marks that can be made by the examiner.

Useful websites

Topic	Website
Diversity and fairness in the Jury System	http://webarchive.nationalarchives.gov.uk/20100505212400/ http://www.justice.gov.uk/publications/docs/JuriesReport2-07-webVersion.pdf
Are juries fair?	www.justice.gov.uk/downloads/publications/research-and-analysis/moj-research/are-juries-fair-research.pdf

Table of key cases referred to in this chapter

Case	Area of Law	Principle
AG v Fraill & Sewart [2012] EWCA Crim 1570	Example of social networking mediums being used by members of the jury to discuss jury room deliberations.	Parties to the discussions were held in contempt of court.
Attorney General v Scotcher [2005] UKHL 36	A case involving allegations of racist behaviour of jury members in a criminal trial.	Secrecy of the jury room is paramount.
Dpp v Stonehouse [1978] AC 55	This case concerns directions from a judge to a jury.	A judge cannot order a jury to convict.
Gregory v UK (1998) 25 EHHR 577 Sander v UK (2001) 31 EHHR 44 R v Miah [1997] 2 Cr App R R v Qureshi [2001] EWCA Crim 1807	These cases can be used to illustrate the difficulty that the courts have had dealing with accusations of misconduct in the jury room relating to bias and prejudice.	These cases illustrate that the secrecy of the jury room is paramount. A juror wanting to alert the court of misconduct in the jury room must follow strict guidelines if they want to avoid an allegation of contempt of court.
R v (1) Abdroikov (2) Green (3) Williamson [2007] UKHL 37	These cases concern situations in which juries have contained individuals who work within the criminal justice system.	There are situations where those involved in the administration of justice would meet the test of impartiality; however, that does not mean that they are automatically impartial.

R v Danvers [1982] Crim LR 680	This is a case that can be used to illustrate a challenge to the array.	The defence sought to challenge the array on the basis that a black defendant could not have confidence in an all-white jury. The challenge failed.
R v J,S,M [2010] & R v KS (2009) EWCA Crim 1755	Examples of two unrelated cases in which there was a suggestion of jury tampering.	The making of an order for non-jury trial should be the last resort; the statutory conditions of the Criminal Justice Act 2003 must be fulfilled.
R v Karakaya [2005] EWCA Crim 346	Example of material downloaded from the internet being taken into the jury room by a juror.	This was contrary to the general rule that the jury would not rely on privately obtained information or receive the information after it had retired.
R v Mason [1980] 3 WLR 617	This case is concerned with jury vetting.	The checking of criminal records is permitted in order to establish that a potential juror is not disqualified.
R v Mears [2011] EWCA Crim 2651	Evidence emerged that a member of the jury had exchanged text messages with a member of the public gallery throughout the trial.	The Court of Appeal had no option but to overturn the conviction on the grounds of the risk of prejudice.
R v Ponting [1985] Crim LR 318	Illustration of a perverse verdict.	One of the frequently cited advantages of the jury system is that they can act according to their conscience.
R v Twomey (2010)	This case is an illustration of a trial being held without a jury following a successful application under the CJA 2003.	An illustration of a trial held under s 44 of the CJA 2003.

@ Visit the book's companion website to test your knowledge

❖ Resources include a subject map, revision tip podcasts, downloadable diagrams, MCQ quizzes for each chapter, and a flashcard glossary

❖ www.routledge.com/cw/optimizelawrevision

10

Funding of Legal Services

Revision objectives

Understand the law	• Do you understand the principles that underpin the legal aid system?
Remember the details	• Can you remember the key bodies?
Reflect critically on areas of debate	• Have you considered the issues raised in the 'Up for debate' boxes?
Contextualise	• Can you see how the different areas of legal aid work?
Apply your skills and knowledge	• Are you confident in answering the 'Putting it into practice' question?

Chapter Map

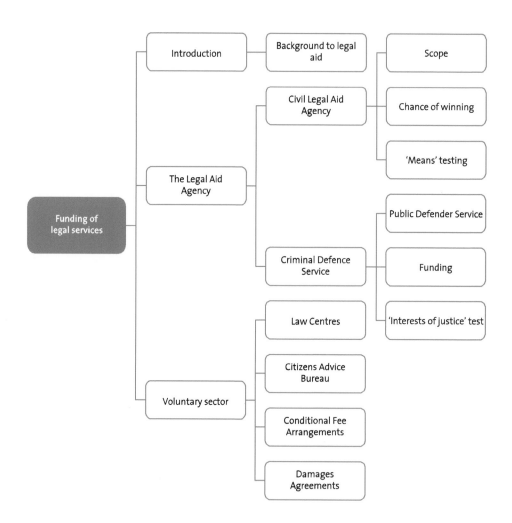

Putting it into practice – example essay question

'Consider the matters a party may take into account when considering a conditional fee arrangement.'

You will find an outline answer at the end of this chapter

Introduction

Since April 2013, and in an effort to save £350 million a year, the funding of legal services has been through some dramatic changes. The Ministry of Justice plans further cuts in the future, so **your first task** when completing assessments is to ensure you are up to date with the changes post April 2013. **Note**: the latest (15th) edition of Slapper and Kelly on the *English Legal System* should be up to date with the new changes.

So you are clear, this chapter will focus on the changes to the system made in April 2013.

Your lecturer should highlight the new rules, and due to its topical nature it may be considered a good area for examination or coursework questions.

This chapter does not cover the history of legal aid.

Aim Higher

Although you are *unlikely* to receive a question about the historical development of legal aid (it may be considered a little too descriptive for an undergraduate question), it is worth being familiar with the background of the system and how it has developed. Most ELS textbooks have a section on this.

For your assessments you need to show an appreciation of why we need legal aid, and what the system is trying to achieve, as well as knowledge of the changes brought about by the recent Acts. When completing your assessments consider the following questions.

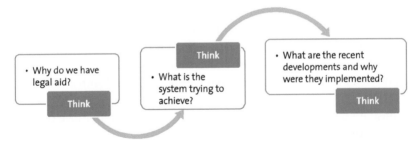

- Why do we have legal aid?

  Think

- What is the system trying to achieve?

  Think

- What are the recent developments and why were they implemented?

  Think

A question on funding may also come up as part of another question, for example when answering a question on accessing the court system, or a question regarding Alternative Dispute Resolution (ADR).

We will begin by looking at the background to legal aid

Legal aid covers both **civil** and **criminal** disputes. It gives those on low incomes or with no income access to legal services. Without legal aid this section of society may be denied access to legal help, for instance from a solicitor.

*NO MONEY = **NO ACCESS TO LEGAL SERVICES***

The scheme was very successful, but with success came an increase in costs. Cutbacks had to be made to stop spending reaching unacceptable limits, **and it is this increase in expenditure that has been the catalyst for the recent changes**.

The need for people to have access to legal services has never been in dispute. The justice system would not be fulfilling its goals if people could not access it. In your assessments you can site Art 6 ECHR, which states that everyone has a right to a fair trial (see the chapter on human rights for further details), which reinforces the right to have access to legal services.

The problems therefore are not in the system itself but in how to provide people with access to legal services without increasing expenditure to unsustainable levels. In your assessments you can state how **conditional fee arrangements** have helped to reduce the financial burden (these are dealt with later) in relation to civil legal aid cases.

So, providing access to legal services is a balancing act between the following:

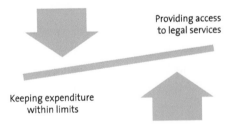

Providing access to legal services

Keeping expenditure within limits

A new Act (the Legal Aid, Sentencing and Punishment of Offenders (LASPO) Act 2012) made changes to the legal aid system in 2013 (mainly by imposing cuts). The Act is in four parts and sixteen schedules. Part 1 covers legal aid and Part 2 covers litigation funding and costs. It is these two parts that we are concerned with in this chapter.

Having considered some background material it is now time to move on to look at the current system.

We will begin by considering the 'umbrella' organisation that oversees the running of the legal aid system.

The Legal Aid Agency (LAA)

This Agency replaced the Legal Services Commission (LSC).

Note: the LSC was created by the Access to Justice Act 1999 (which has now been amended by the LASPO 2012).

The Agency came into force on 1 April 2013.

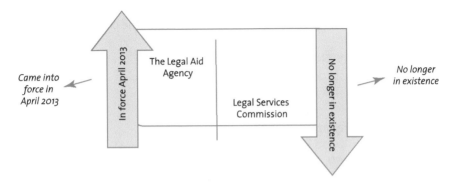

The role of the Legal Aid Agency

The main role of the Agency is to oversee the provision of **civil** and **criminal** legal aid in England and Wales.

Its aim is to deliver a fair, effective and efficient system of legal aid.

In order to achieve the above objectives it has the following priorities:

For your assessments ensure you **understand the role of the Legal Aid Agency and its objectives**.

We will now consider how the system of **Civil Legal Aid** operates.

The Civil Legal Aid system

To be eligible for Civil Legal Aid an applicant must prove the following:		
One: the case must be within the scope for legal aid.	Two: the applicant must have a 50:50 prospect of winning the case.	Three: the applicant must fulfil the financial eligibility criteria.

We will work through these headings as we work through the chapter.

One: is the case within the scope of legal aid?

To answer this we must consider the new Legal Aid, Sentencing and Punishment of Offenders Act (LASPO) 2012.

The Act made three important changes:

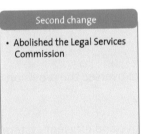

First change
- It reversed the position under the Access to Justice Act 1999 which stated legal aid was available for any matter not specifically excluded, thus reducing the scope of cases eligible for legal aid

Second change
- Abolished the Legal Services Commission

Third change
- Made various provisions in respect of funding and costs

LASPO came into effect on **1 April 2013**. From the diagram above you can see these changes concerned the amending of the financial eligibility criteria, and that (controversially) it took many areas out of the scope of eligibility. The Act brought into effect changes for the scope of civil legal aid. These are contained in Sched 1, Part 1.

Do not worry if these do not mean much to you at present. By the end of this chapter you should be familiar with the significance of these changes.

Civil Legal Advice (CLA)
(Old name: Community Legal Advice)

The role of the CLA

Its primary role is to provide **civil advice** to those who qualify for legal aid.

Work your way through the chart below to familiarise yourself with the areas **now eligible for legal aid** (remember that the Act removed large areas of law that were no longer eligible – **refer back to the chart on page 238**).

Benefit appeals
- ❖ appeals to the Upper Tribunal, Court of Appeal or Supreme Court

Debt (if your home is at risk)
- ❖ court action by mortagage lender due to mortgage arrears, court action by creditor forcing the sale of a home

Special Educational Needs
- ❖ appeals against Special Educational Needs assessments by the council, asylum applications, applications to stay in the UK as a victim of trafficking

Housing
- ❖ eviction due to rent arrears, rented house in serious disrepair, antisocial behaviour

Discrimination
- ❖ discrimination by employers, education providers, housing or service providers

Family issues
- ❖ adoption, child abduction and unlawful removal from within England and Wales, enforcement of international child maintenance

Clinical negligence
- ❖ only where the child suffers a neurological injury resulting in them being severely disabled during pregnancy, child birth or postnatal period (eight weeks)

Civil Legal Advice Helpline

Telephone gateway

LASPO also created a mandatory **telephone gateway** for three categories of work (at Legal Help level):

- ❖ debt
- ❖ special educational needs (SEN)
- ❖ discrimination.

Unless the client is exempt.

The exceptions are when the client:

❖ is in detention (including prison, a detention centre or secure hospital), or
❖ is under 18, or
❖ has been previously assessed by the gateway as needing face-to-face advice, has received this advice within the last 12 months, and is seeking further help to solve a linked problem from the same provider.

In summary,

Telephone gateway used for:	Unless exempt
• debt • special educational needs (SEN) • discrimination	• in detention • under 18 • has been assessed as needing face-to-face advice

Exceptional cases

The good news is that if a case falls outside Sched 1, it may still be eligible under s 10 (exceptional cases). The bad news is that strict rules apply here (and these rules fall outside the scope of this chapter).

Refusal of legal aid where alternative avenues are available

Legal aid may be refused if alternative funding is available, such as conditional fee arrangements (we cover these later).

We have now covered those areas eligible for legal aid. Next we will consider how they work in practice.

The different types of civil legal aid

Civil legal aid can help with the following matters.

Legal help
• Advice is given regarding legal rights and negotiation

Help at court
• Someone helps at court by speaking on the client's behalf (note: this is not the same as legal representation)

Family mediation
• Help in resolving family problems through mediation. Money, children and disputes over the family home are often solved this way (see the chapter on ADR for more on this)

> **Family help**
>
> • Other help, for example drawing up an agreement

> **Legal representation**
>
> • representation at court by a solicitor or barrister

You may wish to include in your assessments some of those matters now **excluded** by the new Act. A list is below.

❖ consumer and general contract;
❖ Criminal Injuries Compensation Authority cases;
❖ employment cases;
❖ education cases, except for cases of Special Educational Needs;
❖ housing matters, except those where the home is at immediate risk (excluding those who are 'squatting'), homelessness assistance, housing disrepair cases that pose a serious risk to life or health and antisocial behaviour cases in the county court;
❖ legal advice in relation to a change of name;
❖ actions relating to contentious probate or land law;
❖ legal advice on will-making for:
   ❖ those over 70
   ❖ disabled people
   ❖ the parent of a disabled person and
   ❖ the parent of a minor who is living with the client, but not with the other parent, and the client wishes to appoint a guardian for the minor in a will;
❖ private family law (other than cases where criteria are met regarding domestic violence or child abuse);
❖ tort and other general claims.

Aim Higher

You do not need to remember all of these but to include a few will demonstrate you have an understanding of how legal aid has changed.

For example, a question may contain an element of asking you to assess 'Is the legal aid system is achieving its aims?' To show knowledge of the reforms and one or two items now excluded will help show you understand how the scope of legal aid has changed over time. You can ask the question 'Is the legal aid system still working if those bringing a claim in tort are now excluded from the legal aid system?' Here it would be appropriate to discuss the role of the CFAs and DBAs (discussed below).

Aim Higher – suggested reading

A thorough account of the historical context for legal aid can be found in Slapper and Kelly, (2013) *The English Legal System*, 15th edition, London: Routledge.

Two: does the client have a 50:50 chance of winning the case (the 'merits' test)?

See the chart on page 238 to see where this fits in.

The Civil Legal Aid (Merits Criteria) Regulations 2013 are relevant here.

They contain the rules the Legal Aid Agency must apply when determining whether an application qualifies for legal aid.

The important regulations are Regulation 4 (prospects of success) and Regulation 5 (prospects of success test).

It is unlikely you will be required to know these regulations in detail on the basis that this would be too descriptive, and more applicable to those in practice.

You will need to know that in order to receive funding the case ought to have at least a 50 per cent chance of success. Those which are classed as 'poor' – where the individual is unlikely to receive a successful outcome – should be refused.

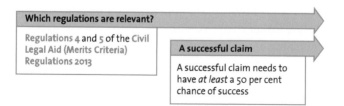

Which regulations are relevant?

Regulations 4 and 5 of the Civil Legal Aid (Merits Criteria) Regulations 2013

A successful claim

A successful claim needs to have *at least* a 50 per cent chance of success

Three: does the client fulfil the financial eligibility criteria (the means test)?

This is the final test a client claiming legal aid must satisfy (**See chart on page 238**).

The 'means test' reinforces that only those on a low income will benefit from the system.

In essence the test calculates a client's disposable income (this is the amount left after essential living expenses) and disposable capital (amount left after essential items, e.g. a home). Legal aid is awarded if the amounts of disposal income and capital fall below certain limits.

Some examples of current limits are given below.

To gain access to all levels of service	For access to legal help, help at court and legal representation for immigration purposes	Family mediation and other legal representation
• Gross monthly income cap of £2,657 • This increases by £222 for every child in excess of four • Capital limit of £8,000	• Disposable income must not exceed £733 per month • Cap of £3,000 on capital	• Disposable income must not exceed £733 per month • Capital limit of £8,000

Those with a disposable income in excess of £315 per month will pay a contribution on a sliding scale.

Those with a disposable capital exceeding £3,000 will be required to pay a contribution of either capital exceeding that sum or the likely maximum costs of the funded service, whichever is lower.

One of three outcomes is possible:

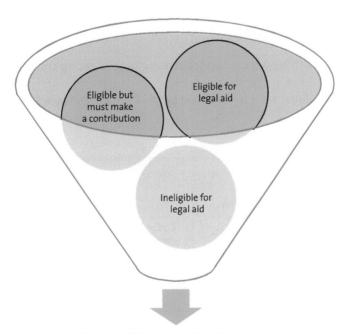

A claimant will fall into one of these three categories

The Act also made three important changes to eligibility.

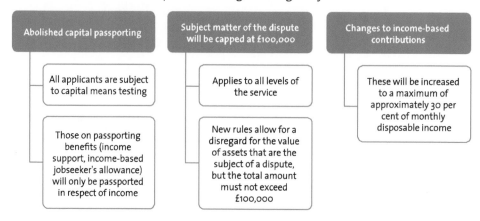

Up For Debate

Consider the fairness of the legal aid cuts. Are those who are now not eligible being deprived of access to the legal system? Are there alternative measures that are available to meet their needs, e.g. conditional fee arrangements? Is the legal aid system an ideal that nobody can afford?

This concludes the section on civil legal aid. We will now look at criminal legal aid.

Criminal Defence Service

This service assists those who are under investigation or facing criminal charges.

If a client requires legal aid it is organised by the **Criminal Defence Service** (CDS).

Its role is outlined below.

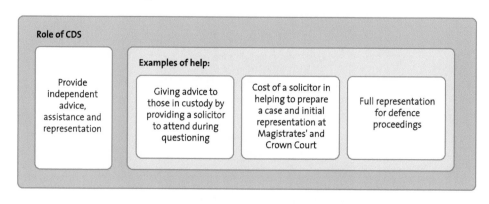

The Public Defender Service

The Public Defender Service (PDS) provides representation by salaried lawyers working under the umbrella of the Legal Aid Agency. The LAA directly employs the PDS staff of solicitors, representatives and administrators.

By helping those accused, it has the effect of helping ensure the police and courts run efficiently.

Eligibility for funding

Two tests need to be satisfied:

Interests of Justice Test
- ❖ Are there any previous convictions?
- ❖ The nature of the offence
- ❖ Risk of custody

Financial Eligibility Test
- ❖ Considers the financial position of the client

Looking further at the 'interests of justice' test, the applicant must satisfy one of the following (this is not an exhaustive list):

- ❖ Is it likely that the accused will lose his liberty?
- ❖ Is it likely that the accused will lose his livelihood?
- ❖ Is it likely that the accused will suffer serious damage to his reputation?
- ❖ Is a substantial question of law involved?
- ❖ Does that case require witnesses to be traced or interviewed?
- ❖ Will expert cross-examination be required?

Once the 'interests of justice' criteria have been satisfied, it is time to consider if the client qualifies on financial grounds.

The 'means' test looks at the client's income. The rules are different depending on whether help in the Magistrates' or Crown Court is required.

Aim Higher

It is unlikely you will be asked a detailed question regarding financial eligibility. So, as with civil legal aid, just ensure you understand the basis of the calculation.

As there are no certainties with these things, check with your lecturer as to the scope of knowledge required here.

The voluntary sector

Having considered the legal aid system, we will now consider how clients are helped in the **voluntary sector** by considering:

1. Law centres
2. The Citizens Advice Bureau
3. Conditional Fee Arrangements (CFAs)
4. Damages-based Agreements (DBAs)

Law centres

Who are they staffed by?	How are they funded?	Examples of work undertaken
• Salaried and trainee solicitors • Non-lawyers including debt managers	• Government and charitable funding • They are free to use (no means testing)	• Landlord and tenant disputes • Representation at tribunals

The Citizens Advice Bureau

Who are they staffed by?	How are they funded?	Examples of work undertaken
• Volunteers and paid staff	• Various organisations including local authorities, charities and individuals • They are free to use (no means testing)	• Provide independent advice on various matters including debts, housing, employment and problems with benefits

Note: the Bar Council supports a **Free Representation Unit** for clients at a variety of tribunals for which legal aid is not available. This is mainly carried out by Bar students (under supervision).

Conditional Free Arrangements (CFA) ('no win, no fee')

What is the role of the CFA?
This is a controversial area. They attempt to reduce the legal aid bill by transferring legal costs from the state to the private sector.

They are available for most types of civil action (excluding family). They are not available for criminal proceedings (see s 58A Courts and Legal Services Act 1990). They gain publicity for their use in personal injury claims (which, excluding clinical negligence, now fall outside of the scope for legal aid).

How do they work?
The litigant's solicitor will get paid only if the claim is successful; they take on the case on the understanding that if they are **unsuccessful** they will not receive payment.

In essence the solicitor arranges to be paid a 'basic fee' and a 'success fee'. The success fee (extra profit) is added to the basic fee and is seen as compensation/incentive for the risk that the solicitor has run by taking the case. The success fee is calculated as a percentage of the normal fees (in a personal injury case, the success fee must not exceed 25 per cent of the damages).

Example

Michael is suing his employer for a personal injury suffered at work.

The basic fee amounts to £1,000.

He and the solicitor agree a success fee of 20 per cent.

If Michael is successful, the full amount payable amounts to £1,200 (the £200 being the success fee (profit uplift). If Michael does not win his case, his lawyers will not receive any money.

The rules changed on 1 April 2013 and now under ss 44 and 46 of LASPO and the **Conditional Fee Agreements Order 2013** clients who enter into a CFA will have to pay the success fee **from their damages**.

One quirk of the system is that the arrangement is not dependent on an individual's personal income. An example of this can be seen by the CFA entered into by the supermodel Naomi Campbell, despite the fact she had enough money to pay for the litigation privately (*Campbell v MGN Limited* (2005)).

Damages-based Agreements (DBAs)
A lawyer working under a DBA will **not be paid** if they lose their case. If they are successful they take a percentage of the damages recovered. The amount that can be paid to a lawyer is capped at 25 per cent in personal injury cases (the same as CFAs).

In summary:

Conditional Fee Arrangements	Damages-based Agreements
• Covers civil actions • If the claim is unsuccessful then no fee is paid • If successful then a 'basic' and 'success' fee is paid	• Covers civil actions (same as CFA) • If the claim is unsuccessful then no fee is paid (same as CFA) • If successful then fees are paid from damages recovered (different from CFAs)

Up For Debate

Are CFAs and DBAs filling the hole left by the legal aid cuts? Does easy access to these types of arrangements encourage litigation from parties with weak claims? Do they encourage people to 'have a go' at making a claim, as they have nothing to lose if they are not successful?

Core issues checklist

In April 2013 the funding of legal services went through some dramatic changes.	✔
Are you up to date with changes that happened after April 2013?	✔
The Legal Aid Agency is the body that oversees civil **and** criminal legal aid.	✔
The Civil Legal Advice agency provides civil legal advice to those who qualify.	✔
Since April 2013 those eligible for civil legal aid have been drastically reduced.	✔
The Criminal Defence Service is the body responsible for assisting those under investigation or facing criminal charges.	✔
The Public Defender Service provides representation by salaried lawyers.	✔
The voluntary sector can also provide advice and assistance to those in need of legal help.	✔

Useful websites

Topic	Website
Legal Action Group	www.lag.org.uk

Putting it into practice – example essay question

'Consider the matters a party may take into account when considering a conditional fee arrangement.'

Answer plan

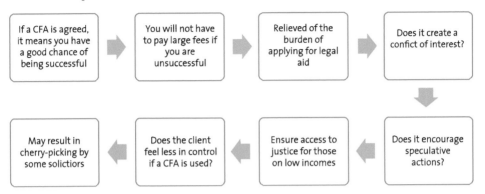

Outline answer

Your answer should consider the following matters.

❖ If a solicitor agrees to take a case it will mean you have a good chance of being successful.
❖ You will be relieved of the burden of paying huge fees if you are not successful.
❖ There will be no need to apply for legal aid, which can be time-consuming.
❖ Access to the legal process is available for those on low incomes.
❖ It may encourage speculative actions (although this is less likely with the more stringent rules).
❖ It may create a conflict of interest between the client and the lawyer. With payment depending on the outcome of the case, there may be a temptation to act unethically.
❖ The client may not have total charge of the case as the solicitor has a vested interest.
❖ Lawyers may pick those claims which are of high value, but refuse to take on good small claims, thereby denying access to justice.

@ **Visit the book's companion website to test your knowledge**

❖ Resources include a subject map, revision tip podcasts, downloadable diagrams, MCQ quizzes for each chapter, and a flashcard glossary
❖ www.routledge.com/cw/optimizelawrevision

11 Preparing for the Exam

Revision objectives

Understand the law
- Do you understand the legal principles surrounding the English Legal System (ELS)?

Remember the details
- Can you remember the key areas?

Reflect critically on areas of debate
- Can you complete all the 'Aim higher' and 'Up for debate' boxes in the chapters?

Contextualise
- Can you see how the different areas of the ELS interact?

Apply your skills and knowledge
- Are you confident in answering all the 'Putting it into practice' questions?

Chapter Map

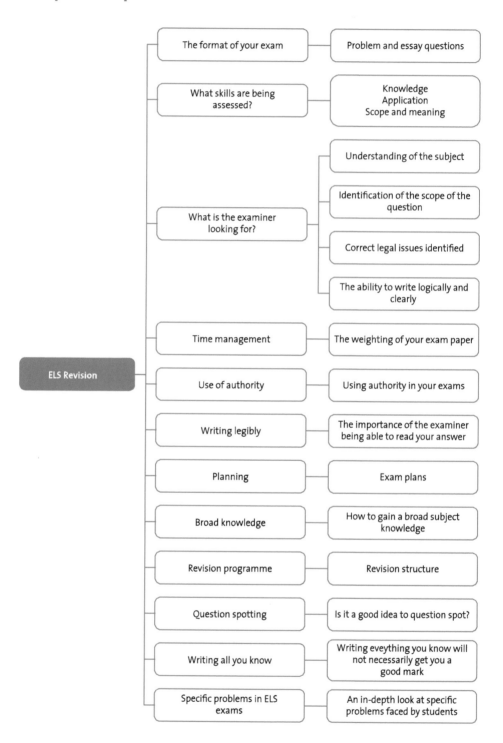

	The format of your exam	Problem and essay questions
	What skills are being assessed?	Knowledge Application Scope and meaning
	What is the examiner looking for?	Understanding of the subject
		Identification of the scope of the question
		Correct legal issues identified
		The ability to write logically and clearly
ELS Revision	Time management	The weighting of your exam paper
	Use of authority	Using authority in your exams
	Writing legibly	The importance of the examiner being able to read your answer
	Planning	Exam plans
	Broad knowledge	How to gain a broad subject knowledge
	Revision programme	Revision structure
	Question spotting	Is it a good idea to question spot?
	Writing all you know	Writing eveything you know will not necessarily get you a good mark
	Specific problems in ELS exams	An in-depth look at specific problems faced by students

Introduction

This chapter is designed to give you advice for your **English Legal System** (ELS) exam.

The topic of the English legal system will be one of the first subjects you will study. If you studied 'A' level law, you may already be familiar with the subject. If this is the case, do not fall into the trap of 'switching off', assuming you have 'done it all before'. 'A' levels and your first undergraduate year will require different skills, and you will need to learn to be more reflective and analytical, which is not generally required on 'A' level courses.

Most students go through a period of adjustment in their first year – adapting to the change from school to university – so do not be disheartened if you find things a little difficult at first; with perseverance you will make the adjustments that studying law at undergraduate level requires.

Although the advice you read in this chapter may be relevant to other exams, it has not been written as a general guide, so we will not be covering advice for all exams, for example your open or seen exams.

Aim Higher – suggested reading

If you wish to undertake additional reading around this subject, and gain advice on among other things, approaching coursework, legal referencing and examples of good and bad essays you may wish to consult one of the numerous skills books that are available. **Steve Foster**'s book *How To Write Better Law Essays* (3rd edition, Pearson 2012) is very good. It gives illustrations of good legal writing and poor practice. It's an excellent purchase and will last throughout your studies.

Although it is very easy to ignore advice on skills, understanding how to answer exam questions is just as important as attending your lectures, participating in your tutorials and completing your revision.

The ability to provide answers under pressure is a skill that will develop as you work through your degree.

Your exams will become more challenging as you progress, and it is a wise student who realises it is not only **what** you write, but **how** you write, that is important.

This chapter should give you a head start in developing those skills.

Note: near the end of this chapter, we have added a section on 'specific problems with ELS exams' – you can see here the areas that most students struggle with.

As a starting point, remember:

The format of your English Legal System exam

Exams are typically divided into essay and problem questions.

❖ An **essay** question will look something like this:

'The Parliament Acts 1911 **and** 1949 **unjustifiably restrict the powers of the House of Lords.' Critically assess this statement.**

❖ A **problem** question will provide you with a set of facts and you have to assess the liability of the parties in the question. An example problem question can be seen at the end of the 'Civil Justice' chapter.

Many students find they like either one style or the other. Some students find essay questions easier; some like problem questions. Students may perceive that essay questions are easier as they believe (incorrectly) they can write everything they know about a topic and receive full marks.

Common Pitfall

BE WARNED: it is not the case that if you write down everything you know about a topic you will get top marks. You will only ever receive marks for 'relevant' material.

Some students find answering problem questions very difficult; applying the law can be quite hard work!

Common Pitfall

When tackling problem questions, **take your time**. Often, students try to reach a conclusion too early. Time should be spent on discussing the relevant legal principles and developing your argument(s). Many place too much emphasis on listing cases, with little explanation of why the case is important or relevant.

Additionally, it is not uncommon for problem questions to be deliberately vague in an attempt to draw the students into a discussion of possible outcomes, and some students can find this confusing at first.

Find out what type of questions you like and why:

Let us continue by thinking about the skills your law exams will be assessing.

Which skills are being assessed?

❖ First, the exam is testing your **knowledge** of a particular subject area; additionally, in some exams it is testing your ability to **apply** that knowledge to a set of facts.

❖ Second, it is testing your ability to identify the **scope** and **meaning** of a question and your ability to provide a well-structured answer.

Consider the following diagram, to see how this works in practice.

What is the examiner looking for?

Understanding of the general subject

Even though you may be asked about a specific area of law, you will gain marks by showing you have an understanding of the 'bigger picture'. For instance, if you are asked a question regarding ADR you can improve your answer by showing knowledge of how this works alongside the traditional court system. Check the 'learning outcomes' on your Module Outline (there should be one for each of your modules) to ensure you are aware (before your start your revision) what your lecturer is expecting from you.

Identification of the scope of the question

You must read your question properly. If the question asks for an analysis of A V Dicey, an analysis of all the theorists will not gain many marks. The examiner in this case will be looking for in-depth analysis of Dicey, not a general descriptive essay about the rule of law.

Identification of correct legal issues

Limit your answer to the relevant law. If you are asked to discuss the law-making powers of judges, do not focus on any other law-making body.

An ability to write logically and clearly

The structure of your answer is crucial to this. Your time management skills will be relevant here.

Your lecturer will consider the following:

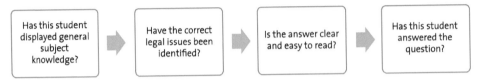

| Has this student displayed general subject knowledge? | → | Have the correct legal issues been identified? | → | Is the answer clear and easy to read? | → | Has this student answered the question? |

Exam time management skills

❖ It is a good idea to have some idea before you enter the exam of the structure of the paper.
❖ This should be provided by your lecturer – do not just assume it is the same as last year's paper.
❖ If you have a two-hour paper and you have four questions to complete, it is easy to work out that you should be spending around 30 minutes per question.
❖ Quite often, ELS papers are divided into parts, and these will not always be equally weighted.
❖ So, let us assume you have two 15-mark questions, one 30-mark question and one 40-mark question. Adding up to 100 per cent overall.

How do you divide up your time?

You have to devote 40 per cent of your time to the 40-mark question, 30 per cent of your time to the 30-mark question and so on. So your time should be split as follows:

40-mark question – 48 minutes
30-mark question – 36 minutes
15-mark questions – 18 minutes **each**

It is important that you stick to the timings allowed for the question. The lecturer will know how long it should take to complete the question, if you are still writing your answer to a 15-mark question after 45 minutes this is a sign that there is a problem.

Likewise, if you finish your 40-mark question in 15 minutes then an alarm bell should be ringing.

> ## Common Pitfall
>
> The vast majority of ELS students who fail the exam will not fail for lack of knowledge, but because they haven't managed their time properly. They spend too long on the first question and run out of time to answer the others.

Answer your questions in any order

Instead of answering each complete exam paper at one time, it is common for examiners to mark all the answers to one question at the same time. They will mark all the answers to Question 1, and then move to marking all the answers to Question 2. This achieves consistency for both students and the lecturer.

As long as you clearly identify the question (both in your answer booklet **and on the front**), it does not make much difference which order you answer your questions in. In our experience, most students tend to work their way through the paper, answering question 1 first and so on.

This may not suit you. When Angela was a student she always liked to tackle the more demanding questions first (the 40-mark question in the example above, for instance). This suited her; it may not suit you. If you are nervous, it may be advisable to answer the smaller questions at the beginning of the exam. Just remember to mark the questions you have done accurately on the front of your exam script and to start each question on a fresh page. This makes it easier to mark and will leave some space between questions for you to add material later, if you wish to.

Use of authority

You **must** use case or other authority in your exam. You would not answer a course work question without authority and you should view your exam in the same way.

> ## Common Pitfall
>
> No Law = No Marks

You are not expected to use footnotes – they are only relevant in your coursework. Following on from this you **would not** be expected to include the case citation, e.g. [2004] EWCA Civ 576.

You will receive marks if you include the principles in your exam; you will **gain more marks** if you give the authority.

Aim for the following:

Due to the time constraints in exams it is worth checking with your lecturer whether he/she expects you to remember the full case name. For example, it would be acceptable for our students to write 'In Halsey, the court decided . . .'. We would not see it as a good use of their time to write out the following: 'In *Halsey v Milton Keynes General NHS Trust . . .*'.

If you demonstrate that you understand the case and the principle flowing from the decision then that should be enough.

If you cannot remember the name of a case (and we have all been there!), then try to indicate something about the case that identifies it.

Common Pitfall

Warning: Forgetting case names too often creates a bad impression and makes your work look sloppy. If we read an exam paper where the phrase 'this was decided in that case where . . .' is littered throughout the exam it looks as though you haven't done your revision properly!

When using Acts of Parliament it always creates a good impression to remember the section numbers, but if you cannot then try to make sure you get the name of the Act correct.

If you have the Act in front of you, do not copy out the sections. It wastes time and you will not get any marks. Include relevant sections and any keywords from the sections, but remember that your lecturer does not need the Act copied out verbatim.

Write legibly

For us, this is the most essential skill of all. If we cannot read it, we cannot mark it.

You will have some idea by the time you embark on your degree as to how your handwriting is perceived by others, so take note of this and if your writing is generally hard for people to read, then now is the time to do something about it.

It is also tempting when you are under a time constraint to take less care with your writing. This is not a good idea.

There should be some allowance made for spelling and grammatical errors, so you should not be marked too heavily on these areas.

However, if your work is generally untidy and messy, for example full of crossings out and bits added here and there, it leads the examiner to believe that you may not know your subject well and creates a poor impression overall.

Planning

It is a good idea to devise a plan before starting to write your answer. We have seen some quite long and involved ones, and some short ones; there is no 'proper or ideal plan', just whatever works for you.

It is a good idea to cross the plans through when you have finished. Examiners do not tend to look at them too closely (we are more interested in your answer than your plan), but it is good to have them to show the structure of your answer and it will help keep you on track.

Gaining a broad knowledge

Earlier we discussed the need for a broad knowledge of your subject. An overall view of the topic will increase your chances of doing well, it will give confidence to your writing and it can help to make your writing less mechanical and descriptive and more analytical.

Although your lecturers will divide teaching up into sections or topics, when it comes to answering questions these separate lecture topics often interact. To address only one topic when three or four are relevant is going to limit the scope of your answer.

Gaining a broad knowledge of your subject can be achieved by:

1. Completing your tutorial questions. This will make life much easier when it comes to the exam. If you do this, then when you start revising it will be the second time you have attempted questions on the topics likely to appear in the exam. Also, if you find a particular area difficult, then you will already know this. Exam success is achieved by engaging with the subject early.

So ask yourself:

> Can I answer my tutorial questions?

> If not, then you need to include them as part of your revision.
> If yes, well done! You have have a head start!

> Lecturers will often use past exam questions in tutorials. This provides students with a clear understanding of what is expected of them in the exam.

2. Attending your lectures. Your exam will be based on what is taught in lectures. If you don't know what has been taught, you will not know what is going to come up in the exam. Crucially, you may miss the emphasis placed on topics by lecturers. Many courses we have taught may have eight to ten topics, but they will all be weighted differently, and this weighting is reflected in the exam.
3. Start your revision early.
4. Practise your questions beforehand. If it is possible, then formulate answers to the previous year's exam paper and ask your lecturer to mark them for you. Alternatively, ask the lecturer if it is possible during the revision period for them to provide outline answers to previous exam questions. Most lecturers should be happy to do this.

Remember to do the following:

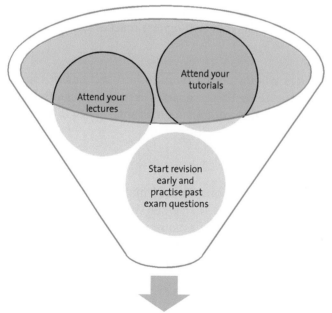

Attend your tutorials

Attend your lectures

Start revision early and practise past exam questions

To gain a broad overall knowledge

There is no way to shortcut your revision

Students often make the mistake of looking for the 'right' answer. We are often asked for a 'model' answer to past exam questions. We do not think there is a 'model' answer to any question. It would suggest that if a student writes something we haven't thought of, then it is wrong. This is not the case. Exam questions can be deliberately vague, and the aim is to draw out of the student as much as possible about the relevant law surrounding the question. There will nevertheless be an outline that most answers should follow.

Aim Higher – revision tip

Gary Slapper and **David Kelly** have written an excellent Question and Answer book entitled *Q&A The English Legal System*, the latest edition of which was published in 2013 by Routledge. This gives a broad range of suggested solutions to essay and problem questions on the English legal system.

Remember: Q&A books are not model answers; they are suggested solutions – one way of approaching a question, not the only way! Many students find these books very helpful in preparing for the exam. Whatever you do, you **MUST NOT** learn solutions from this or any other book as template answers to any question on a specific topic.

Your revision programme

When starting your revision programme, this should (in an ideal world) be the second time you are looking at the law.

Don't assume that because a topic has been covered in coursework it will not appear in the exam. It is safe to say that you probably will not receive it as a main question, but it **may** still form a smaller part of a larger question.

Are all your materials up to date?

Make a list of relevant areas; in particular, has the law been the subject of a new development? If so, make sure you are aware of any changes.

Have you bought the relevant textbook? Some students rely solely on lecture materials, but it is a mistake.

Do you know your exam timetable? Your revision should reflect this. Start revising for your first exam first.

Do not overdo your revision; listen to your body – if it is telling you it needs a break, then it is probably wise to take notice. You can only absorb information if you are in the right frame of mind.

Scan past exam papers for any particular examinable areas. This is no guarantee they will be in your exam, but it will act a guide to the most important topics. This brings us to . . .

Question spotting

It is **not** a good idea to question spot; i.e. assume that because a question or topic has come up for the last four years it will come up again. There are no guarantees. This can be a particularly dangerous tactic if the module leader has changed.

A better approach would be to look at your course outline, your tutorial questions and any advice given by your module leader, particularly during your revision lectures. If you are given any questions to complete as part of your revision, make sure you can answer them. This will also help you with mixed questions (those covering more than one legal topic).

Writing all you know

Do not fall into the trap that catches out many students by writing everything you know about a topic, without addressing the question. Some students feel really chuffed leaving the exam, feeling they have put together a fabulous paper, having written furiously for two hours. Then they discover they have a low mark and are confused. There are two main reasons for this.

1. They have not answered the question.
2. They were asked to 'critically assess' but they have 'described'. When completing a degree, you are expected to provide some analysis. If the question starts with the words 'critically assess' then pay attention.

For instance, if asked:

'Is the role of the courts to interpret and apply the law?'

An **analytical answer** would discuss the role of the courts in a constitutional and legal system, showing understanding of how they resolve disputes, interpret statutes and develop the common law. A very good answer will expand on this by considering, if the above statement is all they do, whether they should or should not go further and actually make the law.

A **descriptive answer** would discuss the rules of statutory interpretation, development of the common law and the doctrine of precedent.

Some 'do nots'

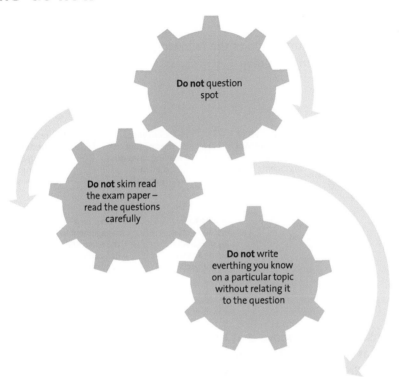

Do not question spot

Do not skim read the exam paper – read the questions carefully

Do not write everthing you know on a particular topic without relating it to the question

Specific problems in English Legal System exams

English Legal System exams can cause a few headaches for students.

During the research for this book ELS lecturers were asked to provide their thoughts on the problems faced by students when studying ELS, and this section of the chapter will summarise the feedback received. **Thus, you are fortunate to be able to read the problems that students face from the lecturers' perspective**.

First, it was noted that students struggle with the **breadth of the subject** (you have no doubt noticed this from the size of your textbook).

Second, studying this subject for the first time may also **challenge some other misconceptions**, such as the idea that law is primarily criminal law or that law is a black and white set of rules.

Next, we can see from the diagram below those topics that lecturers know students struggle with the most.

In addition to the substantive topics the following **skills** have been highlighted as being difficult for students to grasp.

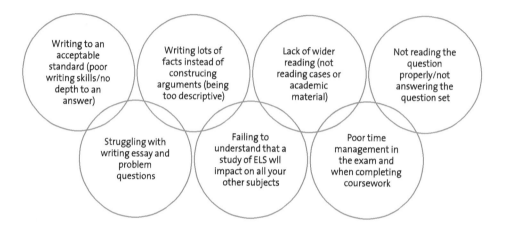

So, we can see from the above that to be a successful law student you need to concentrate as much on skills as you do on the legal rules you will learn in lectures and tutorials. **Remember, lack of skills is increasingly being cited by lecturers as a reason for poor performance in exams**.

There is no magic formula to increase your skills – it is pure practice. For instance, the more cases you read, the better you will be at reading them. The more writing you do, the more likely it is that your writing style will improve. **The failure to write in sufficient depth can be a consequence of over-reliance on lecture handouts, and your lack of wider reading will show through**.

As stated before, most students will prefer answering either problem or essay questions. Bearing this in mind it is helpful to have some idea of the topics that are most likely to be addressed in each type.

The diagram below illustrates how this (generally) works in ELS. As all ELS modules differ, it might be advisable to check with your lecturer, and whether particular topics have come up as essay or problem questions in tutorials.

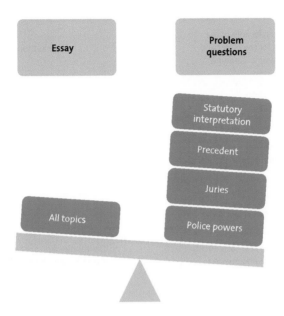

So we can see that all the topics that appear in this book are suitable for essay questions, but only some are suitable for problem questions. With this in mind it would be advantageous to consult past papers to see how your lecturer has dealt with this in previous years. This is not a clear indication of future events but it is always helpful to be aware of past questions (but beware of a change in lecturers, as this often means a change in style of exam paper).

In summary, remember the following

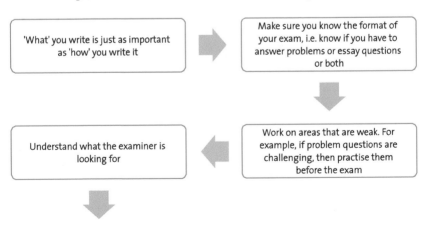

Make sure you take note of the mark allocation for the paper and adjust your time accordingly		Use authority

Do an answer plan in the exam – it will help you with your structure		Write clearly; if your examiner cannot read it they cannot mark it

Start your revision early – attend all lectures, tutorials and revision sessions		Do not question spot – lecturers, examiners and the law change, and your exam paper will reflect this

GOOD LUCK IN YOUR EXAM!

Angela & Odette

Index